T. Harry Williams, *courtesy of Mrs. Estelle Williams*

THE CONFEDERATE HIGH COMMAND

& RELATED TOPICS

The 1988 Deep Delta Civil War Symposium:

THEMES IN HONOR

OF

T. HARRY WILLIAMS

Edited by
Roman J. Heleniak
and
Lawrence L. Hewitt

 WHITE MANE PUBLISHING COMPANY, INC.
Shippensburg, Pennsylvania

This White Mane Publishing Company, Inc. book
was printed by
Beidel Printing House, Inc.
63 West Burd Street
Shippensburg, PA 17257

In respect to the scholarship contained herein, the acid-free paper used in this book meets the guidelines for permanence and durability of the Committee on Production Guidelines for Book Longevity of the Council on Library Resources.

For a complete list of available publications
please write
White Mane Publishing Company, Inc.
P.O. Box 152
Shippensburg, PA 17257

ISBN 0-942597-17-6

PRINTED IN THE UNITED STATES OF AMERICA

Table of Contents

List of Illustrations

Foreword

Roman J. Heleniak

On April 9, 1990, the nation will mark the one hundred and twenty-fifth anniversary of the meeting between the general in chief of the armies of the United States, Lieutenant General Ulysses S. Grant, and his formidable opponent, General Robert E. Lee, commander of the Army of Northern Virginia. The history making conference took place at the McLean home in Appomattox Court House, southwest of the Confederate Capitol. Lee had requested the meeting with Grant to discuss the terms of a possible surrender. Lee's once formidable Army of Northern Virginia, by then reduced to some 50,000 men and outnumbered by at least a two-to-one ratio by Grant's better-equipped, better-fed, and fresher troops, could not flee to the south. Another large Union army, led by the relentless Major General William T. Sherman, was moving towards Lee from that direction and had eliminated any chance of retreat into North Carolina. Except for a possible escape to the west, where Lee's ragged Rebel forces could wage a protracted guerilla war in the mountains, the courtly Virginian knew that he had reached end game.

The two great American soldiers, so different in style and background, but sharing a mutual respect for one another, began their deliberations with an exchange of greetings. After some brief conversation of old army days, Grant got to the business at hand: the terms of surrender. Grant informed Lee that after the Army of Northern Virginia laid down its weapons, the officers would be allowed to keep their side arms; those in the army who owned horses and mules would be permitted to take them home with them for the spring planting. The triumphant Yankees could afford to be generous, for although some scattered Rebel troops did not give up the fight until late June, and the C.S.S. *Shenandoah* did not lower her flag until November 6, 1865, the dream of southern independence, a quest which plunged this nation into its greatest and bloodiest crisis, came to an end that April day in 1865. Appomattox meant more than the surrender of the Army of Northern Virginia. For all practical purposes, the war was over.

The war was over—but the battle rages on. For the more than one hundred and twenty years since the last campaign, historians, journalists, biographers, novelists, poets, participants, and Civil War enthusiasts from both sides of the Mason-Dixon line have been refighting it.

Mercifully, these new campaigns result in few injuries—sprained ankles and insect bites for the most part—because the closest modern day soldiers come to the real thing are the popular reenactments of major battles. At these affairs, "buffs" don ill-fitting Rebel-grey or Yankee-blue uniforms and fire blank cartridges at one another. By day's end, the participants usually retreat to the beer coolers and down ice cold cans of their favorite beverage, an opportunity not available to their ancestors at Gettysburg and Shiloh.

A majority of the post-bellum warriors have rejected the Springfields and Sharps and, instead, have selected the pen, the typewriter, and/or the word processor as the weapons of choice. And, they have been busy since 1865. It is reasonable to state that no other four-year period of American history—even those of the two world wars—has inspired a body of literature comparable to that produced by the United States Civil War. While much of the writing is dreadful, the syrupy romance novels of the late nineteenth century and the wildly inaccurate televised "mini-series" of recent years come immediately to mind, there is and has been a large and eager audience for serious works on the Civil War. No battle, no general, no factor, no angle has been ignored by the scholars and authors who have devoted their efforts to studying the conflict. While biographies of the leading generals and monographs on the major campaigns attract the major attention and remain a staple of Civil War historiography, the writers have not ignored the social, cultural, and economic forces which, in their opinions, influenced the course of the war. Nor have they overlooked such seemingly arcane factors as the Confederacy's lack of salt and the Celtic antecedents of the people of the southern region of the United States as determinants in the Civil War's outcome.

In brief, the Civil War has spawned a small but significant cottage industry in the United States and furnishes scholars and others with a constantly replenishing mine of raw material to be smelted and refined. In recent years, for example, readers have been entertained with new—and major—interpretations explaining why the North won the war and why the South lost. Never mind that many students of the Civil War thought these questions had been addressed many years ago. And, who would dare predict that at some time in the near future some energetic young scholar will not discover yet another reason for the North's supremacy?

This is as it should be, for the final chapter on the history of this nation's fraternal blood-letting has yet to be written; there is still much to be done; questions not yet even asked will have to be answered. Who will author the next major work on the Civil War? While there is no doubt that serious amateurs, many of them lacking the requisite academic pedigree, will continue to make important contributions, the major burden of Civil War historiography will fall on the stooped shoulders of scholars trained in the craft of writing history in the graduate programs of our nation's universities.

Fortunately for the many Americans who possess a deep interest in the Civil War, professional historians, even those toiling in academe, have not divorced themselves from the laity, as is often the case with many other academic specialists. On the contrary, books and articles written by professional Civil War historians are read and appreciated by tens of thousands of readers across this country and in other lands as well—even far away Australia has her share of subscribers to Civil War magazines and newsletters. Additionally, with some notable exceptions, the leading historians in the United States do not possess "household" names and are virtually unknown outside of the profession; most of their monographs are published by university presses and their articles are printed in scholarly journals; the great majority of their readers are other professionals. The Civil War historian is the exception. While the field of Civil War history is a legitimate specialty for scholars, it has a much wider audience than any other area of history. Those who have chosen the war as their major academic interest do not have to rely on university presses and professional journals for publication. Nor do they have to restrict their reading of papers to academic meetings. Civil War historians make frequent appearances before civic groups, patriotic organizations, and the many Civil War Round Tables. A vast network of the latter sprawls across the entire eastern region of the United States and extends into many of the western states as well.

Appearing before these Round Tables and the other groups has given serious scholars the opportunity to cultivate a much wider audience, one not confined to the universities. Conversely, these Round Tables afford the general public the opportunity to see and hear the most renowned historians in the field.

The late T. Harry Williams of Louisiana State University and Frank Vandiver of Rice and Texas A&M University are examples of Civil War writers whose fame extended beyond the university to the secular world, although Vandiver's notoriety at Texas A&M owes as much to the fact that he, the president of that university, briefly, earned less money than the new football coach. Fortunately, the governing board corrected this oversight once the national news media aired the news to an incredulous public. Civil War enthusiasts, however, were less impressed with Vandiver's newly found riches than they were with his tenure at Rice, where his graduate program produced a generation of outstanding historians. Much of what Vandiver passed on to his young charges he learned from his long-time friend and mentor, T. Harry Williams.

The contributions to the study of Civil War historiography made by Williams before his death in 1979, and still being made by Vandiver, in part, provided the motivation for the Second Annual Deep Delta Civil War Symposium at Southeastern Louisiana University, June 24-26, 1988. Williams and Vandiver are names well-known to Civil War buffs, especially in the southern states and especially in Louisiana, a state that claimed Williams as one of her own. Eight prominent scholars joined Vandiver and presented papers in honor of T. Harry Williams; appropriately, all the participants studied either under Dr. Vandiver or Dr. Williams except for Archie McDonald, who has the distinction of having earned a graduate degree under both. T. Harry Williams's widow, Estelle, a native of the Pelican State, graced the symposium by appearing at every session.

The range and breadth of the scholarship presented at the symposium reflects well upon the influence T. Harry Williams had on the writing of Civil War history.

Because of Dr. Vandiver's close relationship with T. Harry Williams, I have selected "Williams and His Generals" as the lead essay in this volume. It serves as an eloquent introduction to the fine papers which follow, papers which reflect well upon the influence T. Harry Williams had on the writing of Civil War history, and, because of its diversity of topics, it provides some semblance of a central theme to the title of this collection: THE CONFEDERATE HIGH COMMAND & RELATED TOPICS.

"Williams and His Generals" is a thoughtful essay on the transplanted Yankee's contributions to historiography, particularly that of the Civil War. While an open admirer of Williams, Vandiver could not resist taking an occasional, albeit gentle, jab at his late mentor's "northern perspective." As Vandiver notes, Williams in his first major work, *Lincoln and His Generals,* made it "acceptable to root for the North." That Williams, a son of the "other side" could do this at a major southern university and become a legend at that school is no small achievement, indeed, for this institution is the same one that adamantly refuses to name a building for its first president, William T. Sherman.

The range of subjects examined at the symposium stretched wide enough to satisfy even those Civil War buffs with the most specialized interests. For example, Dr. Archie McDonald of Stephen F. Austin State University regaled the audience with a presentation of Civil War music, including a stirring rendition of the all-time favorite "Dixie." To be impartial, the Texas native also performed the popular, with Yankees, but not often heard by southern listeners, "Marching through Georgia."

Military history, always a major staple with Civil War enthusiasts, did not go neglected. Both Richard Sommers and Lawrence Hewitt described the protracted hell of siege warfare. In Sommers' case, the Chief Archivist-Historian of the U.S. Army Military History Institute selected the battles fought near Petersburg prior to the eventual Rebel abandonment of the important rail center south of Richmond. As Sommers explained, Petersburg cannot be classed as a true siege because the city was never completely cut off from the outside world by Grant's forces.

Professor Lawrence Hewitt of the host institution, Southeastern Louisiana University, provided insight into what it was like for Confederate troops at Port Hudson, the longest true siege in the history of American warfare. Their backs to the Mississippi, the besieged southern defenders at Port Hudson, according to Hewitt, debated the relative merits of mule and rat meat, with the latter a clear choice of the troops. Given the option of starvation or the eating of strange meat, man will do what he has to do to survive.

The nourishment of the mind is a different matter. This side of the Rebel high command is examined by Dr. Jon Wakelyn of the Catholic University of America in his paper, "Education of Confederate Leaders." He reveals that a great majority of the Confederate command attended college, not only the military academies but civilian colleges as well. Not all of those who attended college could be described as serious students for college men of the nineteenth century were as given to pranks and harassing the faculty as their grandsons and great-grandsons of this century.

More than one Confederate officer studied at the Virginia Military Institute, and who among them could have guessed that the quiet professor of science would go on to earn great fame as the fierce General Stonewall Jackson, chief of Lee's lieutenants and the major reason for Lee's victory at Chancellorsville? Professor Thomas Connelly of the University of South Carolina takes issue with the hagiographers of Robert E. Lee and points out that Jackson, not Lee, came out of the Civil War with the reputation of being the South's greatest general. Eventually a cult of Lee emerged because Marse Robert's character and patrician background made him the better symbol of the "Lost Cause."

Dr. Emory Thomas took mild issue with Connelly and argued that, if anything, Robert E. Lee's nobility of character has been underestimated. The University of Georgia history professor cited the example of Lee's most famous biographer, Douglas Southall Freeman, who after he finished his monumental work, discovered a letter written by Lee in which the great general nonchalantly describes killing a Canadian "snake" as a young officer; the snake was supposedly a Canadian lighthouse keeper. Mortified, Freeman buried the episode in a footnote in a later edition. Thomas credits Robert E. Lee's penchant for writing tongue-in-cheek letters for the confusion.

The revisionism displayed by Connelly and Thomas' defense of the traditional interpretation of Lee, are, of course, in the mainstream of historical writing. Dr. Joseph Harsh of George Mason University in his paper sought to refurbish the reputation of General George McClellan by examining his 1862 Peninsula strategy. Contrary to the widely held view that McClellan lacked the boldness, the capacity to go for the throat, Harsh argues that the Yankee general's plan in Virginia fit the original Lincoln policy of winning the war with a minimum of bloodshed, thus, increasing the chances of a peaceful reconciliation of the two sections of the nation.

The final paper of the symposium, "Jefferson Davis and the Historians," by Dr. Herman Hattaway of the University of Missouri at Kansas City, brought into sharp focus the problems historians have had with the highest ranking member of the Confederate High Command, the President of the Confederate States of America. Hattaway, in his review of the many books about Davis, provides a perfect reminder to those who believe historical questions can be resolved with a definitive answer. Perhaps no other Civil War figure has been the subject of both flattering and unflattering biographies. The permanent place of Davis in the American saga has not yet been established, but several major studies are in various stages of preparation, and, perhaps, some of the ambiguity surrounding Jefferson Davis will be dispelled. Until, and if, that happens, we are left with conflicting interpretations of the Confederacy's only president.

Students of the Civil War would not want it any other way, for in the study of history nothing is final. New evidence found in yet to be discovered diaries or letters and/or new interpretations of existing documents will, no doubt, change the way we think about the men and events of the Civil War and provide the motivation for new books and papers. The Second Annual Deep Delta Civil War Symposium provided a forum for nine prominent scholars to exhibit their most recent works. Since they generated as many questions as they did answers, there will be a Third Annual Deep Delta Civil War Symposium in 1989, one in which thirteen scholars have volunteered to brave enemy fire and read papers. The Civil War is over—but the battle rages on.

Williams and His Generals

Frank E. Vandiver

For students of the Civil War, the 1950s must rank as one of the most important decades. Those were heady days for us Civil Warriors. The Centennial was approaching; public appetites for almost any kind of screed about 1861-65 were voracious; money for research flowed freely; we all had found the gravy train. So a lot of bad books were produced in that decade; so were good ones, and the good ones ranged from purely military accounts of battles to a study of the 20th Maine to an outpouring of biographies. That decade seemed a capstone to rising interest in "the war" which had received great impetus in the 1930s—with *GWTW* and with Douglas Southall Freeman's monumental *R. E. Lee* in four volumes.

In a decade—the 50s—which greeted more than 100 books on the Civil War, few qualified as landmarks. T. Harry Williams' *Lincoln and His Generals* stands at the top of that select group. It is important, first, because of what it was designed to be. Williams said in his Preface: "I have written...the story of Abraham Lincoln the commander in chief. I have not written a military history of the Civil War or a group biography of the principal Union generals or a description of the military organization of the North, although there is something of all of these in the book. My theme is Lincoln as a director of war and his place in the high command and his influence in developing a modern command system for this nation." Not only was the focus clear, it was also different. And from the beginning, the book brimmed with sharp, sometimes controversial analyses of policies, measures, and men. Although Williams denied he wrote "group biography", he did present capsule assessments of every important Union Army commander in both east and west.

Along with his keen perception of Lincoln as war leader, Williams offered an equally important co-theme as the book progressed, the theme that Lincoln not only evolved an efficient, if haphazard, command system, but also one that was modern and likely to last.

There were several significant contributions to Civil War historiography made in *Lincoln and his Generals*. The first, of course, was the enhancement of Lincoln's reputation, even the foundation of a new part of his reputation as war leader. Colin R. Ballard in *The Military Genius of Abraham Lincoln* (1926) had seen some facets of Lincoln's martial perception. But he had failed to see the direction Lincoln's strategic thinking would take and had missed the importance of the command arrangements evolved in the North. Lincoln came from Williams'

1

pages in full-dimensional ways and especially as a strong military thinker.

U. S. Grant, too, emerged much stronger from Williams' pages. Grant seemed the perfect protagonist for the command system Lincoln groped to create. Not only that, but Grant fitted perfectly Williams "modern" mold. Unlike most of his martial contemporaries, Grant had little romance in his soul and less in his thinking. He saw war as an unpleasant business to be dispatched efficiently and he saw force as the best means of doing that business. Williams especially admired Grant's growing appreciation of power, his growing skill in using it.

As Grant grows in stature, Lee diminishes. Williams summed the two up deftly, if perhaps archly: "Lee was the last of the great old-fashioned generals, Grant the first of the great moderns." (p. 314) Lee, too, in Williams' eyes, lacked the breadth of strategic perspective Grant finally achieved. Lee failed to think, Williams asserted, in "global" terms largely beacuse he did not have a "modern" mind. Tactical skill Lee had, even daring in leading the weaker side, but he missed that bold commitment to hard war which Grant and Sherman, even Stonewall Jackson knew.

Among other contributions, *Lincoln and His Generals* also changed the public, and professional, view of the North at war. There had been a fad in both North and South to look on the Confederacy as the respectable side, the side graced with cavaliers and gentlemen, the side overwhelmed by grizzled men of little talent brandishing machines and filthy riches. Grant's reputation, if he had one, was that of dogged butcher, who drank while his men died in Mississippi and the Wilderness. Once Williams had paraded all the Union high command much of the old mythology vanished. They were, all those bearded, blue-clad folk, human and wistful and patriotic and not so boorish after all. Grant, even Sherman, had social presence, if not grace. Williams performed a vital and unappreciated service in making it acceptable to root for the North.

To students of style, Williams taught lasting lessons in unadorned, hence effective, prose and especially in organization so suited to a theme as to appear utterly natural. The book has what might appear to be imbalances, but Williams argued in his preface that readers who thought too much time was taken up with McClellan rather than more competent companions should recall that Lincoln would most certainly agree!

Lincoln and His Generals is important, too, from the standpoint of the author's career. Forty-five when the book appeared, Williams had before published *Lincoln and the Radicals,* plus a collection of Lincoln documents. So this study of men in command was his first real venture in the Civil War. Its impact, its lasting lessons, its trend-setting, make the author's achievement especially impressive. And its best contribution to the future I'm saving for later discussion.

In 1954 Williams published *P. G. T. Beauregard: Napoleon in Gray,* his first direct try at biography. There were various reasons why it was written, not the least of which was location. Williams taught at LSU; his surroundings reeked of Moonlight, Magnolias, and the Lost Cause. Although professing disdain for such archaisms, Williams felt some urge to get right with his surroundings. Beauregard, Louisiana's own, the South's Great Creole, seemed a logical subject for a Civil Warrior. There were other reasons. Williams said he wanted to write of Beauregard because "this paradoxical personality and his dramatic life interested me so much that I was drawn to study him and to analyze him." Then, too, there was the fact that the Great Creole lacked a modern biography. "He was one of the eight full generals of the Confederacy," Williams noted, "he held six independent commands, and for a period he commanded the Army of Tennessee, one of the two principal Confederate field armies. And his postwar career seems to me more fascinating than that of any other Southern general." (Preface)

It was Beauregard's un-Southernness that most appealed to Williams. Especially in postwar New Orleans did Beauregard seem unlike his Rebel contemporaries in making money; worse, even thriving in the welter of Reconstruction. Much of Beauregard's later life fitted him perfectly for a New Southerner mold, and Williams watched, approving. The book is good, the writing, as usual, effortless, clear, frequently especially suited to the combat and excitement. Character analysis comes through and the small, bristly general full of crochets and punctilio crowds off the pages into trouble everywhere. Never quenchable, Beauregard is in good hands with Williams, and emerges alive and brimming.

Writing Beauregard added to Williams' Civil War perspective. He never quite tolerated the South before, saw the Confederates as "the enemy," and found them a posturing, antiquated, almost *opera bouffe* collection of romantics. Beauregard's career touched almost all levels of Confederate efforts, so Williams learned much about Jefferson Davis (who never looks as good as Lincoln!), Lee, all the other generals, and the problems of Southern high command. Although Louisiana's general had strains of toughness that might have made him a bold and effective field commander, he never really got the chance. "His past errors and his personality quirks," says Williams, "had aroused such a distrust of him among the men in the high command that the opportunity was denied. Had things happened a little differently, he might have gone on to become one of the fighting heroes of the Confederacy." (Preface) Still, Beauregard had great battle qualities, his service in defending Charleston ranked spectacular, and his entire career stood a credit to his cause. How does Williams rate him? "Perhaps," he said, "a New York reporter who interviewed him after the war had it right. He said that Beauregard was not a first-class military man but a first-rate second-class man. Maybe the tragedy of the Confederacy was that it did not have enough first-class generals to go around." (Preface)

Beauregard enhanced Williams' modern war thesis. The Creole represented a strain not strong in the South; had there been more like him, like Stonewall Jackson, the South might have waged a more modern, more efficient, harder war. Seeing Beauregard as atypically Confederate, watching him work on the fringes of the war, made him, in Williams' mind, nearly respectable. He liked the way Beauregard fought. Readers will like the way Williams fights Beauregard's actions. Williams once wrote that any historian who is writing of a battle that D. S. Freeman had already written about will find his work much easier. So, too, for those following in Williams' wake. He learns the battles fully before he writes about them; he clarifies problems in his own mind so they do not confuse readers; he analyzes tactical and logistical problems skillfully and his strategic sense is superior. His battle writing ranks among the best. Nor does he miss a dramatic scene.

In the afternoon of July 21, 1861, the situation on the Confederate left looked desperate. Federal strength piled up relentlessly near the Henry House hill, not far from Manassas. Confused, broken, Southern units crowded back toward the hill; Jackson's brigade stood "like a stone wall," but few others seemed as resolute. Beauregard, whose complex plans had fortunately fizzled, went to the hill to rally his army. "As he rode among the men, he made brief speeches to them to stand fast or shouted dramatic statements. Encouraging the commander of the Washington Artillery of New Orleans, he said, 'Then hold this position, and the day is ours. Three cheers for Louisiana!' When the standard of a South Carolina unit fell, he cried, 'Hand it to me, let me bear the Palmetto Flag.' To a Georgia regiment he shouted, 'I salute the Eighth Georgia with my hat off! History shall never forget you!' One thrilled observer said later that if Beauregard were ever painted it should be as he appeared that day: eyes flaming, the sallow face blazing with enthusiasm, the drawn sword pointing to the enemy." (p. 85)

Lessons of the book were in character and personality analysis and, again, in style. Beauregard was a fine biography but not a trend-setting book. It seems, in fact, almost a reluctant one—Williams found it hard to think well of a Rebel.

Work on the Civil War had whetted his interest in wars, especially American wars. In 1960 he published *Americans at War: The Development of the American Military System*. The book was an outgrowth of the J. P. Young lectures at Memphis State University, delivered in 1956, and the central essay was "The Military Systems of North and South." Here Williams used Clausewitz' dictum that a nation will fight a war in ways that resemble its social system to point up the modern, almost industrially-oriented, command structure of the north, and to show weaknesses in the unorganized Southern system. Modernity remained a major theme, along with the special nature of American soldiers. They were tough, full of initiative, reliable in battle, not always easy to command, eager to get home when the war was won—and they were children of victory, save for 1812 and Korea, and Vietnam. Clearly Williams' own perception of what he meant by "modern" had changed. He quoted Churchill admiringly to the effect that "modern war is total, and it is necessary that technical and professional authorities should be sustained and if necessary directed by heads of government, who have the knowledge which enables them to comprehend not only the military but the political and economic forces at work and who have the power to focus them all upon the goal." (p. 5) The Civil War fitted perfectly into the total war mold. Another theme crowds Williams' mind in these essays, one which had precursors in *Lincoln and His Generals*, even faint echoes in *Beauregard*—the matter of a democracy making war. Again, the question is seen through the perspective of command: How does a democracy command its legions? The Continental Congress worried about this problem, was concerned that too large an army might threaten the state. This worry colored a good deal of Washington's thinking, surely, as it did the thinking of many following presidents. Not only did the possibility of martial dictatorship seem serious, but also the matter of raising and supporting armies. How regimented could a democracy afford to become?

Williams found a unique answer—or an avenue to an answer—as he surveyed the sweep of American military experience. He put his tentative solution in a provocative conclusion to *Americans at War*, a solution which really constituted one of the major themes of this book: the influence of the American genius for improvisation. This quality seemed vital to Williams, one which helped make the Yankee warrior in any war so fearsome and aggressive. If Napoleon thought that every French soldier had a marshal's baton in his knapsack, every American soldier carried stars or the gumption to question anyone who wore them. This precious independence leads Williams to conclude his essays with an important plea to future American war planners. "Surely the historian has something of value to say to the men who will have to deal with these problems (in later wars)....Some of the most serious shortcomings in our military policy have come about because soldiers and civilians have had an inadequate or inaccurate appreciation of our history. The historian can emphasize that no system will work well that breaks too sharply with the American past or ignores too much the Americn experience. And finally, he can remind his fellow countrymen that extemporized arrangements expressing the American spirit may be superior to blueprint charts, and—citing the examples of Washington, of Polk and Scott, and, above all, of Lincoln and Grant—he can show that men are vastly more significant than the structural perfection of any system." (p. 126)

This small book rose rapidly in popularity; it appeared as a secondary text in many college history classes. But its real importance seems to have been missed by most. Here, in full dress, Williams paraded the Global War thesis which he first unveiled in *Lincoln and His Generals*. He used global in the sense of total, in the sense of a war that broke beyond armies to engulf populations and potential, if not real, allies; a war, too, that had international impact. A war so vast demanded new techniques for waging, and the command system Lincoln finally reached with Grant as his General in Chief and Halleck as a kind of Chief of Staff fitted the need for the North. The system evolved; Lincoln never could sit down and draw an organization chart and say, here, this is the system I want. The system came into being because it was logical and because the men who could make it work reached prominence and competence. And that system, according to Williams in *Americans at War,* set a tone which has persisted in American command structures to the present.

Williams rightly worried about democratic command problems as wars became complex and sprawled across continents. So huge were the efforts that Gargantuan command structures would be needed to manage them; size might erode democratic control, might enhance totalitarianism. So he urges, through the last part of his book, the constant reminder of civilian management and stresses that strain of improvisation which is the essence of everyman his own general. Those concerns were vital to America as it began its venture in Vietnam and as it sought ways to control forces scattered the world round.

After *Americans at War* appeared, Williams' interests in command suffered some change. He was moving slowly but fully beyond the Civil War in his thinking and research, even beyond military history. For some time a Louisianian a bit different from Beauregard—but not as different as it might seem, Williams would say—had been crowding into T. Harry's thoughts. And the Kingfish, the things he did and the way he did them were changing the way Williams thought about war.

It may be that this observation is backwards—it may be that an interest in war, especially in command, shaped the way Williams looked at Huey P. Long. There is, at any rate, a connection. Williams, in 1962, published a short book on *McClellan, Sherman and Grant* in which he revealed his growing, changing interpretations—and affections—pretty completely. What interested him—and did, increasingly, as he concentrated on LBJ—was power and its use. Grant, as a general, Williams recognized as of the Long-LBJ stripe, to a degree—a man who learned he had power and then proceeded to learn how to use it. Grant was, in Williams' view, consequently a "modern" general and man—a man who rose above sentiment and was a doer. Sherman, too, put romantic chivalry aside to do the business of winning a "global" war. I would guess that Stark Young's Sherman suited Williams. For Williams, modernity was the essence, the be-all, end-all of achievement. While he tipped a hat toward romance, he openly admired "realists." I suspect that tucked away in his secret pantheon lurked the hero of heroes, Charles Sanders Peirce.

McClellan? A different beast, entirely. Not only a democrat, but almost a traditional romantic, McClellan was a man still devoted to such past protocols as the "rules of war." Far from being a doer, far from seeing war as something to be won by hard and harsh measures, he cherished the old-fashioned notion that victory might be engineered rather than won. And, truth to tell, he not only had the "slows" in Lincoln's apt phrase, he had the "dont's"—don't do too much changing of things to win; don't win if reconciliation is possible without it; don't be nasty if chivalry will do. McClellan is simply not a Williams type. Nor would he have been Huey Long's type, either—one of the reasons Williams began to eye the Kingfish's career with hope.

A commission to participate in *Life's History of the United States* kept T. Harry in the Civil War for a while yet. In 1963 he published two volumes in that distinguished series *The Union Sundered* and *The Union Restored*—which reinforced his long-running themes of modernity and total war. The heroes were still Lincoln and Grant, and the Civil War, more than ever, was the Central Fact of American history. By now the places of the two protagonists in the Williams hierarchy of efficiency could not be topped. Progress went to the progressive; victory went to those who knew it must be won. The people who organized with individuality were the ones who would win. Ergo, Lincoln and Grant were the biggest possible winners. In *The Union Sundered* the Williams touch is even surer with the pen, the characterizations deft and delightful, the tragedy of war ever clear. The Confederacy receives its loser's mite with its leaders given the due owed to vestigials. These were not original books, were not intended to be, but they elevated the tone of a general readership by offering much interpretation along with solid information. Williams was, in some ways, at his boldly guessing best about the past in these volumes aimed for the public at large.

Probably the most original of Williams' Civil War books received the least notoriety, although the historical profession noted it favorably. *Hayes of the Twenty-third* appeared in 1965. It is a book which reveals the author at his versatile best and it surprised some of his friends, who were amused when they first heard he would attempt a book on Rutherford B. Hayes in the Civil War. It seemed to many as a case of hitting a mouse with a tank, a matter of dabbling, surely as a waste of talent. Anyone who studies *Hayes of the Twenty-third* must be impressed once more by the obvious art displayed, by the fact that Williams simply could not write anything dull or inconsequential. The subtitle of this volume sets the emphasis: "The Civil War Volunteer Officer." Williams uses a biographical study of Hayes at war to write a perceptive, penetrating, zestful regimental history. This regimental history ranks really above John Pullen's *Twentieth Maine* (1957)—above it because T. Harry does more than write simply straightforward regimental biography.

All his regular themes are present, some stronger than ever—the Union Forever rides with Hayes and his men. Good leaders are the doers, and Hayes got to be one. In this work, though, Williams' vision shifts from strategy and high command, to tactics and small unit actions. Here he is looking closely at a regiment, the most important component of a Civil War brigade and division. The regiments were usually fraternal, made up of men from the same towns or counties and had a kind of integrity difficult to find in larger organizations. A good Union regiment always made its commander look successful, and good Union regiments generally took much pride in themselves and their colonels.

Hayes' experience proved these generalizations. His men were solid, offered a variety of talents for the need, and trained him fairly well in the niceties of command. Hayes had no training at war when the conflict began, and hence fitted perfectly into the general scheme of things. Few men on either side were trained for battle; the cadre of West Pointers which sprinkled both armies were too few for small unit billets. Company and regimental officers were going to have to be raised up on their own or by their men. An old practice, cherished in democratic armies, of electing company and field officers was early discredited. Hayes was assigned to the Twenty-third by the governor of Ohio and given a major's commission. With that special ingenuity Williams thinks vital to American armies, Hayes learned by doing. He watched veterans, acted carefully but with native skill and rose to command his unit. Sometimes he commanded a brigade, on rarer occasions a division—but basically he was a regimental commander.

Williams looks at Hayes' career as fairly typical and uses it to illustrate the essential level of leadership that fought the main tactical unit of the Union's armies. "The story of any army of the war," Williams observed, "is the story of its units, from the regiment to the brigade to the division and finally on up to the corps. Unless all of these units functioned, the army would not function, no matter how high the genius of its commander. We need very much to know more about these units, and almost the only way we can secure the knowledge is to come upon a unit officer like Hayes who wrote freely about how he ran his unit." (Preface) Hayes' problems, his ways of solving them, the trauma of losing his men, the confusion of organization and of battle, the daily stress of administration, above all the daily drain of responsibility form the highlights of this book. That fairly typical Americans should shoulder these burdens and make so many regiments function is the glory of Williams' tale.

For the author, though, there is a deeper significance to be seen in Hayes' career. He was a volunteer, a non-professional in an army that somehow glorified those officers who boasted West Point education—or at least boasted earlier military service beyond militia day exercises. Although respecting regulars in their scope and place, Williams is at pains to show the virtues of volunteers, and especially the virtues of volunteer, amateur officers. These men, who trained themselves, were the backbone of the war. The volunteer was, to Williams, the quintessential soldier because he retained an open mind toward every situation. This lack of formalist reaction made possible the jury-rigging that so often solved battlefield problems. The Americans' slap-dash attitude toward going to war and doing his best and going home seems to Williams by far the most useful quality in martial make-up. Certainly the American view is far more effective, he thought, than the stylized conformism seen in European officers, troops and wars.

Professional versus citizen soldier problems fascinated Williams and he explained their differences in describing an encounter between Hayes and regular Jesse L. Reno. One night, he wrote, the Twenty-third made camp and the men took some straw from a farmer's stack. Hays thought a loyal farmer would approve; a disloyal one could be ignored, so he said nothing. General Reno saw the thievery and stormed into the men with epithets and rebukes. Hayes "stepped forward and said he had the honor to command these troops, and he defended their conduct. Reno calmed down a bit and asked Hayes for his name. Hayes complied respectfully, but then, although he knew whom he was addressing, asked Reno for his. Reno said that they were in a loyal state and that he would not tolerate pilfering. This was the play-by-the-old-rules psychology of so many West Pointers that Hayes regarded as soft-minded sentiment, and the colonel (Hayes) bridled up again. 'Well,' he said, 'I trust our generals will exhibit the same energy in dealing with our foes that they do in the treatment of their friends.' Naturally offended, Reno asked what the remark meant. Nothing in particular, Hayes answered, at least nothing disrespectful. Reno was not completely mollified, and his anger was heightened by the cheer the men raised for Hayes as he rode off. Later Reno spoke of putting Hayes in irons. Hayes did not worry about being arrested....He was convinced that he had acted correctly. It had been a classic encounter between the professional and the citizen soldier." (pp. 134-35)

Williams' new insights into the value of volunteers was important in his work. Previous concentration on high command and commanders had denied him familiarity with the Billy Yanks of the war. His new vision seemed almost heady and he may well have over-reacted to the pristine prowess of the untrained. His affection for highly professional commanders does not entirely square with this new passion for martial innocence. But the vigor he gave to his views and the essential soundness of his regimental perspective overshadow any possible imbalance.

Imbalance T. Harry often used for effect. This is especially true in lectures or discussions. In discourse, whether in the classroom, at professional meetings, or his own comfortable living room, Williams never lacked vigor. He taught always—in writing or talking. His messages were sometimes familiar—Lincoln and Grant were modern men; war must be won not wooed; power and its uses are the essence of living; honor is not always kept by the weak—sometimes his messages were new. He talked often, late in life, of LBJ and the emerging nature of the American presidency. There was little in Grant's presidential years to charm a student of LBJ—Grant lapsed from military conjuror to political bumbler and the retrogression held no fascination for a student of effective graces. But in discourse Williams advanced the state of American historiography. Always urging ideas, always impatient with pomposity, written or oral, he pressed colleagues and students to think and present their thoughts in readable form. Research and ideas that go unpublished, unshared, struck Williams as wasteful and indefensible. If you think, you want to test your ideas against other thoughts. Thoughts for their own sake reek of preciousness.

To his own graduate students Williams remains both example and symbol. He was friend and confidant and aider and abettor. As teacher, he flayed and whacked generations of students into thinking and producing ideas for criticism. Although he often sounded doctrinaire, he was the most liberal of mentors.

I suspect that Williams would have denied the label "intellectual historian," as he resisted any labels. But he qualified as a stimulator of intellectual study, especially in his discussions of strategy and the nature of democracy. He was also a qualified political scientist, having devoted much time and work to unravelling the intricacies of Union warmaking and of American ways of warring. To some degree he can be shoved into the social historians' niche because he viewed armies as societies with their own characters and politics. But he is best known as a military historian, and I reckon he would not dodge that tag.

War and its waging shaped and unleashed Williams' thinking; he was even at home discussing complexities of command and logistics and operations, the complexities of running modern conflicts. These activities had, for him, the feel of reality. And as he thought about the Civil War, as well as the career of Huey Long—battler of a special kind—Williams realized that the war had not only impact but meaning far beyond the scope of its histories.

In some ways Williams saw the Civil War as part of the drama of American unification, or rather part of the drama of America's emergence as a world power. Somehow, by some means, the romantic fascination with chivalry and past manners had to be gotten rid of before Americans could reach maturity. So, T. Harry, the war was a necessary scourging to make way for modern times. What was lost in the rubble was lost already; what was won was the future.

If the war came to pave the way for progress, there were precursors of the future who waged it. Abraham Lincoln and U. S. Grant were the clearest precursors, were the least archaic of their breed—there were others without politesse, but these two were the models. Since the war cut so healthily and lastingly, there are about its career important lessons for the future of this country. For that reason, mainly, Williams believed Civil War historians—an especially strident, passionate crew—ought to keep at their war. They will retell a message about the changing nature of the Union which can ill be forgotten.

In a way this concern for the historian's mission is prophetic of concern for Williams' work. How take his measure?

His written work tells part of his stature; his lecturing, his teaching still more. The whole man? A gadfly? Certainly. But so much more. A curmudgeon? Often, and yet sometimes with a purpose to incite, to stimulate, to enlighten. A scholar? Yes, in the deepest, best sense. But without the scholastic overtones that turn so many historians musty. A stylist? Yes. But one without rigidity.

His ideas? Always fresh and stimulating, fashioned to inform and to pique curiosity. Are there weaknesses in his ideas? I think he underappreciated the southern strain in the American character. This led him, sometimes, to misjudge the real nature of American soldiers. When he thought of Americans at war, he thought really of Yankees. Consequently when he assessed the heart and soul of U.S. troops on fields far-flung around the globe, he missed the special leaven of humanity that southerners have brought to the martial spirit. Then too, he often overstressed the "global" theme in talking of the Civil War. It was a modern war, of course, but so is every war, just as every war is almost a shadow of earlier ones. And, too, it was the only war in America at the time. I think, sometimes, Williams hides behind the label of modernity when really celebrating the reality of war.

Then there is the persistent wish to press various of his heroes into the "modern" mold. Lincoln and Grant are, obviously, determined patriots, men of iron who keep a firm grasp of objective in the swirling cosmos that was America in the first half of the 1860s. That they were demonstrably more modern than, say, John C. Crittenden or John C. Calhoun is at least debatable. They were scarcely more devoted to success than Jefferson Davis, whose willingness to sacrifice the social fabric of his nation for victory was never really acknowledged by Williams. The "moderns" in the Confederacy all bear strong resemblance to the Shermans of the North—Stonewall Jackson is a kinsman in soul to the great scourge of Georgia; so, too, is Jubal Early, who torched Chambersburg, Pennsylvania, in quest of ransom and hence marked himself pitiless enough for military immortality. But Early and Jackson were simply patriots, too, men fully a part of their own heritage who warred harder than their comrades. The same is true of Grant, who scarcely could be said to outdo Sherman in zeal— but who did not offer the generous surrender terms that Sherman tendered to Joseph E. Johnston.

All of which is to argue that "modernity" and "global" war are relative terms with different meanings to each user. They are terms which tend, on occasion, to give the Civil War a false scope. While it was a "total" war in the sense that it involved civilians as well as soldiers, it lacked the "global" impact of a true "world war."

These caveats about Williams are really nit-picking. He was ever more right than wrong in his generalizations, his guesses, his insights. The very weaknesses I've described spring from one of his unusual strengths—the strength to take new interpretive ground.

Another of his strengths is bold conception of his subjects, which leads to a point I deferred in discussing *Lincoln and His Generals.* You will recall that I said of that book that I was saving its best contribution for later development. The point that interests me I have not seen mentioned by any reviewer, never heard talked about by readers, and am sure is wholly ignored. I submit that *Lincoln and His Generals* is one of the most liberating books ever to appear in Civil War historiography—liberating in that it not only changed the course of professional thinking about the war, but also broke old bonds of interpretation. Until Williams' book appeared, virtually all military accounts of the war were forced into a lingering mode of description. All historians wrote tactically. Many of them believed they were writing strategically because they were following in the footnotes of B. H. Liddell Hart and General J. F. C. Fuller and Sir Frederick Maurice. But these eminent English students of the American Civil War were themselves trapped in the tradition of nineteenth century Grand Tactics passing for true strategy. Williams, perhaps because he hewed hard to his own interpretation, never wallowed in old literary traditions any more than he did in historical traditions. For whatever reason, he broke completely free of tactical bonds when he wrote *Lincoln and His Generals* and gave all followers a clear vision of strategy. Lincoln and his commanders are never permitted to sink into the mire of deployment and wagon needs and petty matters of brigade or divisional movements—the president and his generals are seen at their highest levels of concern. Williams rose above generals to see them as instruments of national policy. Strategy is a thing of the highest levels. Williams set all of us Civil Warriors free of that old trap—and our debt is far larger than we seem to realize. Suffice it to say that *Lincoln and His Generals* really did change the course of Civil War writing.

That bequest alone would qualify Williams for lasting gratitude; his fertile thinking also would mark him as one of the most significant American students of the war. Those qualities combined with his constant searching for new interpretations, his constant goading of others to originality, make his life in Civil War history one of the most important in the last half century.

The Civil War in Song

Archie P. McDonald

The warm glow of the camp fire drew the men a little close. The day's march had been hard, and before supper there was a crust of dust to brush where it had gathered on the clothes, on the skin, and sometimes it seemed, on the soul. It especially settled into the lines around the eyes, and drifted snow-like into the nostrils so that the throat felt dry from breathing through the mouth. Shoulders ached from the weight of packs, feet hurt from picking them up and laying them down a million times or more, legs felt large and expanded from exertion, and there was a gnawing feeling in the mid-section from too much work, too little water, and too little food.

But the fire was warm, the sounds and the smells of the supper being prepared was encouraging, friends were near—at least for a while—and for a moment the war seemed light years away. Someone began to play a jew's-harp, another tapped rhythm on the side of his boot, someone began to hum. Presently a banjo appeared, and the clear precision of its staccato harmony, each string easily distinguished even in a chord, gave a bouncy turn to a familiar ballad. First one and then another began to sing, softly, then overcoming the natural shyness that tightens the throat when first hearing one's own voice, gradually grew more confident. Soon the chorus of camp mates joined in a strong rendition of "Tenting Tonight on the Old Camp Ground." They would sing awhile, until each would be captured by his thoughts; then they would fall silent, and gaze, half-seeing, into the fire.

The music had helped. It had uplifted, sustained, cheered, reindoctrinated, saddened; it had, in short, run the gauntlet of emotions for those who had sung or heard. Music was as much a part of their soldiering as the sergeant's curse or the officer's starch.

In the dim light we have not been able to determine what color their uniforms are, Blue and Grey. It could be one as easily as the other because both sides in the American Civil War enjoyed and used music. They used it naturally, but also deliberately for psychological or morale purposes, as all wars, and even the all too brief periods of peace, have spawned and used music. From "Yankee Doodle" to "The Battle of New Orleans" and the "Star Spangled Banner," through "Over There," and "Praise the Lord and Pass the Ammunition," and more recently, "The Ballad of the Green Berets," Americans had played and sung to boost morale, to convince themselves of their righteousness, to keep the home front in support, and just to get through it.

Music was then, as it is today, a part of every American's heritage and of his way of life. Richard Harwell cites an issue of the *New York Herald* in 1862 that claimed that music was as indispensable to warfare as money. Money, it said, was the sinew of war, but music was its soul:

> Good martial, national music is one of the great advantages we have over the rebels. They have only bands of guerrillas and bridge burners, and are as destitute of musical notes as they are rich in shin plasters. They have not one good national theme, if we except the Rogue's March, for Dixie belongs to our own....Having no music in their souls, they are, as Shakespeare says, "only fit for treason, rebellion, stratagems, masked batteries, spoils and knaverie...."

Confederates would, of course, dispute this monopolistic claim, and with good reason. But there was a need for Southern-based music and it was as eagerly met as the need for Southern textbooks. Verse, easily set to music, soon poured from Southern pens to justify and defend "the Cause" and to urge Confederate soldiers to the heroic efforts of which they alone were capable. Southern music houses such as Blackmar, and Schreiner, began to grind out the sheet music to spread the word.

Both sides called on memory for popular songs to sing in camp and at home. "Home Sweet Home," "Lorena," "All Quiet Along the Potomac To-Night," and "The Girl I left Behind Me" were joined by such compositions as "The Bonnie Blue Flag" and "Maryland My Maryland" in the South, and in the North by the great "Battle Hymn of the Republic." The publishers, of course, had a profit motive, but an emotional element was high on the list of reasons for bringing out the music. The aforementioned pieces were popular, but "Dixie" caught the imagination of the South and went straight to the heart. A band striking it up even in the modern South can evoke an emotional response, and it became the favored song of many football enthusiasts who heard it each Saturday in many Southern cities until recently. Even though it suggests suffering and hardship to many, its bouncy, happy aire causes the foot to pat, the pulse to race, and sometimes the tears to flow.

In the North the moldering condition of John Brown and the lament of the young soldier in "Just Before the Battle, Mother" proved that Yankees also could cry and remember. For both sides it was a great emotional indulgence, and music was used deliberately by both sides for specific purposes. The traditional marching songs were, of course, retained for rhythm and cadence, happy songs were encouraged to cheer the troops, sentimental songs were permitted to remind them of home and why they were fighting, patriotic songs were sung to give determination, novelty songs and parodies inevitably sneaked in to amuse, topical songs appeared to celebrate battles and personalities, and so forth. Service in the

the regimental band or the battalion glee club were considered a major part of army life, and it seemed as if every unit had its favorite drummer boy or its brave, youthful bugler.

Perhaps one reason why music was so important to the war effort was so many people could perform it in some way. A great variety of reed and string instruments traveled along in the bedrolls and knapsacks of the soldiers, and many enjoyed participating in vocal musical expression. With electronics and amplification we are much more vicarious in music; they created their own, and the performance was always "live."

Perhaps now, though unprofessional of voice and finger, we can recapture something of the sound and the spirit, as the announcer used to say, "of those thrilling days of yesteryear." I have prepared a few representative songs that were sung during the war. Some are starkly partisan; others are so appropriate that they could be, and often were, sung by partisans of either side. So long as we remember that the war has been over a long time, either can be fun now. If you happened to know some parts of them, please feel free to join me on the chorus.

LINCOLN AND LIBERTY

As we know, few topics have been so adequately investigated as Abraham Lincoln. Even in music, his cup runneth over. "The Vacant Chair," "Old Abe Lincoln Came Out of the Wilderness," "He Is Gone But We Shall Miss Him," and even musical versions of "Captain, My Captain" testify to his impact. I like this simple piece, "Lincoln and Liberty." It came out of his first election and was used for the second because its alliteration made it a catchy tune for campaign workers and supporters. The words are by Jesse Hutchinson, and the tune was an old one in politics, previously used by several candidates. Irish in origin, it is best known as an instrumental fiddle piece under the title, "Rosin the Beau."

C
Hurrah for the choice of the nation,
             Am
Our chieftain so brave and so true,
C
We'll go for the great reformation,
F C   C
For Lincoln and Liberty, too!
                  C
We'll go for the son of Kentucky
             Am
The hero of Hoosierdom through,
   C
The pride of the "suck-ers" so lucky

```
    F C        G      C
```
For Lincoln and Liberty, too!

They'll find what by felling and mauling,
Our railmaker statesman can do;
For the people are everywhere calling
For Lincoln and Liberty, too!

Then up with the banner so glorious,
The star-spangled red, white, and blue,
We'll fight till our banner's victorious,
For Lincoln and Liberty, too.

THE BATTLE CRY OF FREEDOM

One of the great rallying songs for the Union was "The Battle Cry of Freedom." The words and music are by George F. Root. Its "springing to the call" and denunciation of the traitor were quite effective in recruiting and in rousing a martial spirit.

One testimony will illustrate what effect such songs as "The Battle Cry of Freedom" could have on those who heard it, as well as on its singers. Harwell quotes a Confederate major who stated shortly after the war:

> I shall never forget the first time that I heard "Rally Round the Flag." It was a nasty night during the "Seven Days Fight," and if I remember rightly, it was raining. I was on picket when, just before taps, some fellow in the other side struck up that song and others joined in the chorus until it seemed to me the whole Yankee Army was singing. Tom B...., who was with me, sung out: 'Good Heavens, Cap, what are those fellows made of anyway. Here we've licked 'em six days running, and now on the eve of the seventh, they're singing Rally Round the Flag.' I am not naturally superstitious, but I tell you that song sounded to me like the knell of doom, and my heart went down into my boots; and though I've tried to do my duty, it has been an uphill fight with me ever since that.

THE BATTLE CRY OF FREEDOM

```
        G             Em            C        C
```
Oh, we'll rally 'round the flag boys, we'll rally once again
```
G                        D7       A
```
Shouting the battle cry of freedom;
```
   G                            C
```
We will rally from the hillside, we'll gather from the plain,
```
   G                    D7    G
```
Shouting the battle cry of freedom.

We are springing to the call of our brothers gone before,
Shouting the battle cry of freedom;
And we'll fill the vacant ranks will a million freemen more,
Shouting the battle cry of freedom.

We will welcome our numbers the loyal, true, and brave,
Shouting the battle cry of freedom;
And although they may be poor not a man shall be a slave,
Shouting the battle cry of freedom.

So we're spring to the call from the East and from the West.
Shouting the battle cry of freedom;
And we'll hurl the Rebel crew from the land we love the best,
Shouting the battle cry of freedom.

Chorus

C
The Union forever, Hurrah, boys, hurrah!
                                        D
Down with the traitor, Up with the star;
G   Em
While we rally 'round the flag, boys,
C   G
Rally once again,
G   D7   G
Shouting the battle cry for freedom.

THE YELLOW ROSE OF TEXAS

"The Yellow Rose of Texas" was one of many songs that featured state pride. Like other popular pieces of the day, it was born on the minstrel circuit, first being published in 1853 by an anonymous author. It was, of course, a favorite of the Texas troops serving in other states because it gave them an opportunity to swagger a bit in song, something Texans will do any way they can. The original version probably contained the identification of the singer as a "darkey," and the "yellow" may have referred to a mulatto girl friend. It will be presented both ways here for flavor. The final verse illustrates how the song lent itself to parody as it laments the appointment of John B. Hood to replace Joseph E. Johnston in command in the West.

THE YELLOW ROSE OF TEXAS

G
There's a yellow rose in Texas that I am going to see,
     D7
No other soldier knows her, no soldier, on-ly me;
G
She cried so when I left her, it like to broke my heart,

<pre>
        D7   G   D7   G
And if I ever find her, we nev-er more will part.
</pre>

Where the Rio Grande is flowing and the starry skies are bright,
She walks along the river in the quiet summer night;
She thinks if I remember, when we parted long ago,
I promised to come back again and not to leave her so.

Oh, now I'm going to find her, for my heart is full of woe,
We'll sing the song together, that we sung so long ago;
We'll play the banjo gaily, and sing the songs of yore,
And the Yellow Rose of Texas, shall be mine forevermore.

Chorus

<pre>
        G   (Darkie)
She's the sweet-est rose of col-or this sol-dier ev-er knew,
                          D7
Her eyes are bright as dia-monds, they spar-kle like the dew;
        G
You may talk a-bout your dear-est May and sing of Ro-sa Lee,
        D7   G   D7   G
But the Yel-low Rose of Texas beats the belles of Ten-nes-see.
</pre>

And then the wag wrote...

Oh, now I'm going southward, for my heart is full of woe.
I'm going back to Georgia, to find my Uncle Joe.
You may talk about your Beauregard, and Sing of Gena Lee.
But the Gallant Hood of Texas, played Hell in Tennessee.

LORENA

One of the most frequently sung of all Civil War songs, largely because of its wide popularity on both sides, was "Lorena." It was published in 1857. The lyrics were written by the Reverend H. D. L. Webster and J. P. Webster supplied the music. It went through several editions and gradually has become more associated with the South than with the North. Perhaps it is its somberness, its lilting sadness that makes us think of it more in Confederate, greyish ways. It is typical, also, of the nineteenth-century romance and sense of melodrama that can be seen in so much of its music. Like "Aura Lea" and "Annie Laurie," it speaks of lovers and their painful separation by the war. But perhaps "Lorena" did wait.

LORENA

<pre>
        G   G7   C
The years creep slow-ly by, Lo-re-na,
        D7   G
The snow is on the grass a-gain;
</pre>

<pre>
                G7   C
</pre>
The sun's low down the sky, Lo-re-na,
<pre>
    D7   G
</pre>
The frost gleams where the flow'rs have been.
<pre>
    Em   Am
</pre>
But the heart throbs on as warm-ly now,
<pre>
                              Em
</pre>
As when the sum-mer days were nigh;
<pre>
D7   G   G7   C
</pre>
Oh!—the sun nev-er dip so low,—
<pre>
    D7   G
</pre>
A-down af-fec-tion's cloud-less sky.

A hundred months have passed, Lorena,
Since last I held that hand in mine.
And felt the pulse beat fast, Lorena,
Though mine beat faster far than thine.
A hundred months, 'twas flowery May,
When up the hilly slope we climbed,
To watch the dying of the day,
And hear the distant church bells chime.

WHEN JOHNNY COMES MARCHING HOME

"When Johnny Comes Marching Home" is a happy song because it is bringing the soldier home. It was written by Patrick S. Gilmore, bandmaster of the Union Army Band. At the time Gilmore used the pseudonym of Louis Lambert. The tune, by Gilmore's testimony, came to him from a Negro, but it is unlikely that it is a traditional piece of that race. It sounds quite Irish, although this origin cannot be proven, and sounds much like the Revolutionary aire, "Johnny I Hardly Knew Ye," which was used during the Crimean War.

Gilmore was an Irishman, born in Ballygar, Galway County, in 1829. He immigrated in the 1840s and like many others of his countrymen, joined the Army. After the war Gilmore specialized in very large orchestras and choruses, and his "Johnny" became more popular than ever, perhaps because its mood so fitted the homecoming aspects of Reconstruction. Like other pieces that are essentially Union, its Americanness made it also appropriate for the Confederates, and indeed, Johnny is usually thought of as a Rebel. It has been used widely in other wars in which the United States has been a party.

WHEN JOHNNY COMES MARCHING HOME

<pre>
            Em
</pre>
When Johnny comes marching home again,
<pre>
    D
</pre>
Hurrah, Hurrah!

      Em
We'll give him a hearty welcome then,
      G   B7
Hurrah, Hurrah!
      Em   D
Men will cheer and the boys will shout,
      C   B7
The ladies they will all turn out,
      Em D   C   B7   Em
and we'll all feel gay when Johnny comes
marching home.

The old church bell will peal with joy,
   Hurrah, Hurrah!
To welcome home our darling boy,
   Hurrah, Hurrah!
The village lads and lassies say,
With roses they will strew the way,
And we'll all feel gay when Johnny comes
   marching home.

Let love and friendship on that day,
   Hurrah, Hurrah!
Their choicest treasures then display,
   Hurrah, Hurrah!
And let each one perform some part,
To fill with joy the warrior's heart,
And we'll all feel gay when Johnny comes
   marching home.

GOOBER PEAS

One of the best-loved and most remembered novelty numbers from the 1860s, "Goober Peas," deals with the Southerners' alleged weakness for peanuts. It was sung during the war and passed on orally, and finally reached print in 1866 when it was published by A. E. Blackmar. This version claimed that the words were by an A. Pindar while the music was assigned as the work of a P. Nutt. The pseudonyms "goober" and "pinda" are Gullah dialect words referring to the peanut, so it is probable that Blackmar compiled the music after hearing it sung by soldiers. It speaks of the good-natured rivalry between infantry and cavalry, of the boredom of camp life, and it pokes fun at the Army itself.

GOOBER PEAS

      C   F   C
Sitting by the roadside on a summer day

                                       G7
Chatting with my messmates, passing time away,
G   F   C
Lying in the shadow underneath the trees,
              F   C   G7   C
Goodness how delicious, eating goober peas!

When a horseman passes the soldiers have a rule,
To cry out at their loudest "Mister Here's your mule"
But another pleasure, enchantinger than these,
Is wearing out your Grinders, eating goober peas!

Just before the battle the General hears a row,
He says "the Yanks are coming, I hear their rifles now."
He turns around in wonder, and what do you think he sees?
The Georgia Militia, eating goober peas!

   Chorus

         C   C   F   F
Peas! Peas! Peas! Peas!
        G7   C
Eating goober peas!
             F   G   G7   C
Goodness how delicious, eating goober peas!

MARCHING THROUGH GEORGIA

   The celebrated march through southern Georgia following the Atlanta Campaign commanded by William T. Sherman excited Northern opinion as did few maneuvers of the American Civil War. And it would be accurate to say that it excited the South as well. One of the most sucessful campaigns of the war, its "live off the land" and "carry the war to the enemy's civilians" aspects made it both memorable and regrettable. These tactics were justified as a measure of total, modern war and ironically they helped to romanticize Sherman. In the long run, as I have often heard Frank Vandiver say, it was a great boon to the South because it helped make poverty respectable. He swears that a former student from East Texas told him that the old family place in East Texas was burned and looted by Sherman's Bummers.

   This is but one of the poems set to music that lionized Sherman's deeds, but it is the best known and the one that still burns, if you will pardon the expression, Southerners the most. I am reminded that when President Grover Cleveland's personal investigator, ex-Congressman James A. Blount, who was also an ex-cavalry commander from Georgia, traveled to Hawaii to report on that province's qualifications for annexation, that he was met by the islanders well intentioned but catastrophic *faux pas* of having the island band play "Marching Through Georgia." Apparently it was the only American song that they knew.

Richard Bales claims that "Marching Through Georgia" was played during both World War I and II, and even used by the invading Japanese in 1905 as they marched through Port Arthur in the Russo-Japanese War.

The song was written by Henry C. Work, and has been borrowed by several reform movements, including women's suffrage. Irwin Silbur says that of all Union songs, this one is the most disliked in the modern South.

MARCHING THROUGH GEORGIA

G   C   G
Bring the good old bugle, boys, we'll sing another song;
         D7   D7
Sing it with a spirit that will start the world along,
G   G   G   G
Sing it as we used to sing it, fifty thousand strong,
D7   G
While we were march-ing through Geor-gia.

How the darkeys shouted when they heard the joyful sound!
How the turkeys gobbled which our commissary found!
How the sweet potatoes even started from the ground,
While we were marching through Georgia.

Yes, and there were Union men who wept with joyful tears,
When they saw the honored flag they had not seen for years;
Hardly could they be restrained from breaking forth in cheers,
While we were marching through Georgia.

"Sherman's dashing Yankee boys will never reach the coast!"
So the saucy Rebels said, and 'twas a handsome boast;
Had they not forgot, alas! to reckon with the host,
While we were marching through Georgia.

So we made a thoroughfare for Freedom and her train,
Sixty miles in latitude, three hundred to the main;
Treason fled before us, for resistance was in vain.
While we were marching through Georgia.

Chorus

G   G   G
Hurrah! Hurrah! We bring the jubilee!
G   D7
Hurrah! Hurrah! The flag that makes you free!
G   C   G   G
So we sang the chorus from Atlanta to the sea,

D7   G
While we were marching through Georgia.

BATTLE HYMN OF THE REPUBLIC (John Brown's Body)

Often familiar melodies have been used by several lyricists as a medium to bring their verse to the attention of the public. This is especially true of the Civil War melody best known as "John Brown's Body." Almost automatically one assumes that this refers to Osawattamie John Brown, also of Harper's Ferry fame. Unquestionably it does to us; and during the war, it was thus assumed by most who sang it. However, the John Brown to whom it originally referred was a sergeant in the Second Battalion, Boston Light Infantry, Massachusetts Volunteer Militia. Brown sang tenor in the battalion glee club, and it was something of an inside joke among his comrades that he shared the name of a famous martyr/villain. The group wrote the parody to the music of an old Methodist tune, and they unceremoniously sprung it on the public while the Massachusetts Twelfth Regiment marched in a parade down Broadway in New York City. Needless to say, it was an instant success. The regiment was named the Hallelujah Regiment and the song swept the country. Here is a verse of one of the best known versions:

> John Brown's body lies a-moldering in the grave,
> While weep the sons of bondage he ventured to all save
> But though he lost his life in struggling for the slave,
> His truth is marching on.

Using the same tune, Julia Ward Howe penned what is perhaps the greatest of all Civil War songs. Indeed, it is for the ages. Mrs. Ward had come to Washington in late November 1861 with her husband, Dr. Samuel Gridley Howe, who was a member of the Sanitary Commission. They attended reviews in the army camps and heard depressing stories of low recruitment. It was suggested that something was needed to bolster lagging spirits, and when they overheard some soldiers singing the already familiar "John Brown's Body," the Reverend James Freeman Clarke, also on the tour, suggested that Mrs. Ward write more appropriate words to the tune. Mrs. Ward was inspired to do so, but could not get started. She returned to Willard's Hotel and tried to concentrate, still with little success. She determined to retire, and upon doing so, fell quickly to sleep. Harwell gives her testimony concerning the composition:

> I went to bed as usual, but awoke next morning in the gray of the early dawn, and to my astonishment found that the wished-for lines were arranging themselves in my brain. I lay quite still until the last

23

verse had completed itself in my thoughts, then hastily arose, saying to myself, "I shall lose this if I don't write it down immediately." I searched for an old sheet of paper and an old stump of a pen which I had had the night before, and began to scrawl the lines almost without looking, as I had learned to do often by scratching down verses in the darkened room where my little children were sleeping. Having completed this, I lay down again and fell asleep, but not without feeling that something of importance had happened to me.

It had. Here is the most inspiring musical legacy of the century, presented without chorus until the end. You know the words; join me when we get to the chorus.

THE BATTLE HYMN OF THE REPUBLIC

G
Mine eyes have seen the glory of the coming of the Lord;
    C   G
He is trampling out the vintage where the grapes of wrath are
    stored.
                                     G   B7   Em
He hath loosed the fateful lightning of His terrible swift sword,
    Am   G   D7 G
His truth is marching on.

I have seen Him in the watch fires of a hundred circling camps;
They have builded Him an altar in the evening dews and damps;
I can read His righteous sentence by the dim and flaring lamps,
His day is marching on.

I have read a fiery gospel writ in burnished rows of steel:
"As ye deal with My contemners, so with you My Grace shall deal;
Let the Hero, born of woman, crush the serpent with his heel,
Since God is marching on."

He has sounded forth the trumpet that shall never call retreat;
He is sifting out the hearts of men before His Judgment Seat;
Oh! be swift, my soul, to answer Him, be jubilant, my feet!
Our God is marching on.

In the beauty of the lilies Christ was born across the sea,
With a glory in his bosom that transfigures you and me;
As He died to make men holy, let us die to make men free,
While God is marching on.

Chorus

G
Glo-ry, Glo-ry Hal-le-lu-jah,
C   G
Glo-ry, Glo-ry Hal-le-lu-jah,
        B7 Em
Glo-ry, Glo-ry Hal-le-lu- jah,
   Am   G D7 G
His truth is march-ing on!

I'M A GOOD OLD REBEL

Now for a little balance, "I'm A Good Old Rebel" really belongs to the Reconstruction Era but obviously was produced by the war. It reveals considerable Southern bitterness at having lost, but if taken tongue in cheek, also shows a good sense of humor. It rolls all the bitter gall of Southern resentment into one lump, and was in Southern thought, appropriately and respectfully dedicated to Thaddeus Stevens. It was written by Major Innes Randolph under the title "The Lay of the Last Rebel," and was repeated at veterans' meetings and at Civil War Round Table meetings ever since under the title of "I'm A Good Old Rebel." It is a perfect companion piece to the familiar "Forget, Hell" caricature so popular during the Civil War Centennial. And for some reason it always makes me think of Jubal Early.

OH, I'M A GOOD OLD REBEL

C   G7
Oh, I'm a good old Rebel, Now that's just what I am,
 F   C
For this "Fair Land of Freedom" I do not give a damn!
   F   C
I'm glad I fit against it, I only wish we'd won,
            G7   C
And I don't want no pardon For anything I done.

I hates the Constitution, This Great Republic, too,
I hates the Freedman's Buro, In uniforms of blue;
I hates the nasty eagle, with all his brag and fuss,
The lyin', thievin' Yankees, I hates 'em wuss and wuss.

I followed Old Marse Robert for four year, near about,
Got wounded in three places And starved at P'int Lookout;
I cotched the "roomatism," A-campin' in the snow,
But I killed a chance o' Yankees, I'd like to kill some mo'.

Three hundred thousand Yankees Is still in Southern dust;
We got three hundred thousand Before they conquered us;
They died of Southern fever, And Southern steel and shot,

I wish it was three million, Instead of what we got.

I can't take up my musket, And fight 'em now no more,
But I ain't a goint to love 'em, And that is sarten sure;
And I don't want no pardon For what I was and am,
I won't be reconstructed And I don't give a damn!

DIXIE

For most Southerners there is really only one Civil War song. Faced with
the loss of the "Star Spangled Banner" and Old Glory, they soon had a new
flag and a new song that symbolized their spirit, their ideals. Many songs can-
didated for the purpose and never caught on. One did seem appropriate, but
it had several things that might have disqualified it if they had been widely
known. For one thing, it was written by a Yankee. Daniel Decatur Emmett,
who often contributed music to Dan Bryant's Minstrels, wrote the gay, fast-
tempoed song in 1859, about two years after he joined the troupe. He had experienced some success already with "Old Dan Tucker," written when he was
only a teenager.

Emmett had ran away from home to join first the Army and then the minstrel
show, and in 1843 he helped to organize the Virginia Minstrels. In 1859 he was
with Bryant, who expressed a desire for a new "walk-around" to use in the streets
as advertisement. "Dixie" was the answer. It was used almost immediately in
the political campaign in 1860, and introduced to the South by Mrs. John Wood
in New Orleans as a marching piece for forty female Zouaves in a review. In
New Orleans it was passed to the organizing Confederate armies and soon
became *the* Song of the South. Many parodies soon appeared, such as the "Union
Dixie," and Albert Pike's "Southreons Dixie." Back in New Orleans, P. P. Werlein
published the song as "I Wish I Was in Dixie's Land," but there were several
other publications under many names available for purchase in sheet music form.
We have all heard the theories of what the term means: Mason's and Dixon's
Line; the good master named Dix whose plantation slaves longed to live upon;
Dix, the French term for ten; and as a pseudonym for "home" in a Negro dialect.
Richard B. Harwell quotes a story about Emmett and his reaction to the Con-
federate appropriation of his piece.

Quoting T. Allston Brown...:"This is the origin of 'Dixie' and you can
swear to it!

"I give it as received from Dan Emmett himself and from my own
recollection. While I was dramatic editor of the *New York Clipper,*
in 1861, Tom Kingsland of Dodsworth's Band, was proprietor of a
famous bar and lunch room in Broome Street, much frequented by

actors, newspapermen, minstrels, etc. D. T. Morgan, having come back from the army, in the winter, dropped in at Kingsland's.

"Sitting at the several tables and all, apparently, having a good time, were about twenty jovial fellows and among them, Dan Bryant. I was soon at a table with him, Nelse Seymour, Dan Emmett and others.

"Morgan told Emmett that, at night, he could hear the Confederate bands playing Dixie; and that they seemed to have adopted it down South, as their national air. Emmett replied warmly:

" 'Yes: and if I had known to what use they were going to put my song, I will be damned if I'd have written it!' "

Whether or not Emmett wanted Southerners to have his song, they got it. It is the symbol of all that the Confederacy might have been, and its happy sound summons us all, Yankee and Rebel alike, to a recollection of those wonderful, terrible, happy, sad, memorable days of the Civil War. It is the only way I could end such a program in Louisiana.

DIXIE

        C   G7
Oh I wish I were in the land of cotton,
F
Old times there are Not forgotten,
      C   G7   C
Look away! Look away! Look away! Dixie Land.
                  C7
In Dixie Land where I was born,
   F
Early on one frosty mornin',
      C   G7   C
Look away! Look away! Look away! Dixie Land.
    C   F   D7   G7
Then I wish I was in Dixie, Hooray! Hooray!
    C   F
In Dixie Land I'll take my stand
    C   G7
To live and die in Dixie,
    C   G7   C   G7   C
Away, away, away down south in Dixie.
Away, away, away down south in Dixie!

Bibliographic Essay

More than twenty years ago T. Harry Williams arranged for me to present a program to the Baton Rouge Civil War Round Table. Since I had addressed that group already and told them everything I knew about the Civil War, and further, since I recently had acquired a guitar, I suggested that I do a series of songs associated with the war. T. Harry agreed, then grew apprehensive. When I arrived at the meeting, he quickly came over to me and snorted, "You *really* aren't going to *sing*, are you?" "Yes Sir," I replied, "At least I am going to try." I never knew if that was his way of saying "good luck," or if he was truly concerned. After performing my program at the symposium in Hammond, Louisiana, in June 1988, Stell Williams relieved my mind. "Harry is proud of you right now," she said. I hope he was then, too.

What I presented to the symposium was intended for a live audience and I am aware that much is lost when such a program is adapted for print. So if the reader wishes to recreate the music, guitar chords are provided with the first verse of each song. This may not make "Harry" just as proud, but it is the best that can be done under the circumstances.

When I hastily prepared this program for Dr. Williams, I drew upon the resources of the music library at Stephen F. Austin State University, my employer, but I expect the sources that appear below, and more, can be found in any university and many municipal libraries. The introductions were prepared so long ago, and intended for oral presentation only, that I failed to note specific page numbers and sometimes even what information came from this or that book. Therefore, please be assured that the introductory material is wholly the original work of my betters in this field and that my debt to them is complete whether or not it is presented with traditional footnotes. I claim no original research in this subject; I am merely a "busker" of an event that has fascinated me for all of my life. More, however, is required for me to accompany my scholarly colleagues in this record of our proceedings. So, for those who are interested in the music of the American Civil War, and in what scholars have said about it, please see the following works.

Bernard, Kenneth, *Lincoln and the Music of the Civil War*. Caxton Printers: Caldwell, Idaho, 1966.

Child, Francis James, *War Songs for Freemen*. Ticknor & Field: Boston, 1863.

Enurium, E. K., *Stories of the Civil War*. W. A. Wilde Co.: Natick, Mass., 1960.

Glass, P., ed., *The Spirit of the Sixties*. Educational Publishers: St. Louis, 1965.

Harwell, Richard B., *Confederate Carrousel: Southern Songs of the Sixties*. Civil War Round Table: Chicago, 1950.

Harwell, Richard B., *Songs of the Confederacy*. Broadcast Music: New York, 1951.

Harwell, Richard B., *The Confederate Search for a National Song.*

Harwell, Richard B., Confederate Music. University of North Carolina: Chapel Hill, 1950.

Heaps, Willard A. and Porter W., *The Singing Sixties.* University of Oklahoma Press: Norman, 1966.

Howard, John Tasker, *Our American Music.* Thomas Y. Crowell: New York, 1951.

Mitchell, Mrs. M. L., *Songs of the Confederacy and Plantation Melodies.* George R. Jennings & Co.: Cincinnati, 1901.

Moore, Frank, *Personal and Political Ballads.* George P. Putnam: New York, 1864.

Moore, Frank, *Rebel Rhyme and Rhapsodies.* George P. Putnam: New York, 1864.

Moore, Frank, ed., *Songs and Ballads of the Southern People.* D. Appleton: New York, 1866.

Moore, Frank, *The Civil War in Song and Story.* P. F. Collier: New York, 1889.

Oldroy, O.H., *Good Old Songs We Used to Sing From 61-65.* Osborn H. Oldroy & Co.: Washington, D.C., 1902.

Pearson, E. W., *The War of Rebellion in Song and Story.* Republican Press Association: Concord, N.H., 1874.

Porter, D., *Lyrics of the Lost Cause.* D. Porter & Co.: Cascade, Ore., 1914.

Ripley, F. H., *War Songs for Schools.* Oliver Aitson Co.: Boston.

Silber, Irwin, *Songs of the Civil War.* Columbia University Press: New York, 1960.

Silber, Irwin, *Soldier Songs and Home-Front Ballads of the Civil War.* Oak Publications: New York, 1964.

Stanton, K. E., *Old Southern Songs of the Period of the Confederacy.* Samuel French Co.: New York, 1926.

Westcott, Mrs. W. H., *Songs of the Good War.* Entertainment Publishing Company: New York.

Wharton, H. M., *War Songs and Poems of the Southern Confederacy,* W. E. Scull: Washington, 1904.

Williams, Alfred M., *Studies in Folk-Song and Popular Poetry.* Houghton Mifflin Co.: Boston, 1894.

Williams, H. L., ed., *War Songs of the Blue and Grey.* Hurst & Co.: New York.

Petersburg Autumn:
The Battle of Poplar Spring Church

Richard J. Sommers

Beauregard was gone. From early May until late September, 1864, that distinguished Confederate general, whom Professor T. Harry Williams so aptly termed "Napoleon in Gray," had defended Petersburg, Virginia, against five Federal onslaughts. But as summer ended, so did Beauregard's service in the Eastern Theater. On September 23, the Louisianian departed on an inspection tour of the lower Atlantic coast; he would never return to the fighting front in Virginia. Ahead of him lay theater command in the West. Behind him remained the continuing Siege of Petersburg.[1]

For the Southerners, the defense of Petersburg was imperative. In 1860, this "Cockade City," as Petersburg was called, was one of the largest cities in the South. It was the site of lead works crucial to the war effort. But, most of all, Petersburg was the rail center of Richmond. From northeast, southeast, south, and west, railroads entered Petersburg. From the city, a single rail line ran north through Chesterfield County to Richmond. The capital's link to the Atlantic ports, to which blockade runners brought badly needed supplies, and to Lynchburg and the head of the Great Valley of the Appalachians, with its wealth of natural resources, thus ran through Petersburg. Only one other railroad, the line heading southwest through Danville to the Carolina piedmont, connected Richmond to the Confederate interior. Even that Danville line, moreover, would be imperilled if Petersburg fell. Saving the Cockade City was thus essential to saving Richmond itself. Capturing the communications center would correspondingly compromise the capital.

Ever since early May, 1864, Northern armies had tried to take Petersburg. Often they came close, but always they failed. In mid-June, Lieutenant General Ulysses S. Grant himself, the Union General-in-Chief, struck at Petersburg with the main Federal force in the East. In four days of fierce fighting, he nearly captured Petersburg, but Beauregard held on long enough for General R. E. Lee's main Confederate army to arrive and save the city.

Lee's complete repulse of the final Yankee attack on June 18, indeed, was what at last convinced Grant that frontal attacks, which had served him so well in the West from 1861 to 1863, just were not working against Lee and the Army of Northern Virginia in the East in 1864. Thereafter, the Illinoisan not only refrained from such frontal attacks but explicitly forbade them.[2]

His tactics thus changed, but his strategy remained the same as when he first broke camp in central Virginia on May 4: to throw his left beyond the Secessionist right. He accordingly sent two corps against the Weldon Railroad south of Petersburg. They were completely defeated on June 22-23. With that debacle, the mobile warfare of spring gave way to the stagnation of summer, and the Siege of Petersburg began.[3]

It was, to be sure, not a pure siege in a classic European sense: a close investment, in which the beleaguering army attempts to scale, batter down, or blow up the city's ramparts while trying to starve its surrounded garrison into submission. Yet the Petersburg operation was nonetheless a siege in the grand-tactical and strategic sense. Strategically, within the overall course of the Civil War and the course of the war in the East, the Bluecoats confronted Lee with the compelling imperative of saving his capital and its communications center, fixed him in place for the immediate defense of those cities, and thus denied him the strategic mobility which had been the hallmark of his success in 1862 and 1863.

The Yankee siege lines east of Petersburg, within rifle range of the Confederate works, were the means for pinning the Butternut army in position. With their incessant shelling and sharpshooting, moreover, those siege lines wore down the defenders psychologically as well as physically. And, of course, they represented the potential threat that if the Southern garrison grew too weak, the besieging army might attack it directly. But the most important grand-tactical function which the siege lines served was as a great entrenched camp in which the Union army could rest from the rigors of spring and from which Federal forays could sally around both Confederate flanks: northward across James River directly against Richmond and southwestward into the open country below Petersburg against the remaining supply lines.[4]

In late July and again in mid-August such forays punctuated the siege. Three of them the Confederates checked after heavy fighting. But on August 18, the Northerners finally cut the Weldon Railroad at Globe Tavern. Repeated counterattacks by Beauregard and then by Lee himself shook the Yankees but could not shake their clutch. A week later, however, the Graycoats did drive back a Union effort to tear up those tracks south of the tavern.

The Weldon Railroad thus remained in Confederate hands as far north as Stony Creek Depot, sixteen miles south of Globe Tavern. From the depot, supplies were transshipped by wagon over the backroads of Dinwiddie County into the Boydton Plank Road and thence into Petersburg. Containing the western Federal salient at Globe Tavern and protecting the wagon roads and the last rail line—the Southside Railroad running west across the Danville Railroad to Lynchburg—were Lee's main challenges grand tactically as summer ended. Breaking out from Globe Tavern, breaching the forward Butternut defenses, cutting those last supply lines, and putting Petersburg under close siege became the corresponding Northern objectives.

Another five weeks of relative quiescence went by, but by late September, in this beginning of Petersburg autumn, Grant was again ready to strike. Federal victories in the Shenandoah Valley on September 19 and 22 caused him to attack a week ahead of schedule in order to prevent reinforcements from being sent from Petersburg to the Blue Ridge or else to take advantage of the absence of any that did leave.[5] And intelligence that Richmond itself was vulnerable led Grant, for the third time in two months, to launch nearly simultaneous attacks on both sides of the James instead of making a massive drive below Petersburg as originally intended.

To prepare for—or to guard against—that original massive drive, both sides kept most of their forces south of the Appomattox River around Petersburg as autumn began. Out of Grant's overall command of 102,000 men, three-quarters served on the Petersburg sector: the entire Army of the Potomac and the X Corps and Cavalry Division of the Army of the James. Another 15,700 men of the latter army occupied Bermuda Hundred on the left bank of the Appomattox northeast of Petersburg, and 4,300 more troops held two outposts on the Peninsula: the northside of James River. The remaining 6,900 Bluecoats garrisoned Grant's headquarters and main supply base at City Point as well as three posts down the James from there.

The Confederates correspondingly concentrated around the Cockade City. Some 37,000 of Lee's 53,000 troops served there. Another 7,500 manned the trenches and water batteries in Chesterfield County. The remaining 8,600 were stationed north of the James, 4,400 on the front lines and the rest back near Richmond itself. Nearly 5,000 of those soldiers on the Peninsula were inexperienced reserves, militia, local defense troops, or heavy artillery.

With its garrison weak in numbers and quality, Richmond looked a tempting target to Union intelligence officers and planners. To seize this prize, Major General Benjamin F. Butler massed 26,000 men of his Army of the James, including the X Army Corps and Cavalry Division, which had been south of the Appomattox, as well as most of the Bermuda Hundred garrison. Early on Thursday, September 29, he threw a second bridge across the James and unleashed a devastating two-pronged attack which breached or rendered untenable the entire Southern front line.

The ensuing Battle of Chaffin's Bluff threw Richmond into the greatest clear and present danger of capture by a major army which could have held her that the city ever faced right up to the day of her downfall. That her downfall came half a year later, on April 3 of 1865, instead of September 29, was due to Union miscalculations and mistakes, on the one hand, and to the almost incredible heroism and skill of the Graycoat defenders, on the other. The combination gave time for reinforcements from Richmond and the Southside to arrive. Three brigades from the capital, one from Chesterfield, and eight from Petersburg were rushed to the front: some 15,000 men. Four more brigades, 5,500 strong, from Petersburg headed for the Peninsula but were recalled before reaching the James. To meet this grave danger, Lee himself shifted his headquarters to the threatened sector.

So many troops concentrated on the Northside primarily to contain the Federals and save the capital. Yet, as throughout the war, Lee pursued a defensive strategy through offensive tactics. On September 30, he launched a major counterattack to drive the Northerners back. That attack, however, was totally repulsed, and over the next two days the battle rapidly wound down. For virtually the rest of the Petersburg Campaign, the Army of the James remained on the Peninsula, threatening Richmond directly.

While fighting for Richmond raged on the Northside, the armies around Petersburg readied themselves for action. Grant placed Major General George G. Meade's Army of the Potomac on stand-by, September 29, with orders to take advantage of any perceived reduction of Secessionist strength and strike for the Southside Railroad or even the Cockade City itself.

Throughout the day, Thursday, signs of such reduction proved contradictory, however. Union lookouts, to be sure, readily spotted numerous enemy columns marching toward Richmond. Yet those same observers also detected sizable Confederate forces massing in the main works of Petersburg. Two reconnaissances in force further suggested that not only those main works but even the forward line along the Squirrel Level Road just west of Globe Tavern were still held in strength. And when the one remaining Union cavalry division probed the open country south of the city, through which Confederate supply lines ran, it provoked a counterattack which pushed it back almost to the Weldon Railroad.

That cavalry probe caused two Confederate mounted brigades which were marching toward the Peninsula to remain in Dinwiddie County. Yet basically Lee was bluffing. His shows of force on the Southside were designed to mask his weakness. Of his 37,000 men south of the Appomattox River, he sent 10,000 to the Peninsula and issued orders for another 5,500, including those two cavalry brigades, to stand by to follow. Indeed, so desperate was the situation north of James River that Lee was prepared to abandon Petersburg if necessary to save Richmond.[6] Yet, as so often in the war, he did not equate danger with disaster. When possible, Lee did not fall back; he fought back. He, therefore, tried to retain the communications center as well as the capital.

With his own presence required on the Northside, Lee entrusted the defense of Petersburg to his senior subordinate. Now that Beauregard was no longer present, Lieutenant General Ambrose Powell Hill, commanding the III Army

Corps, received that mission. Hill let the Cavalry Corps cover the supply lines south of town, including putting one dismounted cavalry brigade in the advanced line along the Squirrel Level Road. The two infantry brigades which had manned that line moved northward into Petersburg's main defenses. Hill concentrated his forces right around the city to create the appearance of strength and to be ready to counterattack or to withdraw, as circumstances required. A mere 20,200 infantry and artillery and 6,900 cavalry were all that Lee could spare to Hill, and even a fifth of them were under orders for the Peninsula. Yet with that weak a force, the lieutenant-general prepared to defend the army's communications.

His shows of force almost bluffed the Unionists down. At 10:30 P.M., Meade wrote City Point that:

> I do not see indications sufficient to justify my making an attempt on the South Side Railroad....I can throw a force out to Poplar Spring Church, and engage the enemy, if you deem advisable, but this will only be extending our lines without a commensurate object, unless engaging the enemy is so deemed.[7]

The Pennsylvanian thus seemed on the verge of recommending that the attacks be called off. As much as he respected his subordinate, however, Grant did not cancel the operation. He understood the desirability of forcing battle—not in order to inflict casualties but in order to develop opportunities. "When you do move out," the General-in-Chief wrote Meade, "I think it will be advisable to maneuver to get a good position from which to attack, and then if the enemy is routed follow him into Petersburg, or where circumstances seem to direct." The Illinoisan correctly sensed that the Butternuts might well abandon the Cockade City itself if pressed. He determined to press.[8]

The lieutenant-general, however, prudently directed that the attack be temporarily postponed from daylight, September 30, until he could confer with Butler on the Peninsula. After that meeting, Grant at 8:25 A.M. telegraphed Meade that "You may move out now and see if an advantage can be gained. It seems to me the enemy must be weak enough at one or the other place to let us in."[9] About half an hour later, the army commander sent word to his strike force to advance.

That force had begun massing inside the western salient at Globe Tavern as early as September 27. It consisted of seven brigades and six batteries of the V Army Corps under Major General Gouverneur K. Warren and five brigades and four batteries of the IX Army Corps under Major General John G. Parke. To those 20,000 infantry and artillery were added Brigadier General David M. Gregg's two cavalry brigades and two horse batteries, 4,300 strong, which concentrated from one-half to two miles south of the Union works.

Some 24,300 men represented a powerful strike force indeed. Yet they amounted

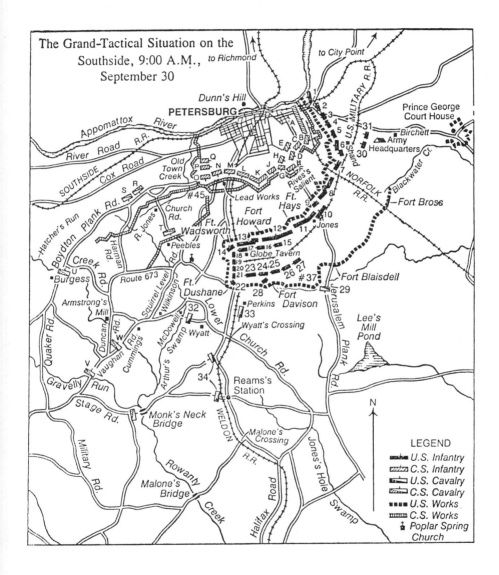

The Grand Tactical Situation on the Southside, 9:00 A.M., September 30 from *Richmond Redeemed.*

to barely 38 per cent of Meade's total command of 63,000 men. The remaining 39,000 under Brigadier General Samuel W. Crawford, Major General Winfield Scott Hancock, and Brigadier General Henry W. Benham held the trenches running east from Globe Tavern to the Jerusalem Plank Road, north from that thoroughfare to the Appomattox River below Petersburg, and around City Point, respectively. Leaving so many soldiers behind made clear how Grant suffered from his own war of attrition. In the course of compelling the Graycoats to stretch themselves thinner and thinner to hold their works, he had to leave more and more of his own troops behind to hold his corresponding works.

Still, Meade managed to concentrate at least a significant portion of his army into the strike force. Now it was moving out. The cavalry spent the day reconnoitering toward Hatcher's Run. Except for minor skirmishing, it saw no action. Friday would prove to be the foot soldiers' day to fight—once they could get to the front.

Reaching there was no easy matter. Only one road ran west from Globe Tavern past the little country meeting house called "Poplar Spring Church," which would give its name to the ensuing battle, toward the forward Confederate defenses along the Squirrel Level Road. Moving 20,000 men over that road would present serious logistical problems under good conditions. And conditions were far from good. The road was narrow. Dense woods—which could conceal Confederates—surrounded it on both sides. Butternuts were reported to be in the area, but how many and just where they were, Warren did not know. What he did know—what the whole course of operations in 1864, from early May to mid-August had made painfully clear—was the danger of surprise counterattacks by the Southerners. Beyond considerations of prudence and practicality, though, Warren was also afflicted with what he acknowledged to be "the anxiety of responsibility" which bore down so heavily upon him.[10]

These three factors internal to the Union situation, far more than the negligible resistance from Secessionist skirmishers, explain why it took Warren two hours to advance the two miles from Globe Tavern to the Squirrel Level Road and then two more hours to deploy just the three brigades which led his column.

To relieve congestion on the Poplar Spring Road and to cover the right flank, his Second Division turned northward up the Vaughan Road. The IX Corps meantime tried to work its way leftward to envelope the Graycoats' right flank. The best way to break the log jam, however, was to break out from the Poplar Spring Road and break through the Squirrel Level Line. Warren's lead division, Brigadier General Charles Griffin's First, received that mission.

Griffin formed his line of battle under cover of the ravine of Arthur's Swamp, a stream which flowed southward west of the church. Ahead of him lay Peebles's farm, the main stronghold on the Squirrel Level Line. Union intelligence indicated that two Confederate infantry brigades held that line. Griffin did not

The Battle of Peebles's Farm from *Richmond Redeemed.*

know that, overnight, they had been replaced by two or at most three regiments of dismounted cavalry. That weak force, moreover, held a weak position. The fortifications were incomplete; the moat did not cover the entire front; and only part of the obstructing frise had been laid.

The garrison proved no match for one of the best combat divisions under one of the best fighting generals in the Army of the Potomac. At 1:00 P.M., Griffin attacked. He handily overran Peebles's farm and captured its redoubt, 59 prisoners, and one cannon— the first gun which the V Corps had taken in the entire 1864 campaign.[11] As a Confederate rearguard tried to make a stand in the upper corner of the farm, the disorganized but victorious Bluecoats went "rolling over the field like a large wave," as a sergeant of the 155th Pennsylvania put it, and chased them away.[12]

In less than half an hour, the Yankees had broken out of their road jam, breached the forward Secessionist line, and seized a road junction of great strategic significance. From Peebles's, the Squirrel Level Road ran north to Petersburg and south to where Gregg's cavalry operated. Also from the farm, Route 673 headed west toward one of the main north-south wagon routes, the Harman Road. Most importantly, the Church Road angled northwest from Peebles's to the Boydton Plank Road itself, barely two miles away.[13]

Though presented with this big breakthrough and the resulting avenues for advance, the Union army took up a defense perimeter around Peebles's farm and went on the defensive. As the other three Yankee infantry divisions joined Griffin, they simply extended the defense line. Such measures were understandable, to be sure. There was no way the Northerners could know the magnitude of their opportunity and the vulnerability of their enemy. What they did know was that victory in Civil War battles disrupted the victors almost as much as the vanquished and hence that Griffin's division was now too disorganized to pursue effectively. And they also knew that every Union attack at Petersburg had provoked a major and often damaging Butternut counterattack, so the fresh divisions were justified in guarding against that expected danger. Yet, ironically, the precautions and the resulting delay were what gave the Confederates time to recover from the potential disaster and to bring up forces for the very counterattack against which the defensive measures sought to guard.

The only Southern troops initially in the area were the defeated garrison of the Squirrel Level Line. Some of those horsemen fled northward up that road. They were soon joined by sharpshooters from Petersburg, who helped them skirmish with the few pursuing Bluecoats. Most of the Confederate brigade meantime retreated up the Church Road. Major General Wade Hampton, commanding the Cavalry Corps of the Army of Northern Virginia, rallied them in a primitive line of logworks crossing that road and covering the vital Boydton Plank Road, just a half a mile beyond. Further to protect that thoroughfare,

Hampton dismounted the Third Cavalry Division and put it too into the logworks.

Dismounted cavalry could make a show of resistance, but to stop Union infantry, Hampton needed Confederate infantry. He, accordingly, notified Petersburg of the disaster and ungently requested infantry reinforcements. His messenger first reached Major General Cadmus Marcellus Wilcox, commanding the right sector of Petersburg's defenses. One of Wilcox's brigades had already gone to the Peninsula, and he was leading two more there on Friday until halted by word that the Army of the Potomac was striking west from Globe Tavern. He, therefore, reversed march through Chesterfield, and by 3:00 P.M. he was back at Petersburg. An hour later, he received Hampton's dire message and immediately led his two brigades down the Boydton Plank Road toward the Church Road, two miles away. Major General Henry Heth soon followed with two brigades of his division and Lieutenant Colonel William J. Pegram's artillery battalion.

This was as many men as Hill felt he could spare. His other eleven infantry brigades and nine artillery battalions were pinned down right around Petersburg to guard against Hancock and Crawford.[14] Even so, the lieutenant-general managed to send a powerful force into the field. By 5:00 P.M., some 9,000 Secessionist infantry, cavalry, and artillery barred the route to the plank road. As ranking officer, Heth assumed overall command of the Church Road sector.

While Confederates concentrated, the Yankees fragmented. Although Warren and Parke "cooperated" with each other, neither was in overall command. Nor did Meade accompany the strike force. He started the day at his permanent headquarters behind the Union right, and he did not reach the front until about 3:00 P.M. By then, the Bluecoats were finally resuming their advance against the plank road. He issued orders to spur the drive: the IX Corps would lead the way; Griffin's division would move up the Church Road to cover Parke's right flank; and the Second Division/V Corps would face north across the Squirrel Level Road to secure the right-rear.

Yet neither Meade's orders nor his presence guaranteed coordination or celerity. Griffin, for one thing, began concentrating his division back on Peebles's farm but did not actually advance up the Church Road. The IX Corps, moreover, did cautiously grope its way northward through the fringe of trees separating Peebles's farm from Oscar Pegram's farm, but then that unit too began fragmenting. Parke himself remained on Pegram's with two separated brigades of Brigadier Orlando B. Willcox's First Division.[15] Willcox's other brigade meantime headed northwest up a fork of Arthur's Swamp toward Dr. Boisseau's house. Preceding Willcox, Brigadier General Robert B. Potter's Second Division crossed Pegram's and halted in another fringe of trees separating that farm from Robert Jones's farm farther north. Potter's skirmishers ranged out across Jones's toward the primitive logworks on the far side of Old Town Creek. Just beyond those works lay the coveted Boydton Plank Road.

Cutting that highway would no longer be easy. Combative Confederate sharp-shooters were proving more than a match for the Union skirmishers. Behind those sharpshooters, the veterans of Cadmus Wilcox, Henry Heth, and Wade Hampton were massing. If Parke were to reach the plank road now, he would have a real fight of it. Yet the Federals no more grasped their present danger than they had recognized their earlier opportunity. When boldness had been in order, they were cautious. Now that prudence was dictated, they proved rash. Evidently exasperated by the slowness of the advance, Parke ordered Potter "to push on...without reference to any one else." Willcox was still back on Pegram's; Griffin was still back on Peebles's; but Potter was to press ahead, no matter what.[16]

Even then, Potter allowed his division to break apart into four demi-brigades. One halted in the middle of Jones's field while its commander scouted off north-west to look for Confederates. Another demi-brigade moved straight north and found Confederates. From army to corps to division to brigade to demi-brigade, the strike force had fragmented. Out of 20,000 men who had sallied from Globe Tavern that morning, barely 1,200 actually moved against the plank road—one of the Southerners' most sensitive sectors, sure to be heavily guarded.

Cadmus Wilcox saw his opportunity. He unleashed his two brigades, rolled up both Union flanks, and routed the lead demi-brigade. "The rebels...were bear-ing down on us, like a fleet of war ships—in front and on both flanks," reported an officer of the 11th New Hampshire; "they advanced in splendid, unbroken lines."[17] A second Yankee demi-brigade moved up to try to retrieve the defeat, only to be swept away itself. Wilcox, reinforced by one of Heth's brigades, then knifed westward through the woods between Jones's and Pegram's and routed a third demi-brigade. Now aware for the first time that something was desperately wrong and coming under increasingly heavy pressure, Willcox's brigade at Dr. Boisseau's barely managed to extricate itself before that place too was overrun.

The fall of Boisseau's completely isolated the remaining demi-brigade. It fled westward to escape the pursuing infantry, only to fall into the clutches of Hamp-ton's dismounted cavalry. The 45th Pennsylvania, 51st New York, and 58th Massachusetts were captured almost in entirety, some 600 prisoners. Only about 50 men managed to escape, among them the brigade commander himself, Colo-nel John I. Curtin, nephew of the Pennsylvania governor.

While Wilcox was mopping up on Jones's, his South Carolina brigade con-tinued south across Pegram's farm. As it moved up a ridge, another of Willcox's brigades charged up the other slope. In the short, sharp shock of battle, the Bluecoats lost and went streaming back, lucky to barely save their battery. Still the Carolinians pressed on.

By now four of Parke's brigades had been defeated. A few of the survivors rallied around Willcox's final fresh brigade for a last stand in Pegram's yard. The South Carolinians challenged that stand, too, but after three handsome successes

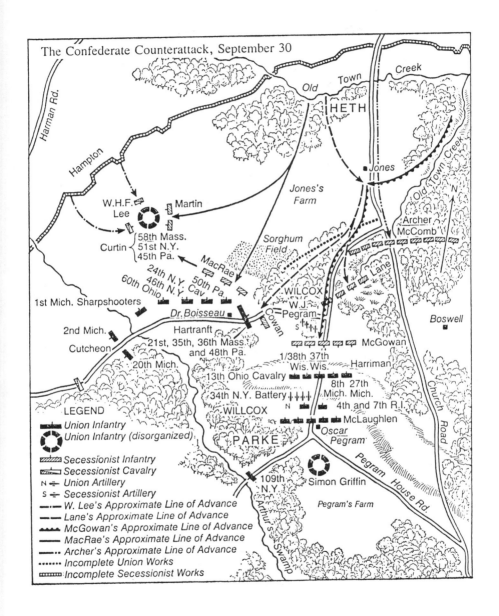

The Confederate Counterattack, September 30 from *Richmond Redeemed*.

they were fought out. Their wave lapped up against the Northern bulwark and soon receded. The final Federal line had held.

Or so it seemed. Heth, too, had a fresh brigade, and he sent it straight down the Church Road to turn Parke's right flank in Pegram's yard. That brigade, however, bogged down in swampy thickets. By the time it could emerge, Charles Griffin had at last moved up from Peeble's and prolonged Parke's line eastward across the Church Road. Until long after dark Heth kept fighting, but he could not crack Griffin's stalwart defense. Finally the Butternuts pulled back to Jones's farm. The big day of battle was over.

Despite these two final checks, the Graycoats had gained a handsome victory. They had not only contained the Federal breakthrough but had hurled it back, routing and almost crushing a whole army corps. At the cost of perhaps 600 casualties, they had captured 1,300 prisoners and inflicted an additional 1,000 killed and wounded. They had saved the supply lines and the city. With a little more effort, they might even be able to regain the strategic intersections around Peebles's farm and restore their original front line.

At least, the prospect was worth a try. Overnight, Confederate commanders prepared to renew their attack on Saturday. Wilcox's two brigades, regrouping back on Jones's farm, would spend the night there. Then on October 1, his 2,400 men were to resume attacking the Federal front on Pegram's farm. Meantime, Heth led his two brigades back up the Boydton Plank Road into the main Confederate works, where his other two brigades rejoined him. This reunited force, 4700 strong, would strike straight south down the Squirrel Level Road into the right-rear of the Unionists on Pegram's. During the preceding big battle at Petersburg, Globe Tavern on August 19, a similar Southern thrust into the Yankee right-rear came close to cutting off Warren's strike force. Now a stronger drive against a more isolated Blue column might well crush it.

Unlike in August, however, this time the Northerners were alert to such a threat. They left only a strong skirmish line, reinforced by one brigade, on Pegram's farm. Overnight their main body withdrew through the woods to Peebles's farm. Willcox secured their left. Potter and Griffin, in the center, occupied and reversed the captured Confederate trenches. Most significantly, Brigadier General Romeyn B. Ayres's Second Division of the V Corps, guarding the right flank, ran west to east across Chappell's farm just northeast of Peebles's. Ayres thus faced north astride the Squirrel Level Road, squarely athwart Heth's path. If the Virginian were to penetrate the Federal right-rear, he would first have to fight his way through heavy opposition.

A. P. Hill and Heth were willing to make an effort. Warren and Parke were quite content to let them try. The V and IX Corps commanders had gotten their fill of fighting on Friday. For October 1, they were inclined to remain on the defensive, strengthen their works, recover from the rough handling, and await developments.

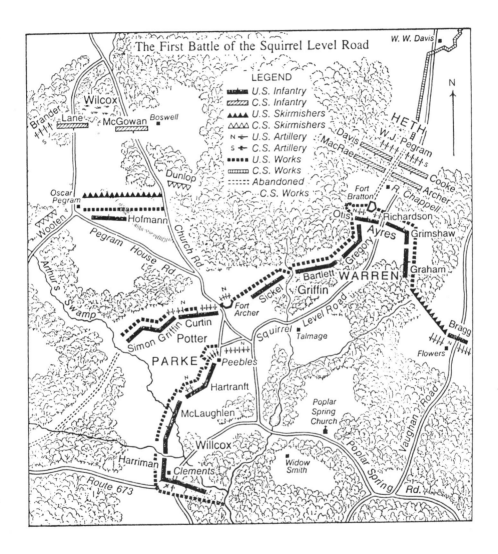

The First Battle of the Squirrel Level Road from *Richmond Redeemed*.

Their attitude contrasted with Meade's intentions. Although the reverses late September 30 initially led the army commander, too, to favor standing on the defensive, he changed his mind overnight on receiving confirmation that two Confederate divisions had arrived on the Peninsula from Petersburg.[18] He therefore ordered Warren and Parke to make a strong reconnaissance in force, October 1, and if opportunity presented, to convert such probes into a full-scale drive for the Boydton Plank Road. To bolster this operation, he directed Gregg's cavalry to join the advance on the IX Corps' left flank, and he further ordered a division of the II Corps to leave the works east of Petersburg and reinforce the strike column in the field.[19]

Meade, though, did not deliver those directives to his subordinates at the front. Rather did he issue them from his permanent headquarters deep within the Union lines, where he had returned overnight. As on the previous day, the army commander would be far from the fighting front when operations resumed on Saturday. The course of these operations thus would depend less on his orders than on his corps commanders' preferences and personalities. Those subordinates were quite content to stay on the defensive.

They thereby left the initiative to the Secessionists, who were quick to seize it. About 8:00 A.M., Wilcox attacked the Yankee picket line on Pegram's farm. As his two sharpshooter battalions rolled up both flanks, the line crumbled and fled back to the main Federal force on Peebles's farm, with the loss of 200 prisoners. The Butternuts pursued as far as the fringe of woods between the two farms. From there, they skirmished with and shelled Potter's and Griffin's line, but they did not attack it. Their mission was to fix the Bluecoats in place, while Heth attacked the right-rear.

The Virginian advanced down the Squirrel Level Road around 8:00 A.M. He readily drove in the Yankee pickets, but he was evidently surprised to discover the enemy ready for his "surprise" attack. Behind those pickets stood not an exposed flank but Ayres's fortified battleline directly across his path. For a time, Heth hesitated. Then he sent his forces forward. In what was becoming all too common in Confederate tactics in 1864, he lost control of those forces. Instead of a coordinated onslaught by his whole division, his drive broke down into separate jabs by three brigades; his fourth brigade did not attack at all. "Oh, it was an awful time Saturday," wrote a soldier of the 55th North Carolina, "charging the Yankees in the rain through the woods and swamps and thickets, and the balls flying thick and fast in every direction, and men getting killed, and wounded hollering all over the woods."[20] An awful time it truly was. Ayres handily repulsed all three thrusts. Within half an hour, Heth was completely defeated, with a loss of 400 men. He too then fell back on the defensive half a mile north of the Federal works.

Later that day, Wade Hampton fared no better in attempting to move up the lower end of the Squirrel Level Road and the Vaughan Road into the left-rear of the Union infantry on Peebles's farm. Although the gray horsemen initially drove in the Yankee rearguard on those highways, they succeeded only in drawing down upon themselves Gregg's main body, which called off its advance out Route 673 toward the Boydton Plank Road in order to meet this new threat. In heavy fighting along the Vaughan Road throughout the afternoon, the Federal troopers repeatedly repelled Secessionist attacks. In maintaining his own position, Gregg accomplished the even more important mission of preventing Confederate cavalry from penetrating Meade's left-rear up on Peebles's farm.[21]

The sturdy defense by Gregg and Ayres thus helped the Bluecoats maintain their position at Peebles's. Meade, though, wanted to do more than just secure that farm. Throughout the day he remained committed to attacking. Yet also throughout the day, the V and IX Corps commanders remained committed to defending; the Confederate assault that morning, although defeated, evidently confirmed their determination. The subordinates' preferences prevailed, at least in part because Meade was not present to prod them. Just as on Friday, he did not reach the front until mid-afternoon.

Even the army commander, moreover, made the advance contingent upon the arrival of reinforcements. Those fresh troops, Brigadier General Gershom Mott's Third Division of the II Corps, had left their trenches astride the Jerusalem Plank Road shortly after 1:00 A.M. They were to travel west from that thoroughfare to Globe Tavern on the recently completed U.S. Military Railroad, which ran laterally behind the whole Federal fortified line. The move marked the first time in American military history that the railroad was employed *grand tactically* to move reserves from a quiet sector almost to the fighting line.[22]

Yet because the operation was unprecedented, neither the strategists nor the quartermasters took fully into account the logistical problems of transporting 6,000 men by rail. Such inexperience, together with paucity of engines and cars, prevented moving more than the equivalent of a brigade at a time. For half a day, the soldiers just stood out in the fog and rain, waiting for the train. Not until just after noon did the first contingent finally get aboard. By the time it reached the tavern and marched out to Peebles's, another two-and-a-half hours had elapsed. And by the time the last of the three contingents arrived at the front, it was 5:30—and darkness had already fallen on that rainy autumn afternoon. "This delay is unpardonable," growled Meade's Chief of Staff to the army's Chief Quartermaster.[23] Yet, unpardonable or not, the delay had consumed the whole day. When Mott's entire force finally reached Peebles's farm, it was too late to advance.

Nevertheless, Saturday was not totally wasted. Mott and the Iron Brigade added 8,800 fresh men to the strike force. Virtually half the Army of the Potomac was now in the field west of Globe Tavern. Confederate defenders were outside their main earthworks as well. Meade recognized this opportunity to catch them exposed in the open field, defeat them, and pursue them at least beyond the Boydton Plank Road and perhaps beyond the Southside Railroad. Despite the reluctance of his subordinates to advance and despite even Grant's growing conviction that there was no point prolonging this offensive, the Pennsylvanian remained determined to continue the battle and cut the supply lines. So great was Grant's confidence in the major-general that the General-in-Chief deferred to his front-line commander and allowed Meade to resume advancing on Sunday.[24]

Confederate redeployment overnight October 1-2 appeared to favor Meade's prospects. Hampton retired from Gregg's front to Hatcher's Run and the Boydton Plank Road. Wilcox pulled back from Pegram's not just to Jones's but all the way to Petersburg. Heth, too, left only skirmishers to confront Ayres and withdrew his main body to the city. Two of his brigades remained there; he led the other two down to Jones's, where they apparently joined a dismounted cavalry brigade in the logworks.

Why A. P. Hill shifted his forces this way is not clear. Perhaps he thought the battle was almost over. Perhaps he wanted to remove exposed targets now that he no longer planned to keep attacking. Or perhaps renewed Federal probes to the outskirts of Richmond on October 1 necessitated readying reinforcements from Petersburg for the Peninsula if the capital should be more seriously threatened on Sunday. Whatever the reason, the effect of his rearrangement was that his 14,000-man strike force (54 per cent of his total command) which had operated against Peebles's farm on Saturday was completely broken up. Now two-thirds of his force, over 17,000 soldiers, were back within the main defenses. A mere 16 percent, or 4,200 men, stood between Peebles's farm and the plank road— the very sector which Meade planned to strike.

Yet far from jeopardizing the lines of communications, the Secessionist withdrawal actually saved them. When operations resumed on Sunday, Parke and Warren expected to advance straight from Peebles's and Chappell's, defeat the Graycoats in their immediate presence, and pursue them all the way to the supply lines. The problem was: no Graycoats were there to be defeated. Pegram's farm was entirely abandoned, and only a handful of sharpshooters remained north of Chappell's. Union lookouts saw strong forces manning Petersburg's main defenses, but where had the strike force gone? Was it too back in the city, or was it lurking in ambush, as on Friday? What had been a simple, straight-forward exercise in minor tactics now escalated into a more baffling problem of grand tactics: to run the risks of seeking out a hidden and potentially dangerous foe.

A bold Union commander would have attempted to resolve that uncertainty to his own advantage by pushing four or five divisions toward the plank road and forcing the foe to react to him. Meade, prudent and competent as he certainly was, lacked the boldness to risk forcing battle on those terms. For all his brave words on Saturday, for all his determination overnight, for all his hopes of perhaps driving even as far as the upper Appomattox itself on Sunday, he could not rise to the opportunity when it came. He saw not opening but uncertainty;

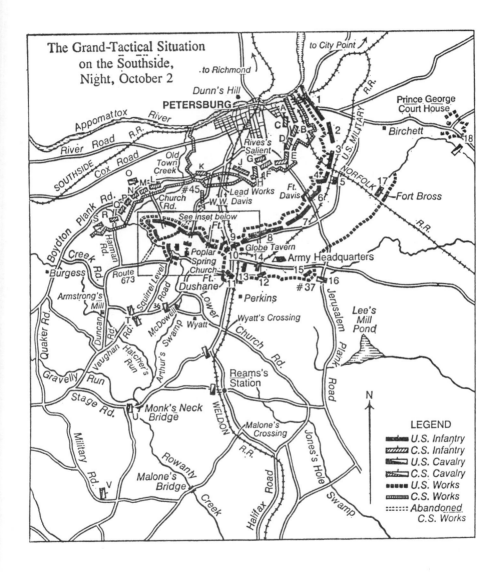

The Grand Tactical Situation on the Southside, Night, October 2 from *Richmond Redeemed*.

he saw not vulnerable communications but manned ramparts. He saw, in sum, no point in continuing the battle. His senior subordinates hardly protested his new analysis. And back on the banks of James River, Grant, who as early as Saturday had thought the current offensive over and who was looking ahead to a new offensive, readily acquiesced in Meade's decision.

With neither side willing to prolong fighting, the Battle of Poplar Spring Church soon sputtered to a close. To the north, Ayres became embroiled with sharpshooters on the Squirrel Level Road. In the center, Heth, whose whole division by now occupied that sector, exchanged shots with Parke and Griffin on Jones's farm.[25] And off to the southwest on the Harman Road, in the biggest action of the day, Mott drove in cavalry outposts but could make no headway against Heth's right. By late afternoon, skirmishing ceased on all sectors, and the Unionists began withdrawing.

They did not retire all the way to Globe Tavern or even to Peebles's, however. Meade rather incorporated the southern half of Pegram's farm as well as Peebles's into his new defense line. Within a matter of days, Ayres's right flank would extend back eastward to connect with the old works on the Weldon Railroad. This new position thus covered the key intersections around Peebles's farm and represented a strong salient thrusting up toward the Boydton Plank Road.

To protect that crucial highway and the railroad beyond it, the Graycoats meantime had to strengthen, prolong, and occupy the inner line of logworks, which were the last barrier to those supply lines. On Sunday night, Wilcox joined Heth in those defenses. Also within days, the soldiers transformed those primitive parapets into formidable fortifications.

Fighting on Sunday and the three preceding days cost the Southerners about 1,300 casualties. Unionists lost more than twice as many, some 2,950 men, including over 1,600 prisoners. To show for such casualties, the Army of the Potomac had broken out from Globe Tavern, destroyed the threatening Squirrel Level Line, captured the strategic road net radiating from Peebles's farm, and compelled Lee to stretch his already attenuated line five miles further southwest to cover his communications.

The Confederate chieftain begrudged such losses. Yet they could have been far worse. His outer line was gone, but his inner line—and the communications which it covered—were secure. And Petersburg itself, which Grant thought within his grasp and which Lee was prepared to abandon if necessary to save Richmond, remained in Secessionist hands. Both capital and communications center, so gravely threatened as autumn began, were saved to the Confederacy for another half year. Such significant successes clearly mark Poplar Spring Church as a strategic victory for the Graycoats.

The battle demonstrates how intermittent heavy combat punctuated the long course of the siege. It shows as well how Grant dominated the strategic initiative at Petersburg. He decided whether, when, where, and why to attack, and Lee could only respond to Northern onslaughts, often unleashed in tandem on both sides of the James.

Yet the Virginian did not simply retreat; he resisted. He masked his weakness, husbanded his strength, arranged for defense in depth, and utilized his knowledge of the ground to launch surprise flank attacks against the more numerous but more unsure aggressors. These counterattacks, as on September 30, often halted the Union drive short of its objective. But rarely any more could the Butternuts drive the Army of the Potomac from the field. Events of October 1 made clear how follow-up attacks simply cost the Southerners irreplaceable casualties and gained nothing. When all the attacks and counterattacks were over, the Confederate supply lines were saved, but the Federals securely retained their latest conquests in their seemingly unstoppable drive westward. Their chokehold upon Petersburg now clutched even more tightly.

Capturing that new territory had proved no easy task, quite apart from actual enemy resistance. Logistical bottlenecks, the difficulty of coordinating large forces in wooded and swampy terrain, the uncertainty of penetrating new country, and the certainty that eventually the Graycoats would strike back bred in Warren and Parke—and to a lesser extent in Meade—slowness, prudence, and precaution which sometimes degenerated into caution, hesitancy, and irresolution. The New Yorker, to be sure, was masterful on the minor-tactical defensive but remained unsure on the grand-tactical offensive. Parke, in this his first Virginia battle as a corps commander, had difficulty controlling his forces. Not until late March of 1865 would he finally demonstrate his fitness for that high an office.

Meade, on the other hand, had long since proven his qualifications for army command. This battle again underscored his stengths—and also his weaknesses. The trust he had earned from Grant, the willingness to press the tactical attack, and the decision to prolong the battle in quest of victory were all to his credit. Yet his vulnerability to be bluffed down on September 29, his inability to rise to the opportunity of seeking out new successes on October 2, and his failure to arrive at the front and exercise more direct control before mid-afternoon of the other two days were characteristic shortcomings that crippled his generalship, as competent as it unquestionably was. To be sure, allowing responsible subordinates to exercise the responsibilities of office was the approved command style of the Civil War. Grant could accord such latitude to Meade, confident that the army commander would use it well, with only an occasional nudge from City Point. But the Pennsylvanian, it seems, gave too much leeway to his corps commanders, and they sometimes abused it to substitute their preferences for his will.

Paucity of surviving Southern sources precludes comparably analyzing Confederate command styles in such depth. Certain themes, however, do emerge: the initiative and resourcefulness of Hampton in meeting—and usually defeating—numerous threats on many fronts, the tactical skill of Wilcox in attacking, the hesitancy and unsureness of Heth in controlling combat troops and his disingenuousness in reporting those operations to higher headquarters.

Like most Civil War battles, this particular fight had this broad spectrum of relative ability and this broad range of tactical operations. It was admittedly neither a great battle like Gettysburg, nor a decisive battle like Cedar Creek, nor yet a Napoleonic battle like Nashville. But it was a *characteristic* battle which typified the combats by which Grant relentlessly tightened his clutch upon the Cockade City and by which Lee for so long fended off repeated danger. Such was this Petersburg autumn at Poplar Spring Church.

Endnotes

1 T. Harry Williams, *P. G. T. Beauregard: Napoleon in Gray*, ch. 13-15.

2 *War of the Rebellion: A Compilation for the Official Records of the Union and Confederate Armies*, ser. 1, v. XL, pt. 2, pp. 156, 268-69, and pt. 3, p. 180 (Hereafter cited as *OR*, with all references being to series 1).

3 For a fuller account of the siege and especially of operations in early autumn, see Richard J. Sommers, *Richmond Redeemed: The Siege at Petersburg*, (NY: Doubleday & Co., 1981).

4 As soon as the Yankees arrived east of Petersburg in mid-June, they cut the railroads running northeast to City Point and southeast into the Blackwater region. Thereafter their tactical objectives became the remaining supply lines: the Weldon Railroad, the Southside Railroad, and various wagon roads.

5 As matters worked out, one Virginia cavalry brigade did leave Petersburg for the Valley on September 27, just before Grant struck. Although he was not aware of its departure and although he did not compel its recall, his operations almost certainly fared better because of its absence.

6 Record Group 109, ch. 6, v. CCCLXII, p. 442, and v. CCCLXIVm p. 501, and v. DCXLII, pp. 89-90, National Archives.

7 *OR*, v. XLII, pt. 2, p. 1094.

8 *Ibid.*, pp. 1094, 1119.

9 *Ibid.*, p. 1118.

10 The corps commander confessed this anxiety in a letter of October 1 to his wife. G. K. Warren Papers, New York State Library.

11 *OR*, v. XXXVI, pt. 1, p. 545.

12 Z. C. Monks to Sarah, October 9, 1864, Monks-Rohrer, Papers. Emory University.

13 In the absence of any known name for the east-west road between the southern end of Peebles's farm and the Harman Road, its modern name is used: Dinwiddie County Route 673.

14 The defenders remaining right around Petersburg consisted principally of Major General Bushrod R. Johnson's Division east of town and Major General William Mahone's Division south of town. Johnson and Mahone thus confronted Hancock and Crawford, respectively.

15 The reader should take care to differentiate Union General Orlando Willcox from Confederate General Cadmus Wilcox, who fought each other that afternoon.

16 *OR*, v. XLII, pt. 1, p. 579.

17 "Return of Staff/11th New Hampshire, October, 1864," New Hampshire Archives and Records Management Commission.

18 These were the divisions of Major General Charles W. Field and Robert F. Hoke, both of which lost prisoners in their unsuccessful counterattacks on Butler's army on September 30. However, Meade dismissed with scorn Butler's claim that Heth and Wilcox had also moved to the Northside. The Pennsylvanian knew all too well that the latter two divisions still barred his path through Dinwiddie County. *OR*, v. XLII, pt. 2, pp. 1121-22, 1144-45; George R. Agassiz, ed., *Meade's Headquarters, 1863-1865*, p. 237.

19 The Iron Brigade of the V Corps also took the field overnight. It moved west from Globe Tavern and deployed astride the Vaughan Road, facing north. That brigade thus lent a little weight to the tenuous picket line linking Ayres's right on the Squirrel Level Road with Crawford's main fortifications back on the Weldon Railroad.

20 James K. Wilkerson to his father, October 5, 1864, Wilkerson Papers, Duke University.

21 In fighting just east of where the Squirrel Level Road entered the Vaughan Road, Confederate Brigadier General John Dunovant, commanding the South Carolina Cavalry Brigade, was killed while leading an unsuccessful charge on Federal lines—the only general on either side to lose his life in the Battle of Poplar Spring Church.

22 Many times during the Civil War, starting with the First Bull Run Campaign in July of 1861, railroads were used strategically to shift troops from a quiet front to an active one. Not until the autumn of 1864 at Poplar Spring Church, however, was a railroad used grand tactically to move forces from a quiet sector to an active one within the same army.

23 *OR*, v. XLII, pt. 3, p. 8.

24 A further measure of the lieutenant-general's confidence in the army commander is that Grant left Meade entirely in charge at the front and contented himself with telegraphic communication between themselves. The latitude which the Illinoisan's absence allowed contrasts with the closer contact which he maintained with the Army of the James. In this Butler's first battle since coming under Grant's immediate control, the General-in-Chief left City Point to visit the Peninsula each day of combat, September 29-October 2.

25 In early afternoon, one stray cannonshot from Heth's line came within inches of hitting Meade, his Chief of Staff, Griffin, and his senior brigadier. The shell, though, passed between the two senior officers mounted, buried into the ground at the feet of the two subordinates—and failed to explode. All four generals escaped unscathed. Andrew A. Humphreys to his wife, October 2, 1864, A. A. Humphreys Papers, Historical Society of Pennsylvania.

"Port Hudson...the nearest to hell you want to go."

Lawrence L. Hewitt

Although nearly vanished and often forgotten, the village of Port Hudson, Louisiana, holds a distinct—if obscure—place in our nation's past. It was at Port Hudson, not Gettysburg, that the full implications of the Civil War became a reality. During the struggle for this Confederate bastion on the Mississippi River, the Union army sent two regiments of black troops on a major assault against the Confederate lines, the first such engagement of black soldiers during the Civil War. The significance of Negro southerners doing battle with white Confederate soldiers, while important to historians, was not that critical to the outcome of the war.

The black soldiers who assaulted the Confederate lines at Port Hudson were part of the Union force that laid siege to the last Rebel stronghold on the Mississippi to surrender, the longest true siege in the annals of American warfare. The *Oxford English Dictionary* defines a siege as "the action, on the part of an army, of investing a town, castle, etc., in order to cut off all outside communication and in the end to reduce or take it...."[1] The Army of the Potomac's siege of Petersburg was not a genuine siege because trains supplied the beleaguered Rebel troops; more than a century later, helicopters did the same for United States Marines at Khe Sanh. For the 7,400 Confederates at Port Hudson there were no trains to bring supplies and food to the men, no road escaped the strangle hold of the Yankee besiegers, not even a pack mule could get through. The Confederates had two choices: one, to accept the inevitable and surrender, or, two, dig in and resist until the last bite of food was gone and the last cartridge spent. The defiant Rebels chose the latter and endured forty-eight days of hell.

Any one of these facts is of such significance that Port Hudson should have a place in the annals of American history. Historians, however, dismiss the Port Hudson campaign in college textbooks with a single sentence at most. The authors of one such volume fail to mention it at all, and even go so far as to omit Port Hudson from their map of the western theater of operations.[2]

Their neglect is inexcusable, because there are other reasons for remembering the struggle for Port Hudson. The late Bell I. Wiley, renowned historian of the Civil War common soldier, concluded that the defenders of Port Hudson endured the greatest deprivation ever experienced in the Confederacy.[3] What qualifies these individuals for such an unwanted distinction?

The man in charge of the garrison was Major General Franklin Gardner. As with any besieged commander, Gardner had to husband those resources that would enable him to accomplish his mission. His goal was to detain as many enemy troops at Port Hudson for as long as possible. He had to hold out. A member of the garrison later concluded that "there was no need of generalship. Our commander...had to exercise only his stubborn courage."[4]

The first thing that changed the Confederates' daily routine at Port Hudson was the almost constant bombardment by Union land and naval guns. One afternoon Gardner was seated outside his headquarters enjoying a brief respite while a servant trimmed his hair. Suddenly, without warning, a shell landed near the general's feet, narrowly missing him as it ricocheted past. Although covered with dirt, the general merely stood, shook off the dust, and resumed his former position. The servant, with the scissors shaking in his hand, was unable to continue.[5]

A Louisiana lieutenant could relate to both of these reactions. "No one can 'get used' to bombardment, though it will not cause a good soldier to flinch. It has the tendency to make a man either a good Christian or a fatalist, according to his early training or latent religious belief."[6] After the war, a youthful Tennessean claimed his premature gray hair resulted from his having endured the bombardment at Port Hudson. Linn Tanner, of Boone's Louisiana Battery, remembered that the bombardment was at first terrorizing; "but after it was seen that such slight damage resulted it soon became monotonous to those on the inside of the earthen breastworks. It was not uncommon to see soldiers with spread blankets playing cards."[7] Checkers was another popular game, but there was no guarantee that a Yankee sharpshooter would not determine the winner. Other soldiers simply lay on the ground facing skyward, watching the burning fuses of the thirteen-inch mortar shells soar high overhead—if they were not falling in their area.[8]

Some of the incoming shells proved to be more dangerous than those fired from the mortar vessels. One eight-inch gun, located opposite the southeastern angle of the Confederate works, fired an explosive round with a reduced powder charge, the result was much like a bowling ball rolling down the alley. In this case, however, the alley ran parallel to, and in the rear of, a section of Confederate breastworks.[9]

Shells fired from the 100-pound Parrott rifle aboard the U.S.S. *Genesee* especially bothered members of the 4th Louisiana, who were stationed on the Confederate right. These Parrott projectiles dropped in on the Louisianians as uninvited guests every fifteen minutes throughout the day. The shells were about eight inches in diameter, two feet in length, and each one weighed over a hundred pounds. Because of their low trajectory, the shells would strike the ground and ricochet repeatedly before exploding, just as stones skipping over water.

Because of this peculiar impact, the Louisianians referred to one of these shells as a "Limping Tom."

After ten days of enduring these rude interruptions, the Louisianians completed a bombproof, which they nicknamed "The Gopher Hole." The shelter was about ten by twelve feet and fifteen feet deep, and was covered by logs. Several feet of dirt covered the logs. Appropriately, the entrance was on the side of the shelter opposite the *Genesee*.[10]

Most members of the garrison ate their daily rations at dusk. The Confederates found a meal to be more palatable if it was served with cordial conversation, and a gathering of friends before dark was an invitation for a Union gunner to send his calling card. One evening, the occupants of "The Gopher Hole" were seated around their dinner table, which was located just outside the entrance of their bombproof. As they began to eat, one of the party cried, "Here comes 'Limping Tom!' "[11] After watching the flight of the shell for a second or two, all of them forgot their manners and scrambled from the table without excusing themselves. The projectile landed right in the middle of the table, sending cow peas and wooden splinters in all directions.[12]

Another constant bother was Union sharpshooters. Hidden within the felled timber fronting the breastworks, they diligently watched for every opportunity to pick off a Johnny Reb. Their bullets usually struck their human targets in the head; consequently, most of their victims were killed outright. It was even risky to expose a hand above the parapet.[13]

The Confederates soon tired of trench warfare. In order to break the monotony, a Confederate would put his kepi on the end of his ramrod or a stick and raise it just above the parapet. This practice became so common that the Yankees soon learned not to waste their ammunition. The failure of the Yankees to be obliging occasionally led a Johnny Reb to raise his hat, while still on his head, above the parapet and take a good look at the enemy's position. Once, when a member of the 4th Louisiana used this procedure for a look-see, a "blind" Yankee shouted, "If you put your head in that hat we'll take a shot at it."[14]

Some Confederates engaged in "crying wolf" or, more accurately, playing dead or wounded in front of their comrades. Jasper Luckett, a Tennessee artilleryman, was particularly fond of the game. One moonlit night, while repairing damage to the breastwork with sand bags, a minie ball struck his belt buckle. He fooled no one this time, for he died shortly thereafter.[15]

The tedium of life in the trenches also bred carelessness. One tragic victim of such thoughtless behavior was Newton Soles, a sixteen-year-old youth in the 1st Alabama. One day, while constructing a "shebang," which resembled a modern two-man pup tent, his tentmate heard a thud and looked up in time

"The Priest Cap," northeastern angle of the Confederate line defended by the 1st Mississippi and 49th Alabama. *Courtesy of the National Archives*

to see Newton roll into a ditch, with blood gushing from a wound in his head. He died because he had carelessly exposed himself to a Yankee sharpshooter beyond the breastwork by standing too erect.[16]

The routine of the siege was broken only once. On June 14, Union Major General Nathaniel P. Banks made a second attempt to breach the defenses. His plan called for a frontal assault from the center of his line against the northeast angle of the Confederate works, known as the Priest Cap, because of its configuration. Banks also ordered diversionary attacks to be made on both his left and right flanks.

The main assault force, an entire division, struck the 1st Mississippi Infantry at the Priest Cap about 4 a.m. Initial Federal success in breaching the Confederate line ended quickly, and the struggle there had almost ceased by the time the right-wing of the assault struck the fortifications to the left of the Priest Cap some three hours later. The Union left-wing failed to make any serious effort whatsoever.[17]

First Lieutenant Frederick Y. Dabney, a member of Gardner's staff, wrote in his report of the siege that the men of the 1st Mississippi Infantry "hurled back from their portion of the line, a force of the enemy ten times greater than their own!"[18] A Texas sergeant, stationed to the right of the Mississippians, described their struggle:[19]

> We are having hard work down near the Rail Road [sic] were it not
> for the smoke we could see it plain—but we only catch a glimpse
> as the smoke is blown away [sic] we know very well that our boys
> are all right from the long and continued yells. They Charge this
> point 4 times today some of their men actually getting upon our
> works but none getting back alive. Scores of their dead lie in 10, 20,
> or 30 yards of the Breast Works. Our men literally mow them down.

Another Confederate recalled,[20]

> By mere physical pressure of numbers some got within the works,
> in front of the First Mississippi..., but were instantly shot down....The
> enemy's hand grenade experiment proved an unfortunate one for
> the assailants, as very few exploded when thrown in—they were per-
> cussion grenades—but when thrown back by the Mississippians, from
> the slightly elevated works, into the midst of the Federals below,
> they exploded, carrying death to their former owners. The fight
> lasted, with great severity, for about two hours, when the [Yankee]
> infantry fell back, but a heavy artillery fire was kept up all day. About
> one hundred prisoners were captured in the ditch near the Jackson
> Road, being unable to retreat.

Brigadier General William N. R. Beall bombarded Gardner with messages
all day. "The First Mississippi is scarce of [percussion] caps; can you send any?
Our loss thus far small; that of the enemy large. Most of our guns (artillery)
are disabled on this line." "The loss of the First Mississippi Regiment in today's engagement is very severe—18 killed and about 14 wounded. The command is much reduced."[21] One such dispatch concluded: "P.S. The Breast works
[sic] near the pieces of art[illery] are much in need of repairs—please send an
engineer officer to have it done to-night."[22]

At one point Beall was informed that Gardner[23]

> does not understand how it is that so many prisoners not wounded
> are picked up in your front & that he is rather suspicious that this
> is a *trick* fixed upon to get a large number of men inside & He wishes
> you to state how it is so many are coming in.

Beall responded, "They couldn't get away so had to come in."[24] The following
day, during a truce, 161 bodies were removed from the moat and abatis directly
in front of the 1st Mississippi and 49th Alabama. One Yankee was found to be
still alive.[25]

Once again, the Federals had failed to breach the Confederate fortifications.

The siege continued while Banks prepared for a third assault, an assault that never materialized. Although it can be argued that the Confederates could not have repulsed another onslaught, it can also be argued that with morale at such a low ebb in the Union army, Banks wisely declined to order his men to charge the fortifications a third time.

As the siege continued, Confederate infantrymen constantly violated the order to conserve ammunition by exchanging fire with concealed Yankee snipers. Several Confederates were shot in the head as a result. Despite the risk, they continued to shoot back.[26]

One such Rebel was armed with a rifle of British manufacture that fired a bullet weighing one and a half ounces, approximately twice the normal weight. After covering himself with Spanish moss, he would climb a cypress tree. From his perch approximately forty feet above the ground, he wounded Yankees more than three-quarters of a mile off. At that range the bullet lacked the velocity to kill, but because of its size it made a nasty wound.[27]

Another celebrated Confederate sharpshooter was nicknamed "Arkansas Joe"

Fort Desperate detached redoubt on Confederate left flank defended by the 15th Arkansas.
Courtesy of the National Archives

by members of the 128th New York. Although conspicuously dressed in a red shirt, "Arkansas Joe" harassed the New Yorkers for weeks before they managed to shoot him out of his tree.[28]

As time wore on, men on both sides began to tire of the endless sniping. Firing was occasionally suspended along a section of the line. These informal truces allowed for the exchange of information for an obliging Yank to provide a craving Reb with a plug of tobacco. Hostilities resumed as soon as an officer on either side noticed the lull in the firing and came to investigate.[29]

Neither bullets nor gunpowder proved to be a problem. An immense supply of gunpowder was available because shipments destined for the Trans-Mississippi Department had been held at Port Hudson because Union forces controlled navigation on the Red River. Bullets were provided by scavenging the battlefield. Thousands of Yankee bullets were melted down, recast, and fired back at the blue-clad soldiers by the Confederates.[30]

Items which Gardner desperately needed and could not replace included, men, cannon, artillery shells, medicine, and food. Despite these shortages, Gardner never despaired. He divided his perimeter defenses into zones, with an engineer in charge of each. The soldiers strengthened the fortifications and constructed loopholes in the top of the parapet for sharpshooters. They made Quaker guns, logs cut and painted to resemble cannon.[31]

The Rebels also placed booby-traps along the fortifications, particularly at the Priest Cap and in the rear of the "Devil's Elbow." To strengthen the Priest Cap, the Confederates planted sharpened stakes that slightly angled toward the enemy. Wire was stretched between the stakes approximately eighteen inches above the ground to trip any assailant. These innovative Rebels were the first to use wire as a tactical device on the battlefield. Behind the "Devil's Elbow," which was located where the breastworks overlooked the Mississippi River below Port Hudson, bridges were constructed over ravines that were designed to collapse when used. The attackers would plummet downward and be impaled upon sharpened stakes. The Yankees repeated failures to capture the "Devil's Elbow" influenced them to nickname the area "the Citadel."[32]

During the final days of the siege, Union sappers reached the base of the Citadel. Protected by the crest of the ridge, these men were secure from Rebel bullets. As a demonstration of their own version of Yankee ingenuity, members of the 12th Louisiana Battalion Heavy Artillery constructed a chute on the crest of the parapet above the approach trench. When it was determined that the Yankees were moving up the say toward the entrance of the mine, one of the Louisianians would lift a recycled Union thirty-two pound artillery shell over his shoulder. Another man standing behind him would light the fuse and shout "Let go!" The shell rolled down the chute, landed at the entrance of the tunnel, and exploded amidst the miners.[33]

Prior to the assault on May 27, surplus rifles secured from the sick in the hospital and from the arsenal enabled Colonel William R. Miles to provide his men with three rifles each. After that attack, rifles dropped by the enemy enabled each man in the 39th Mississippi to have three apiece as well. Members of the 12th Arkansas, who had repulsed the enemy on May 27 armed with a variety of shotguns, managed to replace these weapons of limited range with Enfield rifles. Soldiers in the 1st Alabama had carried flintlock muskets when the siege commenced. These men soon had two weapons, the Enfield for the "long taw" and the flintlock for close quarters.[34] This increased firepower helped compensate for the loss of manpower.

Land mines or "torpedoes" made from unexploded Union thirteen-inch mortar shells also increased the killing power in front of the breastworks, as did grenades. The Yankees used grenades that were designed to explode upon impact with a solid object, including a man's body. The Yankees had to hurl these grenades up and over the parapet from the moat below. The Confederates would pair off, both men holding a corner of a blanket in each hand. Lacking velocity when they cleared the parapet, the Confederates could safely catch the grenades in the blanket. These grenades were then hurled back at the attackers, their downward flight usually providing sufficient momentum to achieve detonation upon impact. The Yankees deemed them "curses coming home to roost."[35] The Confederates made additional grenades from unexploded enemy projectiles.[36]

Gardner ordered the cannon positioned where their fire would have greatest effect. He also had his men dig pits in which to place the guns when not in use in order to protect them against incoming shells. At least three of the guns along the river lay on center-pivot carriages, which enabled their crews to swing them around and fire at the Federal army. The ten-inch columbiad in Battery No. 4 proved so menacing that the Yankees christened the gun "The Demoralizer" and erroneously believed, because of its wide range of fire, that the Confederates had it mounted on a railroad car.[37]

Outgunned three-to-one, Confederate cannon became choice targets for enemy gunners. Captain L. J. Girard was responsible for maintaining Gardner's cannon, and if any individual deserved special recognition for his performance, it was he. Almost singlehandedly and without proper tools or materials, Girard kept the cannon firing. He had to work day and night, because the enemy's cannonade disabled, dismounted, or destroyed virtually every gun at least once during the siege. Despite Girard's superhuman efforts, many of the guns were in such a state by the end of the siege that the Confederates finally loaded them with canister and placed them atop the parapets. When fired, they would recoil and fall to the ground, useless, but at least they could spew death into the enemy's ranks one final time.[38]

An inadequate supply of artillery ammunition, particularly that of explosive shells, proved somewhat of a problem. Unexploded Union projectiles of suitable caliber were recycled by the Confederate cannoneers. The Yankees were not hospitable enough, however, to provide every size needed. Although the Southerners had expended most of their canister on May 27, this shortage did not prove insurmountable. The soldiers tore off their shirt sleeves and filled them with spent bullets and pieces of iron, such as links of chain and broken bayonets, to provide round of canister for the cannon.[39]

Endless labor, exposure, and improper diet sapped the soldiers' health. Too few in number to allow for any regular rotation from the perimeter, the Confederates had to remain in the trenches, day after day, week after week. After a month of such constant vigilance, the officers of the 1st Alabama determined that two men from each company could be safely detached daily. These individuals made their way to the bank of the river for a day's relaxation, only to have their rest constantly interrupted by incoming artillery shells.[40] No place of quiet solitude existed within the besieged bastion.

During attacks and sorties, the Confederates had to run along the breastworks to the threatened point, repulse the attackers, and then hurry to the left or right to repel other assailants. The Southerners were so short-handed that every man in the garrison was provided with a musket and ammunition. The men detached to the Commissary Department were assigned a place in the trenches. And during the second assault on June 14, even Gardner's staff fought in the rifle pits.[41]

The men endured the heat of the day and the heavy dews of the night. At the beginning of the siege, the men escaped the scorching rays of the sun by erecting makeshift shelters. Some of these structures consisted of blankets stretched over barrels. Later, the men burrowed into the earth for greater protection from enemy artillery shells. Others constructed shelters similar to "The Gopher Hole." An Arkansas soldier remembered such a bombproof as being the only possible place to sleep.[42]

The hardships that the defenders suffered took their toll. Fatigued, the men often fell asleep at their posts. After an hour or two in the sun, many woke up delirious; many did not wake up. At least one Tennessean died of blood poisoning, which he contracted from an encounter with the thorns which enveloped the abatis. It is probable that he sustained the injury by stumbling over a Union artillery projectile and falling into the briars while picking blackberries.[43]

The number of sick increased daily. Colonel Isaiah George Washington Steedman, commander of the Confederate Left Wing, commented, "Six ounces of quinine would save the army, as the mass of our diseases are intermittent and bilious fevers, with their many complications."[44] The lack of medicinal stimulants and nourishment augmented the fatality rate from wounds and other debilities. Three members of the already diminished Maury Tennessee Light Artillery died in the hospital from the want of medicines; a fourth died of chills on his way home after securing his parole; and five others were promptly discharged from service following the siege for physical disability. Surgeons forced to amputate without chloroform were lucky if their patients did not die of shock.[45]

One such victim was Captain Richard Boone, of Boone's Louisiana Battery. Described by one unmarried woman as "the handsomest man in Louisiana,"[46] Boone had a leg amputated. Before he died, he requested that his detached limb be fired at the Yankees from a cannon.[47]

One particularly attractive target for Yankee gunners was the gristmill. Its destruction left the Confederates in dire straits until Captain C. H. Jones, the post commissary officer, came up with an ingenious idea. Gardner had retained the single locomotive of the Clinton and Port Hudson Railroad within the fortifications. The Southerners blocked up the locomotive, passed a belt from the drive wheel to a grinding stone, and in this way the engineer "furnished meal at the rate of several miles an hour."[48] Although the railroad depot turned gristmill was in plain sight of the Federal fleet down river, not a single shell struck the locomotive despite repeated attempts by three Union vessels.[49]

One incoming artillery shell proved especially beneficial to the garrison. When it exploded in the river one afternoon, seventy or eighty fish rose to the surface, completely stunned. The Confederates went after them in two skiffs and found most of them to be buffalo and catfish, many weighing well over ten pounds. Hungry soldiers paid between five and fifty dollars for the fish, depending upon their size.[50]

By the end of June, birds had learned not to fly near the fort. Daily rations consisted of three small ears of corn nicknamed "pinewoods nubbins" by the soldiers who never lost their sense of humor. When he distributed the rations, the commissary sergeant of Boone's Louisiana Battery would call out, "Pig-gee, pig-gee, pig-goo-ah!"[51] The artillerymen promptly fell in on all fours and began squealing and grunting, keeping up the jollity of the camp.[52]

With food in such short supply, it was not uncommon for the men to gamble for rations. One such game of chance was appropriately named "hazards"; it consisted of pitching coins at a twig. Each man got three tosses; the closest toss won.[53]

Knowing that his men could not subsist very long on such a diet, Gardner had a mule butchered and set the example for his troops; fifteen pounds of the beast were prepared for his mess. When properly cooked, it was quite tender and had a taste between beef and venison. One private believed "that good fat mule (not sore back) is a better and juicier as well as a finer grained meat than beef...." Although he found suitably prepared mule meat palatable, his comrades often imitated a mule by uttering "ye-haw," kicking, or trotting.[54]

Horses were also slaughtered for rations. Although considered to be "very good eating," horse was not as palatable as mule.[55] One partaker of horse meat indicated in 1909 that "no soldier will forget his first horse-meat breakfast."[56]

Colonel Steedman described the desperate situation on July 3:[57]

> For two days a number of horses have been slain and eaten by men and officers. *Rats,* which are very numerous in our camps, are considered a dainty dish, and are being considerably sought after....I have eaten a piece of horse this morning. I do not fancy it, but will eat it as long as I can sustain life upon it, before I will give any consent to surrender. The whole army exhibit the same spirit.

Only snakes were found to be as delicious as rats, both being "quite a luxury—superior...to spring chicken."[58] Sixty barrels of corned beef, miraculously discovered during the final week of the siege, provided sustenance for those individuals who preferred starvation to mule meat. Those who partook were informed after the surrender that their rations were actually carefully corned mule meat.[59]

Even mule meat, however, was preferable to the cow peas issued by the commissary department. The substantial quantity of cow peas that remained at the end of the siege indicated how many of the soldiers found them unpalatable. The cow peas had been stored in the church, which was visible to Union gunners. A favorite target, splinters of wood, bits of plaster, and slivers of glass were soon intermixed with the cow peas. Some of the soldiers used the dried cow peas with grass and salt to make soup; some of the soldiers did not eat peas ever again.[60]

The shortage of food nearly proved the undoing of the garrison. The men preferred mule meat to surrender, but even that delicacy would have been exhausted by mid-July. By the end of the siege, the daily ration consisted of a half pound of mule meat and one ear of corn.[61]

Because the available water was considered undrinkable, the men substituted something loosely described as beer, a concoction made with the abundant stores of sugar and molasses. Barrels of this beverage were strategically placed along the breastworks, and the soldiers had their fill. One junior officer noted: "This was a very pleasant and healthful beverage, and went far to recompense the men for the lack of almost every other comfort or luxury."[62] A Yankee who tried it during the surrender negotiations on July 8 deemed it "really much more palatable than the river water."[63]

Substitutes were not as readily available for other desired items. Coffee was sorely missed. Members of the 4th Louisiana watched each day at dusk as an elderly German private named Neubacher made a "villanous [sic] compound which he called coffee."[64]

One Rebel complained, "I haven't got a single chaw left, not a crumb for my pipe even...."[65] Nicotine addicts anxiously sought a replacement for tobacco. A "tolerable good substitute" for use in a pipe was found in sumac leaves, which were found in abundance in the woods.[66]

Despite all these shortages, morale never became a problem. Notwithstanding their isolated position, southerners felt confident after their success on May 27, 1863, which came as a surprise to them. They became more determined than ever to hold out. The only segment of the garrison that lacked the means of venting their frustrations were the heavy artillerists stationed along the bluff. They had to endure the bombardment of the long-range naval cannon and mortars without being able to reply, because the Union vessels remained beyond the range of their guns.[67]

The soldiers were occasionally reluctant to be transferred to a different section of the breastworks. Such a move had to be perceived as moving from the frying pan into the fire. If they were needed elsewhere, then, the fighting must be hotter there. And there was always the chance they would be stationed in a section of the works that did not afford as much protection as the ones they had constructed and were being ordered to vacate.[68]

Despite all his measures to increase firepower along the breastworks, Gardner could not compensate for the desertions, which steadily increased as the siege progressed. Colonel Steedman noted,[69]

> Our most serious and annoying difficulty is the unreliable character of a portion of our Louisiana troops. Many have deserted to the enemy, giving him information of our real condition; yet in the same regiments we have some of our best officers and best men.

Most of the Confederate deserters belonged to Miles's Legion.

On occasion, Miles's men entered the Federal lines in droves. After eight men of one company and three of another deserted together, Miles rejected the explanations of the company commanders. He thought such blatant action on the part of the enlisted men was the result "in part at least from utter neglect of or careless inattention to duty on the part of officers."[70]

However, there were two additional reasons for the deviant desertion rate in Miles's Legion. More than half of the men in that unit had been conscripted into the army, while the other Confederate units had few, if any, conscripts. Secondly, after the middle of June, portions of the Legion were stationed in isolated trenches on the Confederate right flank that were so close to the Union lines that the Louisianians could hear Yankee soldiers conversing among themselves. In fairness to these Louisianians, it must be noted that the severity and accuracy of enemy fire in this area made it necessary to rotate the troops in these detached works. The exchange had to take place at night, which resulted in a twenty-four hour shift.[71]

Because of illness during the latter part of June, Colonel Miles was forced to relinquish his command, that of the Right Wing, to Colonel Oliver Perry Lyles. In one of the exposed trenches of this sector, Lyles replaced the unreliable Louisianians with English's Mississippi Battery. These artillerymen shouldered muskets in the trenches throughout the siege.

On June 29, these Mississippians were shot to pieces when two Yankee regiments made a night assault on their rifle pit in front of the "Devil's Elbow." Of the three officers present, two were killed, and 2nd Lieutenant P. J. Noland was wounded. He later died in prison. The color, 1st, and 3rd sergeants and the 4th and 5th corporals were wounded. One private was killed and five were wounded. After this disaster, soldiers ordered to this position demonstrated extreme reluctance to relocate. Colonel Lyles finally determined that the position could only be entrusted to officers and men of his own 23rd Arkansas.[72]

The need to hold Union troops at Port Hudson ended with the surrender of Vicksburg on July 4. Upon learning of that bastion's capitulation, Gardner negotiated surrender terms. The end came on July 9, 1863.

A member of Gardner's staff described the 39th Mississippi at the end of the siege:[73]

> I can never forget the heroic deeds of the brave men who fought them. With no shoes, bareheaded, a ragged shirt of jacket, pants in patches, and nothing to eat except sugar, weevily peas, mule meat and rats, they lay at their posts, unprotected from the rays of a June and July sun, and did their duty with honor.

This description would be appropriate for every unit within the garrison. Most of the defenders of Port Hudson managed to survive the ordeal—but they never forgot the hardships they had withstood. The important issue is what motivated these men to endure the greatest deprivation of the Confederacy.

Gardner had trouble persuading his men that their duty was to hold the enemy at Port Hudson. As the siege progressed, more and more of the men began to clamor for a breakout attempt. They wished to join their comrades who were operating in the enemy's rear.[74]

A Yankee who opposed them concluded, "They must certainly attach a deep importance to this stronghold, or human endurance could scarcely hold out against the dreadful ordeal to which we had subjected them."[75] First Lieutenant Frederick Y. Dabney, Gardner's chief engineer, noted in his final report:[76]

> In the early days of the siege strong hopes were entertained of relief

from our forces at Jackson but as time wore on, and no appearance of it, these hopes became fainter and fainter and a spirit of obstinate resistance usurped their place.

Another member of the garrison contended:[77]

This siege was a full test of all the soldierly qualities: personal courage, endurance, and real fortitude. Here the highest qualities of the soldier were tested....This was a fight in which the individual pluck and cunning of the private soldier told. He was largely thrown on his own resources, had to protect himself as best he could, and with deadly aim shoot as rapidly as possible. Commands were rarely necessary.

The garrison's performance supports the accuracy of this appraisal.

Gardner obviously convinced the garrison of the importance of holding the enemy at Port Hudson. Did patriotism alone carry the Confederates through the siege, or had Gardner instilled a sense of professionalism in his soldiers? His men demonstrated their tenacity, but was this a result of their being able to display their individuality? Could some other factor explain the motivation exhibited by the defenders of Port Hudson?

Private J. M. Wolf of the 14th Arkansas Infantry recalled after the war that, for the most part, the siege was a period of boredom and hunger and that once the men learned to avoid incoming shells they were relatively safe in the fort.[78]

Indeed, casualties were few. Only two hundred men were killed and between three and four hundred wounded. Another two hundred died from disease, including sunstroke.[79] Compared with other Civil War engagements, these losses are almost negligible considering the ferocity and duration of the fighting. Possibly the unlikelihood of becoming a casualty enabled the defenders to perform above the norm.

Standing behind the breastwork opposite the smoldering ruins of the Slaughter residence, Arkansas Lieutenant J. M. Bailey never forgot the anxious moments before the enemy advanced on May 27:[80]

It was a magnificent sight, but the great odds against us looked appalling as our line was weak, averaging about one man to every five feet, and no reserve force. Of one thing we felt sure and that was that our men would do all that it was possible for us to do. Every company officer, as far as I could see, stood in line with his men, musket in hand. To facilitate rapid firing, most if not all of the men, placed their cartridges on the works in their front. Varied were the expressions on the faces of the men. Some were serious and silent. Others joked, danced, or sang short snatches of song, but there was an intense earnestness about it all.

All remembered our defeat at Corinth and many remarked that we would now get even. I don't believe any doubted the result notwithstanding the disparity in numbers.

The odds favored the besiegers who eventually outnumbered the Confederates more than five-to-one.

Were the defenders of Port Hudson getting even? Did revenge provide the impetus for these determined men? These were not the victors of Second Manassas, Fredericksburg, and Chancellorsville. As the Port Hudson defenders ate their mule meat at dusk on July 3, their attitudes could hardly have resembled that of "Marse" Robert's men earlier that afternoon a thousand miles to the northeast, before they marched across more than a mile of open ground.

With very few exceptions, not a single Confederate at Port Hudson had ever tasted the sweetness of victory. They were the vanquished of Fort Donelson, Pea Ridge, Shiloh, Island No. 10, Baton Rouge, Iuka, and Corinth. Of the fifteen infantry regiments and battalions that defended Port Hudson, only the 10th Arkansas had participated in a successful campaign, the defense of Vicksburg during the spring and summer of 1862. The same dismal record plagued the garrison's artillery units.

Those Confederates who had not experienced defeat were those who had not "seen the elephant" (soldiers' term used to describe their first combat) prior to May, 1863. Although the war was in its third year when the siege commenced, a sizeable portion of the Port Hudson garrison consisted of green units, including Miles's Legion and the 9th Louisiana Battalion. Did their first taste of victory on May 27 provide the motivation for both veteran and inexperienced soldiers?

What role did the fear of being shipped north to a prisoner of war camp play? Approximately one-third of the defenders had already had that pleasure, including the 1st Mississippi, 1st Alabama, and 15th Arkansas, the three regiments that did most of the fighting during the siege. Following their capture at Island No. 10, in April, 1862, over one hundred members of the 1st Alabama died during their confinement at Madison, Wisconsin. At least one member of the regiment recorded his thanks for being paroled at Port Hudson, praising it as "an act of magnanimity, pure and simple...",[81] an act that was unexpected. The desire to avoid such a fate must have motivated the garrison.

More than one of these factors influenced every man in Gardner's command. In my opinion, however, the psychological need to seek immortality compelled the defenders of Port Hudson, of their own free will, to endure greater deprivations than any other group of Civil War soldiers.

One might argue that the tenacity of the Confederate soldiers at Port Hudson, their refusal to quit, their willingness to endure punishment, are character traits determined either by biological factors or rearing. To read the rosters of the units at Port Hudson is to travel back to some of the great moments in American history. For example, the Maury Tennessee Light Artillery included Andrew Jackson Alexander, Thomas Benton Alexander, Henry Clay Bridgeforth, Patrick Henry Cook, James Madison Dockery, F. Marion Hadley, James Madison Harbison, Oliver Hazard Perry Hight, Thomas H. Benton Johnson, G. W. Robinson, James Madison Sparkman, and James M. Whittaker. Serving in Company K, 1st Alabama, were three men with A. J. for first initials, one T. J., one J. M., four G. W.'s and one man with the last name of Boone.[82] Was the latter a descendant of the legendary Kentuckian? Did the initials of the others stand for George Washington, Thomas Jefferson, James Madison, James Monroe, or Andrew Jackson? Was there a blood link connecting Port Hudson with Valley Forge, the Battle of New Orleans, and the Founding Fathers?

The officers at Port Hudson included W. J. Boone, Daniel Boone, S. O. B. Crockett, and Robert H. Crockett. The blood of Daniel Boone, Jim Bowie, Davy Crockett, and Ethan Allen flowed through the veins of the defenders of Port Hudson.[83] How could they have shown less determination than their ancestors had at the Alamo?

Unfortunately, the historian does not always have the necessary tools to determine why men behave in certain ways during combat. Limited records and a lack of suitable comparisons make it impossible to completely understand the motivation and reaction of the Confederate defenders. It is not conjecture, however, to state that most of the men would have disagreed with Private Wolf's bland assessment of the siege when he stated that the major problems were hunger and boredom. Survivors of Port Hudson did not easily forget the ordeal of 1863.

More than a half century later, a chance encounter in Port Chester, New York, brought together Nicholas Michael Fox, former private in Company H, 28th Connecticut, and J. R. Fellows, a former Confederate captain and assistant inspector general on the staff of Brigadier General Beall. Fox asked Fellows where he had been stationed during the Civil War.

"I served in the campaign in Louisiana and also in Virginia," answered Fellows.

Fox responded, "When were you in Louisiana?"

Fellows replied, "You helped make me a prisoner."

Later in the conversation, Fox asked, "Colonel, during your experience in the war, which did you consider your worst campaign?"

Without hesitation, Fellows answered, "Port Hudson was the nearest to hell you want to go."[84]

Endnotes

1 *The Compact Edition of the Oxford English Dictionary* (Oxford, 1971), p. 2818.

2 James A. Henreta, et al, *America's History* (Chicago: The Dorsey Press, 1987), p. 457.

3 Bell Irvin Wiley, *The Life of Johnny Reb: The Common Soldier of the Confederacy* (n.p.: The Bobbs-Merrill Company, Inc., 1943; reprint ed., Garden City, New York: Doubleday & Company, Inc., 1971), pp. 93-94.

4 Col. E. C. McDowell, "The Siege of Port Hudson," *Confederate Veteran*, V (1987), p. 174.

5 [Howard C. Wright], *Port Hudson: Its History from an Interior Point of View as Sketched from the Diary of an Officer* (St. Francisville, La., 1937), p. 29.

6 *Ibid.*, 22.

7 Linn Tanner, "Port Hudson Calamities—Mule Meat," *Confederate Veteran*, XVII (1909), p. 512; Jill K. Garrett and Marise P. Lightfoot, *The Civil War in Maury County, Tennessee* (n.p.: n.p., 1966), p. 215.

8 John Smith Kendall, "Recollections of a Confederate Officer," *Louisiana Historical Quarterly*, XXIX (October 1946), pp. 1123-24; Charles McGregor, *History of the Fifteenth Regiment New Hampshire Volunteers, 1862-1863* (n.p.: Published by order of the Fifteenth Regiment Association, 1900), p. 515.

9 "Fortification and Siege of Port Hudson—Compiled by the Association of Defenders of Port Hudson; M. J. Smith, President; James Freret, Secretary," *Southern Historical Society Papers*, XIV (1886), pp. 329-30; map in Robert Underwood Johnson and Clarence Clough Buel, eds., *Battles and Leaders of the Civil War*, 4 vols., Vol. III: *Retreat from Gettysburg* (reprint ed., New York and London: Thomas Yoseloff, 1956), p. 596.

10 U.S. Navy Department, *The War of the Rebellion: Official Records of the Union and Confederate Navies*, 30 vols. (Washington, D.C.: Government Printing Office, 1894-1922), ser. 1, XIX, p. 93; Kendall, "Recollections," 1118, 1121-22.

11 Kendall, "Recollections," 1119, 1121-22.

12 *Ibid.*, 1122.

13 Col. E. C. McDowell, "The Siege of Port Hudson," *Confederate Veteran*, V (1897), p. 174; Kendall, "Recollections," 1133.

14 Kendall, "Recollections," 1127.

15 Garrett and Lightfoot, *Maury County*, 64.

16 Edward Young McMorries, *History of the First Regiment Alabama Volunteer Infantry C. S. A.* (1904; reprint ed., Freeport, New York: Books for Libraries Press, 1970), pp. 65-66.

17 Lawrence Lee Hewitt, *Port Hudson, Confederate Bastion on the Mississippi* (Baton Rouge and London: Louisiana State University Press, 1987), p. 171.

18 Dabney to [Gardner], August 24, 1863, Louisiana Historical Association Collection, Manuscript Department, Special Collections Division, Tulane University Library, New Orleans, Louisiana. Hereinafter cited as LHA Collection.

[19] "Diary of Lt. R. W. Ford (7th Texas Infantry), June 14, 1863 (typescript copy), in possession of Russell Surles, Jr., Dallas, Texas.

[20] Daniel P. Smith, *Company K, First Alabama Regiment, or Three Years in the Confederate Service,* (Prattville, Ala.: Published by the Survivors, 1885), p. 71.

[21] U.S. War Department, *The War of the Rebellion: A Compilation of the Official Records of the Union and Confederate Armies,* 128 vols. (Washington, D.C.: Government Printing Office, 1880-1901), ser. 1, XXVI, Pt. 1, p. 147; hereinafter cited as *OR.*

[22] Beall to [Gardner], June 14, 1863, Letters and Reports, Port Hudson, La., 1862-63, 3rd Military District, Department of Mississippi and East Louisiana, Entry 138, Record Group 109, National Archives, Washington, D.C.

[23] [Gardner] to Beall, June 14, 1863, in *Ibid.*

[24] Beall, endorsement of *Ibid.*

[25] Dabney to [Gardner], August 24, 1863, LHD Collection.

[26] Kendall, "Recollections," 1133.

[27] George H. Hepworth, *The Whip, Hoe and Sword or, The Gulf Department in '63* (Boston: Walker, Wise, 1864; reprint ed., Baton Rouge: Louisiana State University Press, 1970), pp. 293-94.

[28] D. H. Hanaburgh, *History of the One Hundred and Twenty-eighth Regiment, New York Volunteers [U.S. Infantry] in the late Civil War* (Pokeepsie, N.Y.: Enterprise Publishing Company, 1894), p. 49.

[29] William L. Haskin, comp., *The History of the First Regiment of Artillery from its Organization in 1821, to January 1st, 1876* (Portland, Me.: B. Thurston and Company, 1879), p. 365; [Wright], *Port Hudson,* 45.

[30] Frank Moore, ed., *The Rebellion Record: A Diary of American Events with Documents, Narratives, Illustrative Incidents, Poetry, etc.,* 12 vols. (New York: D. Van Nostrand, 1861-71), VII, 207; *OR,* XXVI, Pt. 1, p. 146; Deborah Woodiel and Lawrence L. Hewitt, "Archaeological Investigations at Fort Desperate, Port Hudson State Commemorative Area," unpublished report on file at Louisiana Office of State Parks, Baton Rouge, 1980, op. cit.

[31] Hewitt, *Port Hudson,* 134, 168-69.

[32] "Fortifications and Siege," 335, 338; Patricia L. Faust, ed., *et al., Historical Times Illustrated Encyclopedia of the Civil War* (New York: Harper & Row, 1986), p. 837; Caption on back of "Rat Trap" [sketch], Jerrard (Simon G.) Papers, Department of Archives and Manuscripts, Louisiana State University, Baton Rouge; Johns, *Forty-ninth Massachusetts,* 306; Kendall, "Recollections," 1128.

[33] [Col. Paul Francis DeGournay], "D'Gournay's Battalion of Artillery," *Confederate Veteran,* XIII (1905), 32; Henry T. Johns, *Life with the Forty-ninth Massachusetts Volunteers* (Pittsfield, Mass.: Published for the Author, 1864), p. 306.

34 Kendall, "Recollections," 1117; Lawrence L. Hewitt, "Incompetence, Disorganization, and Lack of Determination: The Federal Assault on Port Hudson, May 27, 1863," *Gulf Coast Historical Review,* I (Fall 1987), 82n; Mobile *Advertiser and Register,* December 29, 1863; McMorries, *First Alabama,* 64.

35 Kendall, "Recollections," 1122; Johns, *Forty-ninth Massachusetts,* 306.

36 Kendall, 4th La., 1122.

37 Hewitt, *Port Hudson,* 168.

38 *Ibid.,* 169; John M. Stanyan, *A History of the Eighth Regiment of New Hampshire Volunteers...*(Concord, N.H.: Ira C. Evans, 1892), p. 307.

39 [Wright], *Port Hudson,* 29; Hewitt, *Port Hudson,* 168.

40 Dabney to [Gardner], August 24, 1863, LHA Collection; McMorries, *First Alabama,* 101.

41 [De Gournay], "D'Gournay's Battalion of Artillery," 32; Thomas R. Myers' Memoirs (typescript copy), in author's collection.

42 Dabney to [Gardner], August 24, 1863, LHA Collection; Kendall, "Recollections," 1122; McGregor, *Fifteenth New Hampshire,* 516.

43 Kendall, "Recollections," 1124; Garrett and Lightfoot, *Maury County,* 64; [Wright], *Port Hudson,* 29.

44 Mobile *Advertiser and Register,* August 9, 1863.

45 Garrett and Lightfoot, *Maury County,* 64; Fred Harvey Harrington, *Fighting Politician: Major General N. P. Banks* (Westport, Conn.: Greenwood Press, c. 1948; 1970 printing), 123.

46 Miss Nannie Davis Smith, "Tares among the Wheat," *Confederate Veteran,* XXXVI (1928), p. 127.

47 *Ibid.*

48 Geo. N. Carpenter, *History of the Eighth Regiment Vermont Volunteers, 1861-1865* (Boston: Press of Deland & Barta, 1886), p. 131; [Wright], *Port Hudson,* 30; R. V. Mitchell, "Autographs from an old Album," *Confederate Veteran,* XXXII (1924), p. 176; Hewitt, *Port Hudson,* 169.

49 [Wright], *Port Hudson,* 30.

50 Johns, *Forty-ninth Massachusetts,* 328; [Wright], *Port Hudson,* 23-24.

51 James M. Wolf to Lawrence. Hewitt, March 7, 1988, in author's possession; Linn Tanner, "The Meat Diet at Port Hudson," *Confederate Veteran,* XXVI (1918), p. 484.

52 Tanner, "Meat Diet," 484.

53 Robert H. Langford, "Colonel Billy," *Confederate Veteran,* XXII (1914), p. 110.

[54] Hewitt, *Port Hudson*, 170; "Fortification and Siege," 339; Linn Tanner, "Port Hudson Calamities—Mule Meat," *Confederate Veteran*, XVII (1901), 512.

[55] "Fortification and Siege," 339.

[56] Tanner, "Port Hudson Calamities," 512.

[57] Mobile *Advertiser and Register*, August 9, 1863.

[58] Harrington, *Banks*, 123.

[59] Smith, *Company K*, 77.

[60] Fred Harvey Harrington, "Arkansas Defends the Mississippi," *Arkansas Historical Quarterly*, IV (Summer 1945), p. 116; "Fortification and Siege," 339; Moore, ed., *Rebellion Record*, VII, 207; James M. Wolf to Lawrence L. Hewitt, March 7, 1988, in author's possession; "Capt. William Baker Beeson," *Confederate Veteran*, XXXIII (1925), p. 64.

[61] J. W. Minnich, "With the Louisiana Zouaves," *Confederate Veteran*, XXXVI (1928), p. 425. Hewitt, *Port Hudson*, 170.

[62] [Wright], *Port Hudson*, 51.

[63] Johns, *Forty-ninth Massachusetts*, 323.

[64] Kendall, "Recollections," 1123.

[65] Robert H. Langford, "Colonel Billy," *Confederate Veteran*, XXII (1914), p. 110.

[66] [Wright] *Port Hudson*, 51.

[67] P. F. De Gournay, "The Siege of Port Hudson," in "Annals of the War," [Scrapbook of miscellaneous newspaper clippings, Tulane University, New Orleans, Louisiana.

[68] *OR*, XXVI, Pt. 1, pp. 157-59, 161.

[69] Mobile *Advertiser and Register*, August 9, 1863.

[70] Arthur W. Bergeron, Jr., and Lawrence L. Hewitt, *Miles' Legion: A History & Roster* (Baton Rouge: Elliott's Bookshop Press, 1983), p. 13.

[71] *Ibid.*, 4, 23, 30; Kendall, "Recollections," 1118-19, 1127.

[72] Bergeron and Hewitt, *Miles' Legion*, 14; *Rolls of the Several Military Organizations which entered the service of the Confederate States of America, from the City of Natchez and Adams County, Mississippi* (Natchez, 1890), pp. 1-3; Edward Cunningham, *The Port Hudson Campaign, 1862-1863* (Baton Rouge, 1963), p. 108; Dunbar Rowland (comp.), *The Official and Statistical Register of the State of Mississippi* (Nashville: Brandon Publishing Company, 1908), p. 858; Lawrence L. Hewitt and Arthur W. Bergeron, Jr., eds., *Post Hospital Ledger, Port Hudson, Louisiana, 1862-1863* (Baton Rouge, 1981), pp. 96, 100; Kendall, "Recollections," 1126-27.

73 Crawford M. Jackson, "An Account of the Occupation of Fort [sic] Hudson, La.," *Alabama Historical Quarterly*, XVIII (Winter, 1956), p. 476.

74 Wolf to Hewitt, March 7, 1988.

75 Frank M. Flinn, *Campaigning with Banks in Louisiana, '63 and '64, and with Sheridan in the Shenandoah Valley in '64 and '65* (Lynn, Mass.: Press of Thos. P. Nichols, 1887), p. 77.

76 Dabney to [Gardner], August 24, 1863, LHA Collection.

77 Col. E. C. McDowell, "The Siege of Port Hudson," *Confederate Veteran*, V (1897), p. 174.

78 Wolf to Hewitt, March 7, 1988.

79 Hanaburgh, *One Hundred and Twenty-eighth New York*, 74.

80 J. M. Bailey, "The Story of a Confederate Soldiery, 1861-5," (typescript copy), Texas State Archives, Austin; Hewitt, *Port Hudson*, 158.

81 McMorries, *First Alabama*, 69, 120-23.

82 Garrett and Lightfoot, *Maury County*, 66-76; Smith, *Company K*, 137-43.

83 Rowland, comp., *Official and Statistical Register of Mississippi*, 525-26; Claud Estes, comp., *List of Field Officers, Regiments and Battalions in the Confederate States Army, 1861-1865* (Macon, Georgia; The J. W. Burke Company, 1912), [Part II], 10; Kendall, "Recollections," 1133.

84 Loomis Scofield, *History of the Twenty-eighth Regiment Connecticut Volunteers* (New Canaan, Conn.: New Canaan Advertiser, 1915), p. 24; Adjutants-General, *Record of Service of Connecticut Men in the Army and Navy of the United States During the War of the Rebellion* (Hartford, Conn.: Case, Lockwood & Brainard Company, 1889), p. 857; *OR*, XXVI, Pt. 1, p. 149.

"Civilian" Higher Education in the Making of Confederate Army Leaders

Jon L. Wakelyn

They became the "great lieutenants." The great captains selected them, and the political process confirmed them to rank. The lieutenants' lives of valor and dedication to leader and cause alike became the stuff of legends. To the troops and to the folks at home, their lives grew in importance as those times and later periods required. Today clearer minds discard some of those lieutenants as flawed leaders whose reputations cannot stand up to scrutiny. Others continue to be fascinated with the qualities of leadership that thrust those few above the many.

Why and how did those men make high rank? What leadership qualities appeared in time of war to make those men into the "great lieutenants?" Some no doubt were natural fighters who loved combat. They were fearless, if not a bit foolhardy. Others inspired confidence and trust through their bearing and their powers of persuasion. In that first of modern wars engineering, artillery, organizational and scientific skills brought a number to the attention of their superiors. Still others already knew their commanders, enjoyed strong political support, and came from the proper family or the right state. They had mastered what Thomas L. Connelly and Archer Jones call the "politics of command."

One way to address the question of making army leaders is to ask what characteristics from their pasts the lieutenants and their captain had in common. At first glance their backgrounds were too varied to find any usable pattern for analysis. Most of them had been born in the South, but a number came from the North or abroad. Many belonged to slaveholding wealthy planter families, but many others came from families without means or status. They had a variety of pre-war career patterns and professional military experience. Most of them were young when the War started; brigadiers averaged 36 years old in 1861. But a number were considered too old for military service.

One common factor in their past lives does stand out. Four hundred and fourteen of the 425 general officers chosen to rank attended college or university. One hundred and forty-six graduated from and 10 others for a time attended West Point. A number of West Point graduates also went to other colleges. Nineteen others received some kind of military school training as officers in the regular army. Twenty-three went to the state military colleges such as the Virginia Military Institute and the South Carolina Military Academy. Another 142 spent time at southern private religious colleges or at state universities. A few of them had been to one of the prestigious eastern colleges.[7]

William H. F. ("Rooney") Lee. *Virginia Historical Society*

Almost all of the men who rose to command corps or armies attended the school on the banks of the Hudson. As Douglas Southall Freeman pointed out, the fabled Army of Northern Virginia "could not have been organized or commanded successfully without West Point." Mexican War veterans, Virginia Military Institute students, especially those trained under "Mighty Stonewall," and those who attended the Citadel Freeman classified as "semi-professionals." He marvelled that "civilians" like Wade Hampton and John Brown Gordon held even temporary corps command. What those "civilians" learned, Freeman maintained, "they acquired by reading, by observation in camp, and by the experience in the stern school of combat," even if "battle experience" was "seldom a substitute for professional training in youth."[2]

Yet nineteen of those so-called "civilians" managed to rise above their ignorance and attain the rank of major general. To be sure a number of them did not deserve the rank. A few who should have risen died early in the war. Surely a great warrior like James Johnston Pettigrew would have become a major general for his valor at Gettysburg, if he had not been killed guarding the army's retreat from that misguided adventure. Formidable political powers John C. Breckinridge and Howell Cobb perhaps gained their extra stars for their prewar fame, rather than for their war-time exploits. Dick Taylor, son of President Zachary Taylor, and the fabulously wealthy Wade Hampton eventually attained the rank of lieutenant general. Of course, brilliant officers such as Pat Cleburne and Bedford Forrest did not attend college. Eight other "civilian" major generals who had no previous military experience had attended college or university. They included Matthew Calbraith Butler, John Brown Gordon, and Bryan Grimes from the Army of Northern Virginia, and William Wirt Allen (whose second star was never confirmed), John Calvin Brown, Henry DeLamar Clayton, William Thompson Martin, and John Austin Wharton from the western command.[3] Analysis of those generals' and a few of their friends' "civilian" education could reveal something about the development of those traits which enabled them to make high military rank.

Their preparation for higher education began at home, and not always did it begin with formal schooling. Many studies suggest the importance of the father's influence upon young sons. Both Butler and Gordon described their relations with their fathers. Gordon claimed to have learned obedience and excellent work habits from his father. He gave up the opportunity to achieve high classroom status when his preacher-businessman father asked this most talented young man to leave college. Butler idolized his navy surgeon father, who talked often about the family military heritage and who taught him excellent work habits and early responsibilities. When Butler's father died the young man was sent back from Arkansas to Edgefield County, South Carolina, to live with a famous uncle, Andrew Pickens Butler. Young Butler appeared to shift devotion to that uncle who led him to the life of the law.[4]

When fathers died young, these boys developed extra-close ties to their mothers. Butler's mother had a special pride about her own ancestors, and, after his father's death, often reminded young Matthew of his duties to that past. John C. Breckinridge, another young man whose later life would be intricately connected with some of the eight studied here, also early lost his father and became close to his devoted mother. Breckinridge's mother seemed singularly ambitious for her son to take his rightful place in that powerful Kentucky family. She reminded him of his family heritage and of his duties to her. Other mothers drilled into their sons the will to succeed and to become leaders of their fellow men.[5] How history gained ambition-obsessed leaders because of these stifled flowers of southern womanhood also became the stuff of legends.

Another phase of childhood education, one largely ignored in most biographies, consisted of the extended community which surrounded the home. Not only did the Alabama-raised Henry DeLamar Clayton hear from his father about the family's Georgia political heritage, but his father also entertained great leaders such as the Shorter brothers. Clayton thrilled to be part of that political world. Surrounded by wealth, young William Wirt Allen knew early Alabama's most prestigious leaders. His father, Wade Hampton Allen, often took him back to Edgefield County, South Carolina to visit Hamptons and Butlers. Matthew Calbraith Butler lived with his political uncle, but he also grew up in Wade Hampton's extended household. Butler remembered the pleasure of witnessing his cousins and other important men of the County put on uniforms and drill the local militia.[6]

Formal schooling for these boys usually began with private tutors or in small local school houses. Gordon's father built a field-school on his property to accommodate the children of the community. Young white girls and boys from different strata of that society played, fought, and occasionally studied together. Stories abound of brushes with teacher-authority figures, of teachers beating the youths, and of lockout of the teachers. Few students, as young Kemp Battle claimed, found much to praise about the abilities of often drunken, ill-prepared and transient teachers.[7]

Almost all of these privileged future leaders' ambitious fathers sent them to college preparatory schools, probably to correct the errors of those local schools. At preparatory school the boys learned enough Greek, Latin, and mathematics to pass college entrance examinations. They also gained distance from parental authority, as they went long periods without seeing their families. For example, Clayton's father sent him to school in Georgia, and did not see his son for months on end. Wharton's widowed mother required that he go back east to preparatory school, because the Texas frontier offered no decent education. A few of those boys became quite fond of their teachers, some of whom acted as their surrogate fathers. Legends surrounded the role models who taught, inspired, and frightened those impressionistic boys. The Bingham family of teachers to the well-placed became heroes to fathers who expected their unruly offspring to attend the University of North Carolina. Moses Waddell bestrode the Georgia-South Carolina line, as he alternately cajoled and threatened generations of youths who would later make their marks on southern life. But frightened, mischievous, devious boys miles from home may have been ambivalent about those legends. One need only read Augustus Baldwin Longstreet's neglected masterpiece, *Master William Mitten*, to feel the anger, sorrow, and other tensions in those student-teacher relations.[8]

The boys' prep school experiences went beyond the formal training from their instructors. For they had to learn to live with one another. At the Bingham school in North Carolina, the young boys united around student leaders to present a common front to their faculty adversaries. From those experiences rose their own leaders. Let the small, mild-mannered, sissified future University president and minor historian Kemp Plumer Battle tell of student life at Bingham with Bryan Grimes and James Johnston Pettigrew. According to Battle they stood out in all sports, they protected weaker students against the bullies, and they set codes of behavior which others followed, even into trouble. The poor speaker Battle remarked to his mother that Grimes and Pettigrew also were brilliant students and outstanding debaters. Battle marveled at how their dignified presence elevated those two boys in the eyes of their peers.[9]

With varying preparation, enthusiasm, and ambition these boys went on to southern colleges and universities. Their parents hoped to see them emerge as men. But they arrived at college as quite young men, full of the uncertainty of their age. At college they found variety in student backgrounds, interests, and age groupings. The average age of admission was fifteen, while the average age for those graduated was nineteen. Most students remained at college only one or two years. Of the eight future major generals, the youngest entered college at thirteen, and the oldest graduated at twenty-four. Five remained a full four years, while one graduated after only two years. At least two did not graduate. All would leave college different than when they arrived.[10]

The colleges and universities they attended were diverse in quality, location, and heritage. A spate of state universities emerged in the first blush of post-Constitution enthusiasm. Another kind of enthusiasm around the 1820s led to the founding of denominational colleges in great numbers. The eight future "lieutenants'" choices of college fit this pattern. Four attended the prestigious state Universities, which included the University of North Carolina, South Carolina College, and Franklin College (later renamed the University of Georgia). Two went respectively to Methodist Emory and Henry, near Abingdon, Virginia, and to Presbyterian Centre College, in Danville, Kentucky. John Calvin Brown graduated from the little known Jackson College in Tennessee. The wealthy

William Wirt Allen travelled north to Princeton, a University with strong southern ties. Most of those institutions were embroiled in some sort of controversy based on financial matters, local community tensions, or over the educational product delivered.[11]

The founders placed these colleges in a variety of locations within their states. Some felt that the state capital was an important place for the education of their young men. Perhaps embued with Mr. Jefferson's ideals of nature, others put their institutions in the wilderness. They also may have believed in contemplative silence, or they wanted to remove the young men from temptation, or vice versa. But the best laid plans gave way to change. For example, by the time Gordon attended Franklin College, Athens had emerged from a rural outpost to become a sophisticated urban center. The railroad soon made Chapel Hill close to the center of North Carolina power. Thus, by the time these young men attended school, either a planter or an urban population afforded them polite company, political contacts, and the requisite town-gown frays.[12]

Photos and descriptions of the campuses also reveal differences in size, numbers of buildings, and quality of surroundings. Small colleges had at most three buildings, which included a central administration and classroom structure and two student residences. Each of the state universities had a large, ivy-covered administrative-classroom building, a library, a laboratory or observatory, and a number of student-faculty residences. Overcrowding forced a few students to live off campus and some faculty to live with the students. Students remarked on the dirt, the peeling paint, and the general rundown conditions in which they lived. Of course, they added to the litter, the broken windows and doors, and the horrible state of the dinner rooms. The schools' slaves fought a losing battle against the filth. But the grounds were always beautiful, as those same slaves tended the gardens and the foliage with care. Fences surrounded most campuses either to keep out strangers, or to keep in the young lochinvars.[13]

Most of the colleges convened in five month shifts. The quality of education at many of them barely exceeded today's high schools, while others delivered a product that approximates our graduate programs. Students recited from memory, heard lectures in large classrooms, and the instructors grilled them with questions. Each term included a specific set of education goals. Primary instruction was in classics, mathematics, and natural philosophy, although the larger and better universities had scientific laboratory training. Those who made it to the senior year took instruction from the college president in moral philosophy, ethics, and political economy. All students had to attend chapel.[14] Students thus learned in a rigorous and controlled system.

This close watch on the students and the rigorous curriculum quite obviously contributed to an adversarial relationship between students and faculty. Contemporary commentators and later memoirs remarked specifically on the violent nature of that relationship. Classroom pranks, such as eating, sleeping, reading newspapers, and throwing wet paper balls, often led to a confrontation of wills. Student attempts to punish the non-compliant faculty, such as by breaking residence windows and destroying of gardens, further exacerbated tensions and usually led to more rigorous enforcement of rules to control student mobility. At times those feuds got out of hand. A few extra-proud or foolhardy students brought arms to class. Students and faculty members threatened one another with physical violence, participated in shoving matches, and occasionally fought. Most of those battles between students and faculty tested the patience of both, made an occasional hero of a student among his peers, and kept the students united against what they perceived as attacks on their liberties.[15]

The most outlandish and brutal event in the annals of antebellum southern student-faculty violence took place at the University of Virginia in 1840. Over a small grievance a student from Georgia named Semmes murdered professor of jurisprudence John Davis, himself a graduate of the University. Semmes left school, never to return, and his name disappeared from public view. Other stories of violence involved the young men who became Confederate commanders. While a student at the University of North Carolina Bryan Grimes witnessed a student throw a chair at President David Swain. The student was expelled with the concurrence of his peers. Battle states that the young man eventually redeemed himself by dying for the Confederate cause. Butler himself probably left the College of South Carolina in 1856 because of his participation in the student riots against the unpopular President John McCay, who apparently was unable to handle either students or faculty.[16]

The faculty were hardly guiltless in that adversarial relationship. They were insensitive to their students' needs. Many of them had come from the North. A number like Francis Lieber spent the better parts of their careers trying to leave the South. Others, born and educated in the South, had their own college experiences and codes of behavior to guide them. Those faculty members often taught college in order to make the proper contacts to rise in the outside world. Not a few of them became college presidents, heads of seminaries, bishops, or entered the professions. Frustrated with what they believed were pig-headed, anti-intellectual students who did not appreciate them, many faculty overreacted to student demands. Their instability, frustration, and worries about self-worth no doubt made matters worse.[17]

If the faculty could have seen the students' lecture notes their worst fears about self-worth would have been validated. Young William Cabell Rives, Jr., has left a brilliant and, alas, typical set of notes from his days at the University of Virginia. In George Tucker's political economy class he took copious notes, often paraphrasing that famous economist-historian's words and ideas. But Rives doodled all over his note page, and his subject matter had little to do with Tucker's lecture. He also made written comments in the margins in which he described a teacher who often questioned the worth of his subject and told many jokes to the students. Tucker's lectures on Roman sex codes Rives must have found important. In his notes he underlined the passage that deemed it acceptable to have sex with the wives of slaves. One memorable bit of marginalia discussed Tucker's description of a dream in which "the other night he saw a rat caught by an oyster." Rives wrote an interpretation of that dream, but I will let amateur Freudians figure out what he made of that imagery. Young Rives also copied a poem from his friend John R. Thompson, later the editor of the *Southern Literary Messenger*, which summed up what a number of students thought about their courses. Thompson's poor attempt at rhyme went this way: "And now Latin History may go to the devil, but the trouble it cost me, I'll never forget."[18]

But violence and boredom in class do not tell the whole story of faculty-student relationships. Literal intellectual influence of faculty on students' ideas and values remains difficult to prove. Students did remark on the brilliance of Francis Lieber's lectures, the busts of great southerners in his office to which he invited them for political discussions, and his efforts in behalf of student debate societies. Young Kemp Battle praised the Chapel Hill faculty members who helped him to improve his debate techniques. Breckinridge left many kind thoughts about President Young, who invited him to dinner, and whose Calvinism became a guide to his later behavior. South Carolina College students commented on Professor Maximilian LaBordes and President James H. Thornwell's instructions on the behavior of public figures. A testimonial to faculty importance in student lives was the continued correspondence between them, in which students asked for advice.[19]

Perhaps more important than formal education was how the students learned to get along with older, more powerful men. For students tried to build good relations with those who graded them. At his "civilian" school Gordon impressed the faculty enough to be chosen to give the prestigious class lectureship at commencement. Butler used his family connections to earn the friendship of professors. Because of ties made with older faculty, Wharton chose not to return to Texas after his graduation, but to remain in Columbia and study law with John S. Preston. Martin made a close friend of Robert Breckinridge, uncle of John C., while at Centre College.[20] In short, college life encouraged youth-mentor relationships, which no doubt would assist those young men at another time and in another system where there superiors graded them.

The larger community in which the colleges were placed also contributed to the education of those future leaders. For many of the students the local town represented a break from both classroom tedium and close watch in the dormitories. Grog shops, brothels, and the young town toughs taught these scions a bit about life. Because town was off limits, students had to sneak in at night. They sometimes went armed. The locals waylayed them, and they had to fight their way out. Class, status, and envy toward the students precipitated those brawls. The student code of honor then gave way to gouging, knifing, and kicking the enemy when he was down. From those encounters a number of students emerged as heroes among their peers. They certainly learned the lessons of group support.[21]

The local townsmen and the nearby planter families replenished the students' emotional lives and their stomachs. As guests of relatives, classmates, and family friends and associates the students heard good music, ate well, met members of the opposite sex, and participated in political discussions of the times. At those gatherings some of the young men even found the brides their families wished for them. Breckinridge recalled his uncle Robert's kindness for getting him invited to the homes of Danville's leading citizenry. An alert guest, he joined in the arguments about the abolitionist activities of James G. Birney. Young Butler visited with Wade Hampton and his family at the sumptuous Columbia mansion. There Butler heard in detail about political manipulation in the state legislature. Because of his family wealth, young Bryan Grimes had access to all of the rich folks around Chapel Hill.[22] No doubt those young men benefitted by those connections, both while at college and later in their lives. For in that setting another kind of learning had taken place.

If student-faculty and student-community relations had their physical sides, so did student relationships with one another have violent episodes. Most visitors to the campus, concerned parents, and later analysists have remarked at length on student fights. Contemporary commentators maintained that violence permeated student relations to the detriment of learning. Perhaps this was because they defined learning too narrowly. Some parents worried that harm would come to their sons, while a few sought to protect their sons' rights to harm others. Later scholars declared that student violence reflected the martial behavior endemic to the South. That violent behavior, they claim, simply underscored the fact that most students learned little from their education.[23] They should have looked more closely at how students learned from one another.

It is clear that violence indeed was part of student education. But that violence should be understood as ways students tested the limits of school authority in order to impress each other. Wenching, gambling, drinking, and fighting were ways to resist college rules. J. Marion Sims described the reasons he drank too much while a student at the College of South Carolina in this way: "I did not want to appear before my comrades as if I were afraid of anything or anybody." Despite faculty admonitions, a few well-to-do students treated their campus slaves poorly. One suspects they also needed to pose as typical young planters for the sake of their peers. Young Kemp Battle remarked that students formed a "lawless" club at the University of North Carolina to enforce pledges of mutual assistance against authorities who caught students doing mischievous and destructive pranks. He maintained that the faculty even condoned some forms of violence as part of the ritual of the test of authority.[24]

Other types of student violence reveal much about their relationships with each other. Young John C. Breckinridge fought in class and out, but claimed that most of his violent activity related to campus pranks. He insisted that pranks relieved the students' tensions. John Brown Gordon fought with his college roommate over space until it became clear who was the stronger. They then fought no more. Both later remembered that they defended each other against the rest. Even student duels appeared to test relationships rather than merely reflect a violent community. More often than not, seconds came from the duellers' own states, as students sought familiar support groups for their own insecurities. As to the degree of violence, a wise Linton Stephens knew that student fights could lead to the use of weapons. But his own experience was that they used fists and mostly fought evenly. Stephens himself rarely had to fight, because he forced peer respect through a bluff of physical action and the presentation of a stern public visage.[25]

Students also sought to control what they believed was excessive violence. At LaGrange Military School in Alabama, when a student stood accused of using a weapon against an unarmed fellow, all the students supported the faculty decision to expel the miscreant. Battle also remarked that in several cases where students used excessive violence, other students insisted they leave the University.[26] In those ways, students policed their own behavior.

Student physical courage which tested both authority and each other often led to the creation of campus heroes. Bryan Grimes protected the weaker Battle, which endeared him to that future college professor. That Grimes inherited Pettigrew's mantel as a "hell of a fighter" helped to make him a campus leader. Young John Wharton found much to praise about future Confederate General Martin W. Gary as student leader in the College of South Carolina's 1851 Biscuit Rebellion. Young Matthew Calbraith Butler's ability to defend himself led to his famous role as leader in the 1856 Guardhouse Riot against President McCay's supposed dictatorial powers. The expelled Butler became a college legend.[27]

Other forms of hero-making, which provided an alternative to violence, took place in the classroom itself. There the young men continued to compete, to test and to rank one another. They had many reasons for wanting to excel. Of course, curiosity and genuine intellectual endeavor always drove a small number of students in their studies. Another ambitious group, usually from large families or the middle classes, regarded success at school as a means to enter the professions. Hard work had been a part of their earlier lives, and exertion in class simply was an extension of that experience. This seemed to explain why the

Matthew C. Butler. *Reproduction from the Collections of the Library of Congress*

scholarship student Matthew Whitaker Ransom studied so much and seemed to have an academic chip on his shoulder. He wanted to prove that he was the brightest in his class, and that he deserved the trust others had placed in him.[28]

For most of those who would later become the "great lieutenants," family pride and heritage often mingled with ambition and desire to compete with their peers. One of eleven children, Gordon sought a top place in his class to justify his father's trust in him. The Alabamian Henry DeLamar Clayton wanted to show his father and his peers that he belonged at an eastern college. The coveted Roberson Prize Medal for debate at Emory and Henry was his reward. The rich and brilliant Bryan Grimes carried the burden of a family whose members had always done well at the University of North Carolina. He took pride in his father's acknowledgement that he ranked highest in his class.[29]

Faculty and family recognition of classroom ability seems no more important than the rank the students gave to it themselves. Class notes show the preoccupation with class place. In his notes William Cabell Rives, Jr. listed by name and in order his competition in classics. The small, frail Kemp Battle knew exactly where his competition stood in class. He idolized Grimes and Pettigrew, and he remarked at how a member of the lesser sort like Ransom could soar among his peers.[30] It seems that academic talent and the success that came with it also made some students famous on their campuses.

Of course these were the rare students. Discouraged faculties maintained that the majority of students merely marked time. Students had other things on their minds as their lecture notes readily attested. The overwhelming majority of college students never bothered to graduate. Neither Wade Hampton nor Matthew Calbraith Butler remained to take degrees. Hampton attended the College of South Carolina because his family insisted on it. Even his biographer believed that Hampton would rather have been fishing or riding. Gordon joined a host of students who left college early because their fathers needed them in business or because of family crisis.[31]

For those future leaders who remained in college, non-classroom activities also served to test and to sharpen the skills of student competitors. The Literary Societies provided the setting for student debates. The historian of those societies suggests that education in all its facets took place in those arenas.[32] At their meetings the students presented themselves to one another in dress, manner, and style. They learned to think critically, to write speeches, and to practice the art of public speaking. The use of State newspapers and library collections of famous political speeches and pamphlets, as well as special political guests, made the Societies hothouses of public affairs. In short, that setting trained leaders. The qualities developed would someday be useful on battlefields other than the campaign trail.

Students competed for membership in the Societies. Only through unanimous approval of the members did one gain admittance. Appearance, comportment, family, and ability influenced the selection process. At Princeton Breckinridge joined the prestigious Whig Society, because southerners controlled the Society, because his uncle Robert had influence there, and because Centre College's President Young had taught him how to express himself. The members welcomed a young man who could win at debate. William Starr Bassinger and Jabez L. M. Curry belonged to the literary society at Franklin College, which recruited other young men from their part of the state and from Alabama. At Emory and Henry bitter controversy surrounded election to membership in the literary societies. It seems that the Temperance Society clashed with the drinking literary societies, and the young ministerial students rejected those rowdy organizations. At the University of North Carolina the Dialectic Society attracted young men from wealth and status, many of whom became future leaders in the state and the nation. Zebulon Baird Vance and Leonidas Knox Polk had belonged to it, as had other members of their families. Battle's cousin told him before he went to the "Hill" that he had to join the Dialectic Society. Family ties and leadership abilities contributed to Grimes and Pettigrew joining the Dialectic, and Grimes succeeded Pettigrew as its leader. Grimes also presided over the prestigious "South Building Party," a club within the Society.[33]

A case at the College of Charleston before the faculty judiciary board suggests just how important those literary societies were to the young students. When the board admonished the president of the Chrestomatic Society for keeping members too late at meetings, the response was that no member dared to miss any of the debate. Young Bassinger admitted that he joined a literary society in order to impress his peers, to meet the right people, and to parlay those activities into future gain. John Brown Gordon basked in his peer group's selection of him to give important speeches. He stressed the good conduct and code of proper gentlemanly behavior learned in the Society. Curry summed up the results of what he learned. "Through my college course I gave much attention to my debating society and whatever sucess I have achieved as a speaker is very largely attributable to my training in this school."[34]

Subjects for debate usually reflected current political and moral questions. But the content mattered less than who spoke and who heard the speeches. Long after their specific memories of the topics faded, those young men remembered who rose to the top and what they gained from the competition. Faculty members as advisors, speakers, and part of the audience took the measure of their students, and they in turn were judged for their performances. Successful "old grads" often came to the sessions, where they too judged and were judged. Famous political and intellectual leaders of the South also spoke before the students. Calhoun and William Gilmore Simms chose a number of those gatherings to make important statements to the outside world. Because of the presence of those great men, the students themselves felt part of the larger community. Of course the students competed to impress those men of substance.[35]

Not all student relations centered on the competition in which they tested and ranked their peers. Many students described numbers of examples of mutual assistance. For once they had secured their place and rank, they banded together in the struggle against the common enemy. The ever vigilant Kemp Battle labeled student unity as cheating together. But the record reveals far more than that view. For example, a major part of that mutual assistance was to provide a lecture file for later generations of students. Literary Society members collected notes as well as quizzes and recitation questions, and kept them on file for future use. Another generation of students no doubt gained its first view of the professors as well as much more from the class notes of William Cabell Rives, Jr. John R. Thompson passed on his physical science lecture notes to other students. Rives, Jr.'s letters in the family papers contained lecture notes in many subjects which friends and relatives had given to him. Correspondence between students often ended with the refrain that the notes might prove useful.[36]

Carved out of need, ambition, rank, and true feelings, friendships became a most important part of college life. When Bertram Wyatt-Brown maintains that "the fights led to long-standing male friendships of an intense, fraternal kind," he is only partly correct about how those friendships were made. Lumped together in a sort of prison at an impressionable age students naturally united their resources and skills against the common foe. When the elder Rives asked his son to introduce John C. Calhoun's son to the best kind at the University of Virginia, he knew that both young men would benefit from the connection. Competition in classroom and debate society forged friendships of lasting kinds between Linton Stephens and Jabez Curry, and between Jacob Hunter Sharp and John Brown Gordon. Family connections of wealth and pride and the rank achieved in the struggles for survival as students made longtime friends of Grimes, Pettigrew, and Charles Manly. Mutual respect and need bonded William Russell Smith and Burwell Boykin. Boykin could do math, which Smith could not; Smith could write, and Boykin could not. They merged their talents.[37] A few of those friendships would surface on another field of battle.

Those student friendships also led waves of young men to volunteer for service in the Civil War. Of the 633 students in attendance at the University of Virginia in 1861, 515 joined the Confederate army. Even the border state Centre College of Breckinridge and Martin had half the class of 1860 don the Confederate gray. Faculty and college presidents remarked on the enthusiasm for the Confederate cause the students engendered among themselves. It was as though the young men tried to outdo one another in showing their loyalty to the south. No doubt some found excitement in the hopes that war would open doors to personal advancement. Others acted out of duty to family and identity with the deeds of their ancestors. In his novel *Tiger-Lilies*, Sidney Lanier captured the war spirit which united his fellow students. In the lecture halls, the dormitory rooms and the debate societies, he declared, "an afflatus of war breathed upon us." "Who could have resisted the fair anticipation the new war-tides brought?"[38]

That enthusiasm for group participation in the War relates to the experiences the students had together. The life of college students also made leaders of a few of them. How did the total college environment contribute to the making of those who would become the "great lieutenants?"

If one listens to General Basil Wilson Duke in his life of Transylvania University graduate John Hunt Morgan, too much has been made of the college education of great warriors. Duke maintained that "there was nothing in his boyhood of which any record has been preserved, to indicate the distinction he was to win, and neither friends nor enemies can deduce from anecdotes of his youthful life arguments of any value in support of the views which they respectively entertain of his character." John Brown Gordon's biographer found just the opposite to be true. He concludes that "innate ability explains this unusual record in part, but in part, only. The education he received at the University—reading military biography, public speaking, mastering difficult courses in mathematics, and attaining a place of leadership—probably explains much more."[39] One suspects that the truth of how college education made leaders lay somewhere between those two extremes.

Summary of the ways in which college turned boys into young men and eventually made a few of them leaders of men begins with the many connections the students made at college. Emory Thomas discusses how young Jeb Stuart made important connections while at college. His natural abilities gained the respect of his peers and his professors. Stuart also learned much through his friendship with Custis Lee, son of commandant Robert E. Lee. As a guest at the Lee family quarters, he impressed the elder Lee, who no doubt assisted him in his first appointment under Colonel Philip St. George Cooke. Stuart married Cooke's daughter, and gained a valued cousin in the peripatetic newspaperman John Esten Cooke. The writer Cooke often used his columns to promote the daring military exploits of that reckless young relative.[40]

Most of the young men under review appeared to benefit in ways similar to Stuart. They also had learned to impress both the faculty and the leaders in the local community. Perhaps those informal contacts, or organizations as Connelly and Jones call them, which were forged at college or University, helped to make generals. Wharton married a South Carolina governor's daughter, whom he met at the College. His close friendship with law instructor John Smith Preston, no doubt had significance for his later careers. Martin's rise in the Army of Tennessee could have been connected to such Centre College links as the Breckinridges and the Campbells. John Calvin Brown's brother Neill had preceded him at Jackson College, and Neill became governor of Tennessee. Although Clayton lived in Alabama, he married into the famous Hunter family of Virginia, where he had attended college. John Brown Gordon's close friend at Franklin College was a brother of General William J. Hardee. Grimes was idolized by a prep school student at Chapel Hill named George B. Anderson, his first Civil War commander and a promoter of his military career. Young Matthew Calbraith Butler served under his close family friend Wade Hampton, a member of what Connelly and Jones call the Breckinridge-Preston "concentration bloc." Connelly and Jones also describe an Abingdon-Columbia connection, which this study would extend to Danville, Kentucky and to Edgefield County, South Carolina. Their north-south line actually becomes a square which possibly links a number of colleges and universities to a regional politics of promotion.[41]

Those political contacts made in college suggest one way leaders made rank. Another and perhaps more important role for college life relates to the skills developed through the various forms of training there. By skills I don't just mean the training in violence of student warriors. That seems to acknowledge a unique southern martial tradition, a theory which I hope has been put to rest.[42] Nor do I mean that in class those young men acquired the information to make them leaders. It was the honing of intelligence, the process of learning, not the data itself, that made the classroom, and the extension of class into debate societies, so important to their education. They were forced to memorize great quantities of information. They had to demonstrate constantly their command of the facts. Always on the firing line in class, they were expected to recite with precision and eloquence. Those skills of presentation and the appearance of confidence in their information no doubt for the best of them would be useful in the selection process for another type of firing line.

The political relations and the class training reinforced the most important part of student education. In the many ways they interacted in the total college environment, a few of those young men learned to impress and to stand above their peers. The students selected their own leaders for a variety of reasons. Skill at debate, at athletics, and at manipulation of adults made some stand out. The ability to fight and to protect the weak also placed a small number above their fellows. Mutual assistance in and out of the classroom made a few leaders of their peer group. Thus, the college peer selection process may have revealed the same qualities which led others to make the grown versions of those students into the "great lieutenants" of the Confederate army.

Endnotes

1 Ezra Warner, *Generals in Grey* (Baton Rouge, 1959), xx-xxi, and *passim*; for additional details on military lives see Jon L. Wakelyn, *Biographical Dictionary of the Confederacy* (Westport, Conn., 1978).

2 Douglas Southall Freeman, *Lee's Lieutenants* (3 Vols. New York, 1942) III, xviii-xx.

3 Warner, *Generals in Grey*, passim.

4 Allen P. Tankersley, *John B. Gordon: A Study in Gallantry* (Atlanta, 1955), pp. 17-38, 49; Orville Vernon Burton, *In My Father's House Are Many Mansions* (Chapel Hill, 1985), pp. 106, 117; for a different analysis of the father-son relationship, see George P. Forgie, *Patricide in the House Divided* (New York, 1979), pp. 14-63.

5 See Ulysses Robert Brooks, *Butler and His Cavalry in the War of Secession* (Columbia, S.C., 1909), p. 51; William C. Davis, *Breckinridge* (Baton Rouge, 1974), pp. 11-12. See also Jon L. Wakelyn, "Antebellum College Life and the Relations between Fathers and Sons," in Walter J. Fraser, Jr. (et al), *The Web of Southern Social Relations* (Athens, Ga., 1985), pp. 107-126.

6 Thomas McAdory Owen, *History of Alabama and Dictionary of Alabama Biography* (4 Vols. Chicago, 1921) III, 347, 28-29; *Confederate Military History* (12 Vols. Atlanta, 1899) VII, 385; Burton, *In My Father's House*, p. 97.

7 Tankersley, Gordon, pp. 29-33; W. J. Peele (comp.), *Lives of Distinguished North Carolinians* (Raleigh, N.C., 1897), p. 495; Samuel A. Ashe (ed.), *Biographical History of North Carolina* (IX Vols. Greensboro, N.C., 1907) VII, 251; Owen, *Alabama Biography* III, 347; John Newton Waddell, *Memorials of Academic Life* (Richmond, 1891), pp. 45-55; Jabez L. M. Curry, *Autobiography*, Ms. in Curry Papers, Library of Congress.

8 Augustus Baldwin Longstreet, *Master William Mitten* (Macon, Ga., 1889), *passim*.

9 Lewis Preston Summers, *History of Southwest Virginia* (Baltimore, 1966), pp. 566, 559-564; Peele (comp.), *Lives of Distinguished North Carolinians*, p. 495; Ashe (ed.), *Biographical History of North Carolina* VII, 404; Kemp Plumer Battle, *Memories of an Old-Time Tarheel* (Chapel Hill, 1945), pp. 8, 39, 58, 74; also see letters of Kemp Battle to his mother (Lucy), during the mid-1840s, in William H. Battle Papers, Southern Historical Collection, University of North Carolina (hereafter cited as SHC).

10 See various histories of southern colleges, especially their class lists. Ages of students were computed through an analysis of those class lists. See also the seminal work of Erik H. Erickson, *Identity, Youth and Crisis* (New York, 1968), pp. 128-132, for the analysis of age and student cohorts which informs most of this essay.

11 The best studies of antebellum colleges in the South are Kemp Plumer Battle, *History of the University of North Carolina* (Vols. Raleigh, 1907); Daniel Walker Hollis, *South Carolina College* (Columbia, S.C., 1951); Thomas G. Dyer, *History of the University of Georgia* (Athens, Ga., 1984); George James Stevenson, *An Increase in Excellence* (New York, 1963). For the opinion of many southern people on the state of higher education see *Southern Literary Messenger* XXII (April 1856), 241-253, XXIV (June 1857), 408-409.

12 See the above histories of southern colleges and Universities.

13 Also see the citations listed in footnote #11.

[14] See select college catalogues for information on curriculum, requirements, and dates of sessions. This information changed little over the course of the period under review. For an excellent example of analysis of antebellum scientific study see, Ronald L. Numbers and Janet S. Numbers, "Science in the Old South: A Reappraisal," *Journal of Southern History* XLVIII (May 1982), 163-184.

[15] *Southern Literary Messenger* XI (Feb. 1845), 384-386; Bertram Wyatt-Brown, *Southern Honor* (New York, 1984), pp. 165-166; Charles C. Sellers, *History of the University of Alabama* (Tuscaloosa, 1955), p. 163.

[16] Philip Alexander Bruce, *The University of Virginia* (5 Vols. New York, 1920), II, 309-310, Semmes, probably a member of the family of Raphael Semmes, seems to have had a brother who lost his life fighting for the Confederacy. For the lasting message of that terrible deed, see Alexander Rives to William Cabell Rives, April 21, 1845, William Cabell Rives Papers, Library of Congress.

[17] See for example, Francis Lieber to Samuel B. Ruggles, May 19, 1842, Francis Lieber Papers, Library of Congress.

[18] William Cabell Rives, Jr. Notebook, "Lectures on Greek History, 1842-1843," in William Cabell Rives Papers, Library of Congress; John R. Thompson to William C. Rives, Jr., Dec. 27, 1843, in same.

[19] Lieber Papers, Library of Congress; see the many letters of recommendations in the Moses Waddell Papers, Library of Congress; Lewis Reeves Gibbes Papers, Library of Congress; Davis, *Breckinridge*, p. 14.

[20] Tankersley, *Gordon*, p. 46; Brooks, *Butler and His Cavalry*, p. 52; Ashe (ed.), *Biographical History of North Carolina* VII, 251.

[21] Bruce, *History of the University of Virginia* II, 288.

[22] William Cabell Rives, Jr. to his mother, Nov. 13, 1842, Rives Papers, Library of Congress; Davis, *Breckinridge*, p. 14; Brooks, *Butler and His Cavalry*, p. 51; Ashe (ed.), *Biographical History of North Carolina* VII, 257.

[23] *Southern Literary Messenger* XI (Feb. 1845), 384-386; Wyatt-Brown, *Southern Honor*, p. 167; also see John Hope Franklin, *The Militant South* (Cambridge, 1956).

[24] William H. Battle to Lucy, April 9, 1848, William H. Battle Papers, SHC; Davis, *Breckinridge*, p. 14; Tankersley, *Gordon*, p. 49; Battle, *History of the University of North Carolina*, v. and *passim*.

[25] J. Marion Sims, *The Story of My Life* (Columbia, S.C., 1889), p. 101; James D. Waddell (ed.), *Biographical Sketch of Linton Stephens* (Atlanta, 1870), p. 40.

[26] John Allan Wyeth, *History of LaGrange Military Academy* (New York, 1907), p. 90; Battle, *History of the University of North Carolina*, p. 665.

[27] Battle, *History of the University of North Carolina*, p. 507; Brooks, *Butler and His Cavalry*, p. 50; A. C. Moore, "Alumni of the South Carolina College Who Died in the Service of the Confederacy," *Bulletin of the University of South Carolina* XII (Jan. 1908), 308-309.

28 Maximilian LaBorde, *History of the South Carolina College* (Columbia, 1859), *passim*; Hollis, *South Carolina College*, p. 201; Battle, *Memories*, p. 59.

29 William Garrett, *Reminiscences of Public Men in Alabama* (Atlanta, 1872), p. 659; Battle, *Memories*, p. 78; Tankersley, *Gordon*, pp. 49-54.

30 William C. Rives, Jr., "Lectures on Greek History," in William Cabell Rives Papers, Library of Congress; Kemp Battle in many letters to his mother in 1847, in William Battle Papers, SHC; Battle, *Memories*, p. 93.

31 Manley Wade Wellman, *Giant in Gray: Life of Wade Hampton* (New York, 1949), p. 39; Tankersley, *Gordon*, p. 51.

32 Thomas Spence Harding, *College Literary Societies* (New York, 1971), pp. 1, 26, 89, 93.

33 Davis, *Breckinridge*, p. 15; Curry, *Autobiography*, Ms. in Jabez L. M. Curry Papers, Library of Congress; Stevenson, *An Increase in Excellence*, pp. 160-172; John B. Lewis to Kemp Battle, Aug. 12, 1843, William P. Battle Papers, SHC.

34 Journal of the Proceedings of the Faculty of the College of Charleston, June 8, 1849, College of Charleston Library; Tankersley, *Gordon*, p. 48; Curry, *Autobiography*, Ms. Jabez L. M. Curry Papers, Library of Congress; William Starr Bassinger, "Reminiscences of Life at Franklin College," *The Georgia Historical Quarterly* IX (Mar. 1925), 77.

35 See John Perkins' speech to the Society of Centenary College in *DeBow's Review* XIX (Oct. 1855) 462-465; Jon L. Wakelyn, *The Politics of a Literary Man* (Westport, Conn., 1973), p. 88.

36 John R. Thompson to William C. Rives, Jr., Dec. 27, 1843, "Lecture Notes in Greek History, 1842-43," "Tucker's Moral Philosophy," in William Cabell Rives Papers, Library of Congress.

37 William Russell Smith, *Reminiscences of a Long Life* (New York, 1889), pp. 257-260.

38 Sidney Lanier, *Tiger-Lilies* (Baltimore, 1867), p. 100; Battle, *University of North Carolina*, pp. 690, 720; John L. Johnson, *The University Memorial* (Baltimore, 1871), pp. 439-442; Charles C. Wall, Jr., "Students and Student Life at the University of Virginia, 1825-1861," Ph.D. Dissertation, University of Virginia, 1978, p. 284; see also Wayne Flynt, "Southern Higher Education and the Civil War," *Civil War History* XXII, 211-225.

39 Basil Wilson Duke, A History of Morgan's Cavalry (Bloomington, Ind., 1960), p. 18; Grady McWhiney, "Education in the Old South: A Reexamination," in Walter J. Fraser, Jr. and Winfred B. Moore, Jr., (ed.) *The Southern Enigma* (Westport, Conn., 1983), pp. 169-188. For the other view see Tankersley, *Gordon*, p. 54.

40 Emory M. Thomas, *Bold Dragoon: The Life of J.E.B. Stuart* (New York, 1986), pp. 19-32.

41 Thomas L. Connelly and Archer Jones, *The Politics of Command* (Baton Rouge, 1973), pp. xiii-xv, 52-59.

42 Marcus Cunliffe, *Soldiers and Civilians* (New York, 1968), pp. 335-373; Wyatt-Brown, *Southern Honor, passim*.

Lee and Jackson in 1863; The Shift of Historical Opinion

Thomas L. Connelly

Both men became quite different in the decades after Appomattox, in the years when former Confederates were constructing the mythology of the Lost Cause.

In the case of both Generals Robert E. Lee and Thomas "Stonewall" Jackson, how they were perceived by the Southern people—and the entire nation—changed drastically between even the last year of the Civil War and 1880.

It has been well documented that during the war, Robert E. Lee had a number of rivals for the Southern heart. Other hero symbols included Jackson, Generals Albert Sidney Johnston, P.G.T. Beauregard, Joseph Johnston, and others. General Stonewall Jackson was the most serious competitor for hero symbolism, and a strong case can be made that during the war, he was at least equal in popularity to Robert E. Lee.

Of course, some of Jackson's competition with Lee for hero symbolism can be explained away as the product of a fickle public press. Hungry for hero symbolism and for military victories, the Confederate press in the spring of 1862 seized upon Jackson as the saviour of the South.

But what of the first group of Civil War historians, who wrote immediately after Appomattox? What was their comparison of these two leaders?

During and immediately after the Civil War, three Virginia journalists were the dominant popular Confederate writers. In the books of journalists Edward Pollard and James McCabe, and novelist-journalist John Esten Cooke, there was a consistent viewpoint of the relative military merits of Generals Robert E. Lee and Thomas "Stonewall" Jackson.

Edward Pollard, once temporary editor-in-chief of the Richmond *Examiner*, discussed the two officers in several books, such as his *The Lost Cause: A New Southern History of the War* (1866) and his *Lee and His Lieutenants* (1867). Pollard's 1870 biography, *The Early Life, Public Services and Campaigns of General Robert E. Lee* is exactly the same book as the 1867 volume, except for the addition of five new pages on Lee's post-war career.

Pollard, who asserted that "the war produced no military genius more complete" than Jackson, gave that officer credit for the famous flanking movement at Chancellorsville in 1863. He argued the strategy "originated with Jackson and not with General Lee."

Like other early Confederate historians, Pollard was critical of Lee's generalship in several campaigns, especially at Gettysburg. The earliest group of Confederate writers concentrated their explanation for Confederate defeat on affairs of the first day, July 1. The critical time came that evening, when General Richard Ewell's corps had defeated the Union right wing and had driven it through the streets of Gettysburg. Ahead were the eminences of Culp's and Cemetery hills. If they had been seized, the Federals would have been forced to abandon their strong position along Cemetery Ridge. Instead, Ewell and his division leader, General Jubal Early, developed a case of timidity and called off the attack.

According to Pollard, Lee seemed bewildered and out of control on July 1. He mismanaged Ewell's corps and did not insure that the hills were taken. Also, he disregarded the advice of General James Longstreet, who argued that the Confederate army should shift to the right and flank the Army of the Potomac from its position. Instead, intoxicated by "the animus and inspiration of the invasion," Lee ordered the brutal assaults of July 2-3.[1]

James McCabe, editor of the *Magnolia* weekly, advanced these same basic themes in his wartime biography of Jackson and his later *Life and Campaigns of General Robert E. Lee.* Jackson, not Lee, was "the idol of the South." Stonewall Jackson also was the genius of the Chancellorsville victory. The "bold and brilliant plan" which Lee adopted "was proposed by General Jackson."

Like Pollard, McCabe blamed Lee, Ewell, and Early for the defeat at Gettysburg. On July 1, "a strange hesitation" by Lee prevented Ewell from being ordered to seize the hills. By July 2, Lee had lost his poise, rejected Longstreet's advice for the flanking march, and ordered the disastrous assaults of July 2-3.

The last of this early triumverate of Confederate writers was the popular romantic novelist and biographer, John Esten Cooke. Cooke, already an established historical novelist when the war began, served with General J.E.B. Stuart's cavalry in the Army of Northern Virginia. More important, Cooke wrote three biographies of General Stonewall Jackson. *Stonewall Jackson and the Old Stonewall Brigade* originally appeared in serial form in the *Southern Illustrated News* in early 1863. Later that year, after Jackson's death, Cooke issued *The Life of Stonewall Jackson.* This Richmond publication, so popular that it sold 3,000 copies the first day, was issued shortly thereafter in a pirated edition by a New York publisher. Finally, in 1866, Appleton and Company in New York issued Cooke's larger *Stonewall Jackson: A Military Biography.*

It is obvious that Cooke believed Jackson to be the popular hero and military genius of the Confederacy. To Cooke, Jackson was "Greatest of Generals," "the idol of the popular heart," and the "Man of Fate" in the Confederacy. It was Jackson, not Robert E. Lee, who deserved credit for the victory at Chancellorsville. Jackson designed the famous flanking march to which Lee "speedily assented."

Cooke's view of Lee, like that of Pollard and McCabe, was admiring but critical. Certainly his 1871 biography, *A Life of Gen. Robert E. Lee*, would only infuriate admirers of the General. Like other early writers, Cooke blamed Lee principally for the defeat at Gettysburg. The army was mismanaged on the evening of July 1 and the vital hill positions were not taken by Ewell's corps. Longstreet's wise counsel for a flanking maneuver was ignored. Lee instead suffered from supreme overconfidence, believed his army could achieve any goal, and ordered the disastrous assaults of July 2-3. Hence, Cooke observed, "pride goes before a fall."[2]

Major Northern popular historians echoed these themes, and none was more influential than William Swinton. Swinton, a college professor who served as a war correspondent for the New York *Times*, was the most respected early historian of the Civil War. In 1866, he issued his famous *Campaigns of the Army of the Potomac*, followed in 1867 by *The Twelve Decisive Battles of the Civil War*. In his *Campaigns of the Army of the Potomac*—which remained for years the standard history of war on the eastern front—Swinton placed the primary responsibility for Gettysburg's loss on Robert E. Lee.

Again the events of July 1 were the central focus. Lee was at fault for surrendering to the timidity of Generals Richard Ewell and Jubal Early in their failure to capture Culp's and Cemetery hills. Swinton decribed Lee as off balance and overconfident, intoxicated by the first day's victory. Longstreet's flanking proposal was ignored because Lee had lost "the equipoise in which his faculties commonly moved." He believed his army could do anything—even seize Cemetery Ridge in the assaults of July 2-3.[3]

The opinions of foreign observers were the same. Lieutenant-Colonel Henry Fletcher of the Scots Guards visited the Confederacy and obtained material for his three-volume *History of the American Civil War*. He criticized Lee's tactics at Gettysburg on July 2-3, particularly the failure of Ewell's corps to be used properly. Meanwhile, Lieutenant-Colonel Arthur Lyon Fremantle in late 1863 published his diary account of operations at Lee's headquarters during the battle of Gettysburg. In his "The Battle of Gettysburg and the Campaign in Pennsylvania," Fremantle recorded his stay at General James Longstreet's headquarters during the battle. There was no criticism of that officer, no talk of an alleged early attack on July 2nd. Francis Lawley, later editor of the London *Daily Telegraph*, also viewed the battle from Rebel headquarters. Lawley admired Lee greatly and after the war told General Jubal Early that he had little or no chance of looking "on his kind" again. Still, Lawley blamed Lee and the operations of Ewell's corps on July 1 for the defeat. In an 1872 article, Lawley recounted that Lee appeared overconfident in Pennsylvania, even "too big for his breeches." Generals Richard Ewell and Jubal Early were blamed for not taking advantage of initial success on the left wing on July 1, and Lee was guilty of "maladroit manipulation" of the rebel army for his failure to heed General James Longstreet's advice for a flanking maneuver.[4]

An even more influential foreign commentary appeared eminent. The Comte de Paris, Louis Philippe d'Orleans, had been both critical and complimentary of Robert E. Lee in the first two volumes of his prestigious *History of the Civil War in America* (1875, 1877). In fact, the first volume had so enraged Jubal Early that he published a furious onslaught in an early 1877 volume of the *Southern Historical Society Papers*. Characteristically, the fawning editor, J. William Jones, introduced the diatribe by stating that "...everything from the pen of his able military critic...is noted as of high historic value." Clearly it was a vintage Jubal Early rebuttal. Referring to the Count's "numerous historical errors," Early stormed that he should "consign to the flames all that he has so far published and begin his task *de novo*...."

The poor Comte was so intimidated that he even joined the Southern Historical Society and promised that he would help the South "obtain that fair hearing at the bar of history." The Comte had decided also that in the writings of his third volume—which would include Gettysburg—that he would keep the peace and consult the Lee devotees in Virginia before writing it. In early 1877 he contacted J. William Jones, editor of the *Southern Historical Society Papers*, and sent him a list of five strategic and tactical blunders the Comte believed that Lee made in the Pennsylvania campaign. Only one related to General James Longstreet—destined to become Gettysburg's scapegoat. Mistake Number Five, the Comte said, was that "The heroic but foolish attack by Pickett should never have been attempted." The Comte obviously had been dependent upon William Swinton's work and thus cited that General James Longstreet said that the attack was ordered against his will by General Lee. However, since the appearance of Swinton's book, an article written by Jubal Early—published by the Southern Historical Society—had charged that Longstreet was at fault for not attacking earlier in the day when General Richard Ewell's corps could have cooperated. The Comte stated, "I hesitate very much between these two opinions."[5]

There was no hesitation in Virginia. Editor Jones immediately sent the letter to Jubal Early with the notation that this appeared a good opportunity to give "the true story of Gettysburg." Actually the controversy over the battle had been raging for almost five years before the 1877-1878 public relations campaign by the Southern Historical Society which destroyed the reputation of General James Longstreet.

After the Civil War, General James Longstreet's military reputation was exceptionally good. This had been noted carefully in Professor William Piston's study *Lee's Tarnished Lieutenant*. Piston documented carefully the opinions of major post-war writers, Southern and otherwise.

But Longstreet made three mistakes. He became not only a Republican but an active member of that party in Louisiana's post-war tawdry display of politics. In 1867, he further damaged his rapport with former Confederates by publishing his famous letter in the *New Orleans Times* which criticized Democrats and called for Southerners to embrace Republicanism. Kinsman by marriage to General Ulysses Grant, Longstreet loomed high in local New Orleans Republican circles. Worse, in 1874, when the local White League—many of them Confederate veterans—attempted to overthrow Governor William Kellogg's administration, Longstreet led the predominantly black Louisiana state militia against them.

The General's second mistake was to criticize Robert E. Lee after the Civil War. It is important to note that it was not the criticism itself that was threatening. As mentioned, a host of writers immediately after the Civil War had done the same—John Esten Cooke, Edward Pollard, and many others.

But to the Virginia cult of Lee admirers, Longstreet obviously posed a special threat because of both his credentials as second in command of the Army of Northern Virginia and the fact that immediate post-war historians had praised him highly.

Longstreet, at once vulnerable and potentially damaging to the Lee image, was destined to be the target of the Virginia group.

This was Longstreet's third mistake. During the 1870's, he dared to challenge the literary power of the growing Lee cult in Virginia. Robert E. Lee's death in 1870 had unleashed a flood of both devotion to his memory and determination to rewrite Confederate history. Several powerful groups were organized to perpetuate the General's memory. In Richmond, the Lee Monument Association was led by Generals Jubal Early and Fitzhugh Lee, and former Lee staff officers such as Colonel Walter Taylor. In Lexington, the Lee Memorial Association was controlled by former officers such as General William Nelson Pendleton and Colonel Charles Marshall, and by a local Baptist minister and Lee devotee, Reverend J. William Jones. Meanwhile, Washington and Lee University, with the General's son, Custis, as President, also strove to perpetuate Lee's memory.

Meanwhile, admirers of Robert E. Lee gained control of the Southern Historical Society. Organized in 1869 in New Orleans, the Society had faltered until it was reorganized at a meeting at White Sulphur Springs in 1873. The Virginians literally captured the Society. General Jubal Early was elected President. Under new rules of organization, all members of the executive council must reside in Virginia. Reverend J. William Jones was elected secretary-treasurer. In 1876, when the Southern Historical Society *Papers* began publication, Reverend Jones was named editor of what was to become the South's principal journal of Confederate history.[7]

All of these groups were led by men who were determined to reverse the course of Confederate historical writing. They were unhappy with the current historical image of Robert E. Lee, because literary opinion in two ways prevented what the Virginia writers desired—the image of an invincible military leader.

One threat, obviously, was the consensus view of why Gettysburg was lost. It is important to note here that not only Robert E. Lee's military reputation had been criticized. The explanation of Gettysburg's loss had centered upon the events of July 1. General Jubal Early's reputation also had been damaged by historical criticism, and his enthusiasm for rewriting the battle's history may be viewed in part as a personal desire for vindication.

The second threat to Lee's invincibility was the prevailing image of General Stonewall Jackson. By 1870, Jackson remained more than a rival hero symbol. Some writers described him as the South's greatest wartime leader, while most historians had given him the credit for Lee's greatest victory at Chancellorsville.

* * * * *

Even before the arrival of the Count of Paris's inquiry, the Lee group already had been hard at work to rewrite the story of Gettysburg. Clearly, William Swinton, in his 1866 *Campaigns of the Army of the Potomac*, had leaned heavily on General James Longstreet for his account of Confederate operations. Swinton's book documented "a full and free conversation" with Longstreet in 1865. And the criticisms of Lee offered by Swinton are identical to those made by Longstreet during the 1870's in numerous journal and newspaper articles. Lee had promised Longstreet that he would not fight an offensive battle in Pennsylvania, but became exhilarated with the prospect of combat after the successes of July 1. Meanwhile, Lee mismanaged Ewell's assault of that evening, disregarded Longstreet's flanking strategy, and committed the Army of Northern Virginia to senseless headlong assaults on July 2-3.

As early as 1872, the Lee group began an attempt to reverse this version of the battle. That year, General Jubal Early delivered a long, rambling address at Washington and Lee University, on the anniversary of the General's birthday. One long section defended Early's 1864 campaign in the Shenandoah Valley. Another section sought to reverse the blame for defeat at Gettysburg. Early came up with a new explanation. The battle was not lost due to mistakes by Lee, Ewell, and Early on July 1. Instead, General James Longstreet was to blame for failing to attack promptly on July 2. Lee had intended for Longstreet's corps to attack at dawn, but that officer—opposed to the assault—stubbornly delayed his advance until late afternoon. Had Longstreet attacked at dawn, Lee would have won a "brilliant and decisive victory."[8]

The next year, General William Nelson Pendleton delivered the 1873 Lee birthday address, and embellished the sunrise attack story. Now Pendleton argued that he had made a personal reconnaissance of the Federal left wing on the evening of July 1. Lee, satisfied with what Pendleton reported, ordered Longstreet to attack "at sunrise the next morning."[9]

The concept that Lee planned a daylight attack by Longstreet was absolute fabrication. Obviously Longstreet was late in making his attack on July 2. Yet even a surface examination of the sources revealed that as late as the morning of July 2, Lee himself was confused as to what should be done, and did not even order Longstreet to prepare to attack until about 11 A.M.

Members of Lee's staff knew that Pendleton's story was bogus, and were embarrassed about it. In private letters, several officers denied that any such sunrise attack order had existed. Colonel Charles Venable even thought that General Pendleton was suffering from mental illness, and blamed it on that officer's frequent attacks of loss of memory. Venable characterized Pendleton's story as replete with errors, and regretted that the speech ever got into print. Other staff members, such as Colonels Walter Taylor and Charles Marshall, also denied that such a sunrise attack order was given.[10]

But the damage had been done. Perhaps due to their own rising anger at Longstreet's articles on the battle, these staff members never made public statements as to Pendleton's erroneous speech. Meanwhile, both Early's and Pendleton's speeches were given much publicity. Early's address was printed in both book and article form, and also comprised the first chapter of Reverend J. William Jones's influential 1875 publication, *Personal Reminiscences, Anecdotes and Letters of General Robert E. Lee*. Pendleton toured the South for two years delivering his speech, in order to raise funds for various Lee memorial projects. Later, it was published in the prominent *Southern Magazine*.

Those former members of Lee's staff who could have corrected these accounts did not do so. Apparently they were angered by responses made by Longstreet in various Louisiana and Virginia newspapers. Thus, instead of issuing public denials that the sunrise order existed, staff members joined the rising chorus of Lee devotees who blamed Gettysburg's defeat on Longstreet's delayed assault. Longstreet was blamed in Colonel Walter Taylor's *Four Years With General Lee*, and Colonel Armistead Long's later *Memoirs of Robert E. Lee*. Meanwhile, Taylor and Colonel Charles Marshall repeated the accusation in various articles published in the Southern Historical Society *Papers* and the Philadelphia *Times*.

The 1877 inquiry by the Count of Paris provided the ultimate opportunity to complete the task of rewriting the history of Gettysburg. There were meetings and correspondence between members of the Lee group—Early, J. William Jones, Fitzhugh Lee, Colonels Walter Taylor and Charles Marshall, and others. From these discussions came the famous "Gettysburg Series" which was printed in the Southern Historical Society's *Papers* in 1877-1878.

The series, obviously designed to absolve Lee, Ewell, and Early for any blame for the defeat, was planned by Jubal Early himself. Letters were sent out to nineteen ex-Confederate officers—all selected by Early—requesting them to respond to the criticisms of Lee offered by the Count of Paris. Jubal Early even arranged matters so that all of the articles which appeared in the first issue of the "Gettysburg Series" (August, 1877) were by men he knew would handle Longstreet roughly, such as General Fitzhugh Lee, Colonel Walter Taylor, Early himself, and others.[11]

Jubal Early's concern for his own reputation at Gettysburg was evident when the December, 1877 issue of the Society's *Papers* appeared. Obviously he was frustrated that some of the writers in the first few issues of the "Gettysburg Series" were not saying what he desired them to do—place all of Gettysburg's responsibility upon Longstreet. While there was ample criticism of that officer, some writers continued to place some blame upon Ewell's and Early's failure to capture the vital hill positions on the evening of July 1.

Early's response was to publish an angry, forty-page article in the December issue which both defended his operations on July 1 and repeated his old charges against Longstreet. He said "it is remarkable" that writers even bothered to look elsewhere for reasons for Confederate defeat "when there is an all-sufficient cause staring us in the face...." That cause, of course, was Longstreet's delayed attack on July 2.[12]

A second article by Jubal Early in that same December issue not only displayed insecurity for his own reputation, but demonstrated his manipulative tactics. During the Gettysburg controversy, General James Longstreet had remained relatively quiet except for occasional letters to newspapers. Finally, goaded by articles written by members of the Virginia group, Longstreet consented to write two articles for the popular "Annals of the War" series in the Philadelphia *Times*. The first article, which appeared in the November 3, 1877 issue, was highly critical of Lee, Ewell, and Early for operations on July 1.

It was common practice in that era of journalism—and particularly in the Southern Historical Society *Papers*—to counter unfriendly articles by reprinting them in the magazine accompanied by a strong rebuttal. Now Jubal Early's insecurities motivated him to take his usually unfair tactics to a new low. He ordered his servile editor of the *Papers*, J. William Jones, to print Early's harsh reply to Longstreet in the December issue *without* publishing the article he was criticizing. Instead, Longstreet's article should be published in a later issue. Early explained that by this tactic, by the time readers came to Longstreet's article, they would be well-schooled in his errors.[13]

In October of 1878, the "Gettysburg Series" came to an end. There, in articles in the Philadelphia *Times*, in published memoirs, and elsewhere, the admirers of Lee preached the same message. Clearly, by the end of the decade, the reputation of General James Longstreet was severely damaged, if not destroyed, and the "new" explanation of Gettysburg's loss was accepted generally in the South.

Meanwhile, the Lee circle strove to restructure also the image of General Stonewall Jackson. In the late 1860's, General Robert E. Lee himself had exhibited some irritation with the prevailing Jackson image. In late 1865, Anna Jackson, the General's widow, had asked Lee to read the manuscript of Jackson's biography, written by his former staff officer, Robert L. Dabney. In November of 1865, Lee returned the manuscript with some general criticisms and a cryptic referral to errors made by the author. When Mrs. Jackson appealed to him to list the errors, Lee in January of 1866 replied with a long letter objecting to numerous parts of the book, especially that in which Dabney gave Jackson credit for the strategy at Chancellorsville.

Then, in 1867, Lee again was obviously irritated when an article on Chancellorsville published in the *Southern Review* gave the credit to Jackson for the victory at Chancellorsville. While Lee asserted that he did not wish to detract from Jackson's fame, there was no question that the orders for the Chancellorsville battle and others came from the commander-in-chief, and not from Jackson.[14]

After Lee's death, his admirers in Virginia took every occasion to remind Southerners that Lee, not Jackson, was the genius of Chancellorsville. Thus argued Jubal Early in his 1872 address at Washington and Lee University, J. William Jones in his 1874 *Personal Reminiscences*, and Walter Taylor in his 1877 *Four Years With General Lee.*

Once the controversy with Longstreet subsided in the late 1870's, the group turned more attention to the image of Stonewall Jackson. In 1879, General Fitzhugh Lee delivered a long, powerful address on the battle of Chancellorsville at a meeting of the Association of the Army of Northern Virginia. The speech, soon published in the Southern Historical Society's *Papers*, assigned Lee all of the credit for the famous flanking movement. Jackson was depicted as overconfident, expecting General Joseph Hooker's army to retreat. But Lee's "almost superhuman intelligence" knew better. Instead, Lee designed the brilliant flanking strategy which won the day.

Fitz Lee's "new" version of Chancellorsville was carried throughout the South on a two-year lecture tour (1881-1882) designed to raise funds for the Southern Historical Society. From Galveston to Charleston, from Nashville to Mobile, the heavily publicized tour gave a new image of Stonewall Jackson to Dixie.[15]

In brief, by the eighteen-seventies, the Virginia group of writers determined to rewrite Confederate history and change an image. These Lee devotees, out of fanatical devotion, their own psychological needs, even concern for their own military reputations, determined in the eighteen-seventies to rewrite the history of the war. Lee must emerge better than his peers, better than a "Stonewall" Jackson, Joe Johnston, Albert Sidney Johnston and others. The Lee cultists, such as Jubal Early and J. William Jones, sought to restructure the hall of Confederate icons, so that Robert E. Lee would be elevated above all others. The peerless, stainless Lee also could suffer no defeats. Historical writing had gone hard against Robert E. Lee, these men believed, and so now history must be rewritten.

Perhaps they were successful for two very different reasons. First, they possessed all of the tools needed for their work. The organizational, advertising, and literary resources of the Lee group appear almost inexhaustible. The Lee Memorial and Lee Monument associations were highly organized, with local units in various towns, speakers who delivered fund-raising lectures throughout Dixie, and much printed advertising extolling Lee's reputation. The Lee group controlled as well the South's largest historical organization—the Southern Historical Society, and in turn dominated as well the most prestigious southern historical magazine—the *Southern Historical Society Papers*. Washington and Lee University—headquarters of the Lee Memorial Association group—had its own professional fund raisers, orators, and advertising campaigns.

Beyond all of this were other elements of support. There was the Ladies Lee Monument Association, the large, powerful Association of the Army of Northern Virginia, and the semi-independent Virginia Division of that same veterans' group.

Meanwhile, a generation of former Confederates was emotionally receptive to such symbolism, vulnerable even to the rewriting of history. A defeated South badly needed such symbolism. The Lost Cause mentality had deep religious touchstones, as has been argued by Thomas Connelly and Barbara Bellows in *God and General Longstreet: The Lost Cause and the Southern Mind*, and Charles Reagan Wilson in *Baptized in Blood: The Religion of the Lost Cause*. Both the longtime Protestant ethic and the new Social Darwinism of the late nineteenth century equated success with merit. As Samuel Hill, Jr. observed in *Southern Churches in Crisis*, the success ethic of evangelical Southern religion was especially crucial because the ex-Confederates, by tradition, personalized their relationship to God. God was less a deity to be worshipped than personal companion to provide succor.

So when defeat came, perhaps the former Confederates saw a catastrophe greater than human loss, property damage, or social upheaval. For four years, Southerners had fought believing that God would bring them deliverance, that Jehovah eventually blesses the righteous. In letters, diaries and newspapers, the Confederates described their cause as holy, their civilization better than that of the North, and thus victory an eventual certainty. In 1862, the editor of the *Southern Literary Messenger* boasted that the Southerner "is now, as he has always been and we trust will always be, superior to the Northern man," while an Atlanta newspaper editor described the North as "a swindling race" concerned only for "filthy lucre." And in 1874, George Cary Eggleston published his serialized "A Rebel's Recollections" in the *Atlantic Monthly*. The author recalled that even in the grim campaign of 1864, soldiers in the Army of Northern Virginia refused to consider failure, because "we were convinced, beyond the possibility of a doubt, of the absolute righteousness of our cause, and in spite of history we persuaded ourselves that a people battling for the right could not fail in the end."

Defeat in 1865 thus was a calamity far beyond material loss. On one hand, Southern evangelical religion stressed not only the close personal relationship between man and God, but that one's only evidence of salvation came from an ambiguous, often insecure sense of inner peace. Defeat appeared to jeopardize both. It also juxtaposed the former Confederates against the Puritan ethic that success is a sign of God's grace. The calamity of alienation from one's religious ethos was present even before Appomattox, was there late in the war when nurse Kate Cumming wrote in her diary, "Our sins must have been great to have deserved such punishment."

There was here a sense of intellectual, even emotional displacement, and rationalists of the Lost Cause struck back angrily immediately after the war. The basis for the entire Confederate rationale was expressed by historian and former Richmond editor Edward Pollard in his 1866 *The Lost Cause*. He insisted that Southerners were "the better men," superior "in all standards of individual character over the people of the North."

The "better man" concept of moral superiority buttressed every one of the several rationales for secession or defeat offered by Southern authors in the two decades after the war's end. Early political apologies such as Alfred Bledsoe's *Is Davis a Traitor, or Was Secession a Constitutional Right Prior to 1861?* (1866), beneath turgid, legalistic prose, took the higher moral ground that Southerners had adhered to the principles of the authors of the Constitution while Jacobins in the North had violated them.

Alongside came a torrent of orations and articles comparing the Confederates to chivalric hosts of the Middle Ages, as well as a revival of the tournament as a sport in the eighteen-seventies. Beneath the escapism of such symbolism was a genuine belief in the war as a moral crusade, a saga of Christian knights. At one Confederate reunion, former General W. H. Jackson underscored the similarities of the chivalric code and the Confederate epic, comparing the crusades against Islam with the South's fight against vandal hordes of the North.

The moral issue was present also in the angry post-war military apologies for defeat, penned by former rebel generals such as John Bell Hood, Joseph E. Johnston, Jubal Early, and many others. More often than not, these books were vain, self-serving items designed in part to protect or augment reputations. Literary pyrotechnics between former Confederate officers were commonplace. Still, there was a mutual area of agreement—the "better man" concept.

The theme of moral superiority permeated rebel literature and oratory after the war. Magazines of the Lost Cause era, such as the *Southern Historical Society Papers*, printed articles asserting Northern cowardice and Yankee mistreatment of rebel prisoners. *The Land We Love*, edited by ex-Confederate general Daniel Harvey Hill, bore a masthead which proclaimed that "No nation rose so white and fair, or fell so pure of crimes" as did the Confederacy. In an 1868 article on Southern character, a writer in that magazine stormed that "we cannot believe that a race which gave us Washington, Lee, Calhoun, Clay...can be inferior to the races we have described—to Yankees and Negroes, Germans and Irish. True the United States subdued us. The Huns subjugated the Roman Empire, but was Attila superior to Julius Caesar, or to the race from which he sprang...?"

And shortly after Robert E. Lee's death in 1870, eulogies took the better man approach. Senator Ben Hill of Georgia labeled Lee "a private citizen without wrong....a man without guile," while later the editor of the *Southern Magazine* called Lee "...the noblest type of manhood that this age has produced."

More significant were comments made by Reverend Randolph McKim, a former Confederate soldier, in an 1870 eulogy at Christ Church in Alexandria. McKim's speech foretold much of the ensuing Lost Cause rationale of the eighteen-seventies and beyond. Lee was to be remembered, McKim observed, not just "...because he was a pure and stainless patriot, not merely because he was a model of uprightness and morality. No!" McKim exclaimed. Instead, revere Lee because he was "...as devout as a Christian as he was distinguished as a man— because he was as faithful as a soldier of the cross as he was illustrious as a soldier of what he believed to be the cause or right," one whose life afford an example "of Christian faith as of military genius."

In brief, it was not enough for post-war Southerners to assert moral superiority. They still had the task of explaining how the righteous could lose, how a noble people could fail.

By the eighteen-seventies—as McKim's eulogy indicated—the Lost Cause rationale began to center more upon the Christian interpretation of the Civil War. It provided an opiate to the sense of alienation, that a good people, supposedly protected by Divine Providence, could be destroyed.

Gradually in the eighteen-seventies, the rationale would be well refined. The war became a morale crusade, not unlike those of the Middle Ages. The Confederates also became soldiers of the cross, and endured travail as part of God's eternal plan. A catastrophe such as Appomattox did not prove that God disapproved of the Southern way. In due time, that would be seen, declared the rationale. As General Wade Hampton declared in an early speech, "right *shall* make might, my friends. We may not see it here on earth...but in the last great reckoning ..you who have stood by this right shall on that day find that right shall prevail."

It is important here to note the difference in the theological rationale of a young, self-sure Confederacy of earlier times and a defeated South. The religious ethos of the aspiring Confederacy was more Judaic than Christian, more akin to David's sword than the cross of Christ. Clearly, the evidence is overwhelming that Southerners believed that the Northerners were the Philistines, and the symbolism evoked in the Southern press was not unlike that of the Old Testament.

Defeat changed this. The Old Testament ethic was more akin to the Puritan belief that success was equal to merit. The post-war South could not dwell on the success-merit syndrome, and moved away from the Old Testament symbolism of David to the New Testament symbolism of Jesus Christ. Unsuccessful in the war, the South of the Lost Cause clung to the Christ symbolism, which stressed that good causes can fail in the immediate, though they would triumph in the future.

General Stonewall Jackson had been a wartime David symbol, who smote the Northern Philistines, wielding the sword of the Lord of Hosts. The Jackson image was that of an avenger—stern and inflexible.

But this image of Jackson, more akin to Old Testament symbolism, could not succeed in the post-war South. The more Christian oriented image of Robert E. Lee was more desirable. Lee became positive proof that good men can lose, that righteous causes can fail.

But any Confederate leader selected for a Christian symbol in the Lost Cause era also must have a flawless, invincible image. There can be no Gettysburg to tarnish his record. Likewise, such an individual could have no peers, such as a Stonewall Jackson, but must stand on a plateau above other war heroes.

Perhaps this is why the entire South accepted so freely the rewriting of Confederate history in the 1870's by the Virginia group. Such a reinterpretation was needed. Only then, could Robert E. Lee emerge as the symbol of the Lost Cause.

Endnotes

1   Thomas L. Connelly, *The Marble Man: Robert E. Lee and His Image in American Society* (New York, 1977), 60-61, 58; Edward Pollard, *Lee and His Lieutenants* (New York, 1867), 229, 110-11, 116.

2   James Dabney McCabe, *Life of Thomas J. Jackson, by an Ex-Cadet* (Richmond, 2nd ed., 1864), 191, 179, 196; Connelly, *Marble Man*, 19, 57-60; John Esten Cooke, *Stonewall Jackson: A Military Biography* (New York, 1866) 410, 464; *ibid, A Life of Gen. Robert E. Lee* (New York, 1871), 155, 306-7, 317-18; Richard Harwell, *Stonewall Jackson and the Old Stonewall Brigade* (Charlottesville, n.d.), 49-72.

3   William Swinton, *Campaigns of the Army of the Potomac* (New York: 2nd ed., 1882, 17, 163, 124-25, 142-65; see also *ibid, The Twelve Decisive Battles of the War* (New York, 1867), 352-53.

4   Francis Lawley, "General Lee," *Blackwood's Edinburgh Magazine*, CXI (March, 1872), 361-63.

5   Connelly, *Marble Man*, 85-87; J. William Jones to Jubal Early, March 22, 1877, Charles Marshall to Early, May 24, 1877, in Jubal Early Papers, Library of Congress.

6   For a new account of Longstreet's post-war political activities and ensuing unpopularity, see William G. Piston, *Lee's Tarnished Lieutenant: James Longstreet and His Place in Southern History* (Athens, Ga. and London, 1987), 104-09; see also Charles Marshall to Jubal Early, March 24, 1876, May 24, 1877, in Early Papers, Library of Congress.

7   Connelly, *Marble Man*, 27-56.

8   See Jubal Early, *The Campaigns of Gen. Robert E. Lee* (Baltimore, 1872); Connelly, *Marble Man*, 55-56; J. William Jones, *Personal Reminiscences, Anecdotes, and Letters of Gen. Robert E. Lee* (New York, 1874), 32.

9   William N. Pendleton, "Personal Recollections of General Lee," *Southern Magazine*, XV (December, 1874), 603; Glenn Tucker, *Lee and Longstreet at Gettysburg* (Indianapolis, 1968), 13, 43; Piston, *Lee's Tarnished Lieutenant*, 121-31; Connelly, *Marble Man*, 84-85.

10 Piston, *Lee's Tarnished Lieutenant*, 124-25, 129-30; Tucker, *Lee and Longstreet at Gettysburg*, 13, 43.

11 For a discussion of the Gettysburg Series, see Connelly, *Marble Man*, 86-89. For an examination of the series, see consecutive issues of the Southern Historical Society's *Papers*, from August, 1877 to October, 1878.

12 See "Leading Confederates on the Battle of Gettysburg: A Review by General Early," *Southern Historical Society Papers*, IV (December, 1877), 281; see also pp. 241-81.

13 Jubal Early to J. William Jones, November 19, 1877, in Southern Historical Society Collection, Confederate Museum, Richmond; see also Jubal Early, "Supplement to General Early's Reply—Reply to General Longstreet," *Southern Historical Society Papers*, IV (December, 1877), 282-302.

14 See Mrs. Thomas Jackson to Robert E. Lee, October 20, 1865, January 9, 1866; Robert L. Dabney to Lee, May 14, June 2, 1866, all in Robert E. Lee Papers, Washington and Lee University; see also Robert E. Lee to Mrs. Thomas Jackson, November 11, 1865, January 25, 1866; Lee to Robert L. Dabney, February 13, May 21, 1866; Lee to A. T. Bledsoe, October 28, 1867, all in Lee Family Papers, Virginia Historical Society.

[15] Fitzhugh Lee, "Chancellorsville," *Southern Historical Society Papers*, VII (December, 1879), 545-85. See also Connelly, *Marble Man*, 82-83.

[16] For viewpoints on the relationships between the Confederate Lost Cause mentality and Southern religion, see Thomas L. Connelly and Barbara Bellows, *God and General Longstreet: the Lost Cause and the Southern Mind* (Baton Rouge, 1-38; see also chapters 1 and 2 of Charles Reagan Wilson, *Baptized in Blood: The Religion of the Lost Cause* (Athens, Ga., 1980).

Marse Robert at Mid-Life

Emory M. Thomas

What follows is of necessity a report on work in progress—some discoveries and tentative conclusions from my research on the life of Robert E. Lee.[1] I hope I can offer some insights about Lee and by extention about the human condition. And I want to share my excitement about this extraordinary person. Let me begin by quoting him.

> My experience of men has neither disposed me to think worse of them nor indisposed me to serve them; nor, in spite of failures which I lament, of errors which I now see and acknowledge, or of the present aspect of affairs, do I despair of the future. The truth is this: The march of Providence is so slow and our desires so impatient; the work of progress is so immense and our means of aiding it so feeble; the life of humanity is so long, that of the individual so brief, that we often see only the ebb of the advancing wave and are thus discouraged. It is history that teaches us to hope.[2]

These are stirring words, and it is significant that Robert Edward Lee wrote them in the aftermath of defeat and in the very midst of failure. In the shambles of Southern civilization and culture as he had known it then, Lee could affirm, "It is history that teaches us to hope." Surely in the larger sense in which Lee meant that last pronouncement, he believed that history teaches hope. But when we consider what historians have done with Lee and the history he made, we might suggest that he amend the sentence to read, "It is history, not historians, that teaches us to hope."

Consider some examples of what historians—great historians, near-great historians, would-be-great historians, and not-great-at-all historians—have done with Lee and his history. For certainly portions of the record of Lee in the hands of historians has sometimes raised as many doubts about the hopefulness of history as Southern defeat and failure in 1865. Let me offer some examples.

Professional journals are required reading for historians who want to remain "current" and competent in their teaching, research, and writing. Yet, although they arrive through the mail in a "plain brown wrapper," historical journals are often about as titillating as the white pages of the Cleveland telephone book. The prose in scholarly periodicals is usually as exciting as the obituary notices in the *Minneapolis Tribune*. And, however "solid," the articles read very much like the Pure Food and Drug Act.

Exceptions there are, however. Tucked carefully away in the May, 1977, issue of the *Journal of Southern History*—all but concealed between an exhausting study of the property rights of Southern women during Radical Reconstruction and a 43-page list of about 900 journal articles relating to Southern history published in 1976—is an article of refreshing interest and rare suspense. At first glance "A Historian's Dilemma: A Posthumous Footnote for Freeman's *R. E. Lee*" by John Gignilliat of Agnes Scott College looks as though it might be a conventionally dull tome. Not so.[3]

The piece concerns Douglas S. Freeman, Virginian, scholar, and newspaper editor, who between 1915 and 1935 wrote in four volumes the definitive biography of Robert E. Lee. Freeman's *R. E. Lee* is the standard portrait of the Great Gray Knight as Southern Saint.

Not long after Freeman published his labor of love, however, he discovered a disturbing document—a letter from Lee to a friend in which Lee confessed to an almost casual murder, committed apparently while in the act of trespass and petty theft.

The incident occurred in 1835 when Lee was a young (28) lieutenant participating in a surveying expedition on Lake Erie. In the course of his duties, Lee and another lieutenant sought to use a lighthouse located on Canadian soil as a reference and observation point. Lee described what happened next.

> "The door was locked & we could not gain admittance, but after some time succeeded in getting through the window i[n] rear when we discovered the Keeper at the door. We were warm & excited, he irascible & full of venom. An altercation ensued which resulted in his death. We...gained the Top, attained our object, & in descending I discovered Some glass lamp shades, which we stood much i[n] need of as all ours were broken. I therefore made bold to borrow two of his Majesty....We have nothing to offer in our behalf, but necessity and as we found the Lt. House in a most neglected condition & shockingly dirty, & were told by the Capt. of the Cutter that there had been no light in it for more than a year. I hope it will not be considered that we have lopped from the Government a useful member, but on the contrary to have done it some service, as the situation may now be more efficiently filled & we would advise the New Minister to make choice of a better Subject than a d...d Canadian Snake."

Understandably Freeman was puzzled. Here was an authentic letter in which Lee seemingly convicted himself of mindless brutality. How could his hero be so uncharacteristically characterless? For a long time Freeman resolved his dilemma by ignoring it. Nine years after he first read Lee's self-incrimination, Freeman proposed that the other lieutenant and not Lee had killed the lighthouse keeper.

ROBERT E. LEE, *Courtesy Virginia State Library*

Later still Freeman included the incident in a reprinting of *R. E. Lee.* But he submerged the material in a footnote and referred to the "unhappy incident" as "the accidental death of a Canadian lighthouse keeper." Clearly Freeman was trying to protect the spotless reputation of the noble Lee he had come to know in his research and writing.

Fortunately, however, Freeman was himself a man of character and integrity. He compelled himself to enter the incident, however obscurely, in the Lee record, and he left the original letter with its riddle for posterity to ponder.

Posterity, in this case historian John Gignilliat and editor of the *Journal of Southern History* Sanford W. Higginbotham, found the solution absurdly simple. The events of Lee's trip to the Canadian Lighthouse were as Lee described them in his letter—except the "lighthouse keeper" was a literal Canadian snake, a reptile, not a person. In the letter to his good friend Lieutenant Lee simply sought to relieve the tedium of his mundane assignment by indulging in a mock-heroic telling of a routine incident. He wrote the account tongue-in-cheek to a friend whose sense of humor excelled his biographer's.[5]

In his attempt to protect Lee's sainthood, Freman all but withheld evidence that only enlarges Lee's humanity and thus enhances his statue as hero. In order to understand Lee, I believe it is important to reread what he wrote and said—to look behind his words and rethink their meaning.

Despite evidence that even Freeman did not fully fathom the scope of Lee's personality, *R. E. Lee* remains, after more than half a century, the definitive study of its subject. And in that biography, based upon twenty years of labor and love, Freeman vented his unbridled admiration for his subject. In the final chapter he concluded:

> "Because he was calm when others were frenzied, loving when they hated, and silent when they spoke with bitter tongue, they shook their heads and said he was superman or a mysterious man. Beneath that untroubled exterior, they said, deep storms must rage; his dignity, his reserve, and his few words concealed sombre thoughts, repressed ambitions, vivid resentments. They were mistaken. Robert Lee was one of the small company of great men in whom there is no inconsistency to be explained, no enigma to be solved. What he seemed, he was—a wholly human gentleman, the essential elements of whose positive character were two and only two, simplicity and spirituality."[6]

Freeman's interpretation of Lee as the embodiment of simple virtues and uncomplicated piety has endured among Americans, and especially Southern Americans, with the same tenacity as his biography. Lee, essentially Freeman's "Lee," has held an honored place in the pantheon of American heroes, and below the Potomac he has remained a demi-god.

Recently, however, has come a challenge to the Lee legend so thoroughly accepted by so many for so long. In 1977 Thomas L. Connelly published iconoclasm in *The Marble Man: Robert E. Lee and His Image in American Society*. Connelly's judgements deserve a serious hearing; he is a distinguished Southern historian, probably the nation's preeminent living scholar of Civil War military history. Most of *The Marble Man* concerns not the history that Lee made, but what history has made of Lee. Beginning with his death in 1870, Connelly carefully charts the course of the Lee image in the American mind. Yet an assessment of image necessarily requires an examination of reality, and thus Connelly offers a final chapter about the living Lee.[7]

In contrast to Freeman, whose final sentence proclaimed, "there is no mystery in the Coffin there in front of the windows that look to the sunrise," Connelly portrays Lee as a bundle of complexities and complexes. He writes of "inner loneliness," a "repressed vibrance" and a preoccupation with death. He interprets Lee's piety as an attempt at escape from reality into mystical fatalism. Connelly's Lee responded to difficult situations by invoking trust in "Divine Providence" and not responding. "His life was replete with frustration, self doubt, and a feeling of failure,....He was actually a troubled man, convinced that he had failed as a prewar career officer, parent, and moral individual."[8]

There are stern judgements, and many people have dismissed *The Marble Man* as blasphemy and Connelly as an apostate. Yet it is an important book, and Connelly has opened an interesting debate. A hero is usually a hero because people identify him with qualities and virtues which they admire and to which they aspire. In challenging the "marble" qualities of Lee as hero, Connelly, may have begun a redefinition of Lee's heroism. In trying "to portray him as a human being," Connelly has opened the way for a greater appreciation of Lee's humanity. When the scholarly dust clears, Lee will remain a hero, perhaps even more a hero than he currently is. Freeman's Lee seems too perfect, too divine in an age like ours which is all too aware of human frailty. Connelly's "Lee" is certainly too full of human frailty, but at least he is identifiably human.[9]

Somewhere between Freeman's simple saint and Connelly's collection of complexes was the "real" Lee. The challenge is much more than simply adding Connelly's "Lee" to Freeman's "Lee" and dividing by two, to arrive at an average "Lee." In addition to rereading and rethinking Lee's words, Lee's biographer should think again about the title of Connelly's book. *The Marble Man* as a description of Lee comes from Stephen Vincent Benét's epic poem *John Brown's Body*.

> —And so we get the marble man again,
> The head on the Greek coin, the idol-image,
> The shape who stands at Washington's left hand,
> Worshipped, uncomprehended and aloof,
> A figure lost to flesh and blood and bones,
> Frozen into a legend out of life,
> A blank-verse statue—[10]

Benét, however, was not content to describe Lee as a statue. He suggested that no one could understand Lee by analyzing only what he said and wrote (as Freeman and Connelly have essentially done). Benét pointed out that Lee's words were not always as important as Lee's actions.

> Yet—look at the face again—look at it well—
> This man was not repose, this man was act.
> This man who murmured "It is well that war
> Should be so terrible, if it were not
> We might become too fond of it—" and showed
> Himself, for once, completely as he lived
> In the laconic balance of that phrase;
> This man could reason, but he was a fighter,
> Skilful in every weapon of defence
> But never defending when he could assault,
> Never retreating while he still could strike,
> Dividing a weak force on dangerous ground
> And joining it again to beat a strong,
> Mocking at chance and all the odds of war
> With acts that looked like hairbreadth recklessness
> —We do not call them reckless, since they won.
> We do not see him reckless for the calm
> Proportion that controlled the recklessness—
> But that attacking quality was there.
> He was not mild with life or drugged with justice,
> He gripped life like a wrestler with a bull,
> Impetuously. It did not come to him
> While he stood waiting in a famous cloud,
> He went to it and took it by both horns
> And threw it down.[11]

Lee was and is a hero because he acted out heroism. And anyone who aspires to write his biography must ponder the existential Lee.

Nineteenth-century Americans, like modern Americans, had various formulae of words and phrases which they considered appropriate to various circumstances. Lee, perhaps more than most of his contemporaries, knew the correct words to use, and he was quite sensitive to what he believed he ought to say in given situations. Much of what he wrote and said sounds stylized now. Thus it is important to remember what Lee did, while he was speaking and writing the *pro forma* prose of his time. Sometimes, in fact, his deeds contradicted his words.

In addition to looking behind Lee's words and discovering that the lighthouse keeper was really a snake, I suggest the need to look beyond words and examine Lee's actions which did not always conform to his words. There is a third caveat as well. It is important to remember that Lee was human. Consider the awe one Southerner felt when he discovered that his grandfather had seen and known Lee. "It was as if...he had seen and known the Good-Lord-in-Heaven, because I picture them as almost interchangeable: The Good-Lord as General Lee in a shiny nightshirt, and General Lee as the Good-Lord in a Confederate uniform." Consider the Richmond schoolteacher who turned Lee's photograph to the wall when her pupils misbehaved to "spare him the painful sight."[12]

So pervasive has been the conviction of Lee's sainthood in the American soul, that even so insightful a critic as Tom Connelly has fallen victim to Lee's divine mystique. When he challenges the Lee image, Connelly uses that image as a target for his critique. And by using the image, he gives it unintended credibility- —much like the schoolboy cry "I am *not* a sissy," or the protest of presidential candidate George Bush, "I am not a 'wimp.'"

Lee was a human being. His words are important clues to understanding him, if we are willing and able to think beyond the superficial meaning of those words. And we must think, too, about Lee's actions which were sometimes more revealing than his words. Let me now offer specific examples (1) of looking behind Lee's words, (2) of focusing upon Lee's deeds, and (3) of emphasizing Lee's humanity.

I

Here are some lines from a letter Lee wrote in 1843 when he was thirty-six years old to a young woman he addressed as "Tasy." Her name was Sarah Beaumont; she was nineteen at the time; and she was the daughter of Dr. William Beaumont who was a good friend of Lee's in St. Louis.

> My beautiful Tasy;—I have just returned from Washington where your charming letter followed me. I have brought it back with me to enjoy it. I wish you were here in person, for I am all alone. My good Dame not wishing to leave her mother so soon, even to follow such a spouse as I am.

•　　　•　　　•

> Poor Alex K—I pity him. Comfort him Tasy, for if the fire of his heart is so stimulating to the growth of his whiskers there is danger of his being suffocated. What would be the verdic of a jury in that case ?suicide? It is awful to think of: Inveigle him out to talk French with you. You know that is the language of the heart & you might in that way introduce a little cold water to quench the flame. I hope the sympathy between himself & Miss Louise is not so intimate as to produce the same effect on her, for I should hate her sweet face to be hid by such hairs unless they were—mine.

•　　　•　　　•

...a word of advice. It is translated from Theocritus & is an inscription on a statue of Love

"MILD HE MAY BE, AND INNOCENT TO VIEW,
YET WHO ON EARTH CAN ANSWER FOR HIM? YOU
WHO TOUCH THE LITTLE GOD, MIND WHAT YE DO."

Say not that none has cautioned you

"ALTHOUGH SHORT BE HIS ARROW, SLENDER HIS BOW:
THE KING APOLO'S NEVER WROUGHT SUCH WOE."

If after this Tasy you fall a *victim*, you cannot blame me for it.[13]

Here is a portion of a letter Lee wrote to Martha Curtis Williams (Markie) in May of 1851. "Markie" was in her mid-twenties; Lee was forty-four. The correspondence between the two distant cousins continued for twenty-six years.

> My dearest Markie
> You have not written to me for nearly three months. And I believe it is equally as long since I have written to you. On paper Markie, I mean, on paper. But oh, what lengthy epistles have I indited to you in my mind! Had I any means to send them, you would see how constantly I think of you. I have followed you in your pleasures, & your duties, in the house & in the streets, & accompanied you in your walks to Arlington, & in your search after flowers. Did you not feel your cheeks pale when I was so near you? You may feel pale Markie, You may look pale; You may even talk pale; But I am happy to say you never write as if you were pale; & to my mind you always appear bright & rosy.[14]

Finally, here is part of a letter Lee wrote in 1840 to two young sisters, Elizabeth and Matilda Mason (Bettie and Mattie). He had recently enjoyed their company at White Sulphur Springs were he had lingered en route to St. Louis and duty.

> What then must I tell them of? It shall be of the belles & beaux of this new country & I will commence with what they all wish to come to, bride & bridegroom. A specimen of this species I have before me every day at dinner. He was a loafer about Natchez. She is very pretty, an heiress & just from the altar. She has not yet laid asside the manner she acquired in her belleship, Sits during dinner expanding her large eyes & pouting her pretty lips has all the appearance of one that has not found matrimony what it is cracked up to be. ...Today while busily engaged with his grouse & champagne he was much startled by the announcement of her intention of going to Europe, but moved himself sufficiently after one swallow to beg permission to accompany her. The next in position and first in rank

comes Genl. [Edmund Pendleton] & Mrs. [Myra Whitney] Gaines. They have enjoyed their happiness longer though it is still so new upon them that no wonder they cannot conceal it. She declares that the Genl. has more than fulfilled every promise he ever made her & he that he could not have believed that he could have again experienced in all their freshness the joys of wedded life. I am afraid at seventy they will prove too exhausing to his veteran frame. He already appears to be sinking under them & her prospects are very good of again becoming a happy widow. She is very pretty, affable & lively & is as rapid in her thoughts and speech as he is dilatory & faltering.[15]

This, of course, is a tiny sample of Lee's correspondence, even of his correspondence with young women. On the surface these letters seem fairly straightforward. Lee sought to amuse the young women to whom he wrote with flattery, gossip, and wit. Avery Craven who edited a published edition of the "Markie" correspondence says that the letters "abound in that good-natured banter that characterized his manner with young folks...." Craven also finds "wholesomeness of his spirit," "a rather appalling sense of duty," and "respect for authority."[16] Douglas S. Freeman concluded:

The company of women, especially of pretty women, he preferred to that of men. In the presence of the other sex, he displayed a gracious, and sometimes a breezy gallantry; but no suggestion of a scandal, no hint of over-intimacy, was ever linked with his name. His conversation with his younger female friends was lively, with many touches of teasing and with an occasional mild pun, but it was not witty.[17]

Freeman "lived" with Lee much longer than I have; but with all due respect I believe Lee was quite witty. And I believe that behind the words in these examples was a sensitive, warm, sensuous man.

Lee's analysis of the two pairs of newly-weds in his letter to the Masons demonstrate his keen understanding of human relationships. His discussion of the "joys of wedded life" and his description of the woman who had "not found matrimony what it is cracked up to be" — "expanding her large eyes" — "pouting her pretty lips" — are downright tittilating.

His opening lines to "Markie" are tender and caring. At the same time they tell the young woman that she is an object of Lee's fantasy.

To Tasy, Lee writes of fantasies and then offers a poem which is plainly erotic. I have searched the works of Theocritus in vain for the poem. But whether Theocritus or someone else wrote it matters not; Lee used it; maybe he wrote it. Even though Lee wrote the letter before Sigmund Freud was born, the Freudian implications of "touch the little god" and "short be his arrow, slender his bow" are clear. And I suspect that Lee himself had a sense of the erotic significance behind his words.[18]

I do not suggest that Lee was a "dirty old man." He was sensitive, warm, and sensuous—none of which adjectives do I mean pejoratively. His written repartee was subtle and witty. He could and did tittilate and fantisize, and he employed an occasional erotic double entendre. I suspect his correspondents appreciated Lee's cleverness; I hope they responded in kind.

I am not prepared to explain why Lee carried on this lively correspondence with young women. I suspect it had something to do with the frustration he felt in his marriage and with the compulsion he felt for control. Mary Custis Lee was never as lively as Markie Williams or Tasy Beaumont seem to have been; but as long as his relationships with these and other young women lived primarily in letters, Lee could be confident of his capacity to control himself. Whether or not Lee ever lost control of himself I do not know. I do know that he worried about losing control.

The double entendre appears not only in Lee's letters to young women; he was capable of risqué rhetoric in conversations with men. The best example I have found occurred in 1843 or 1844 when Lee was serving at Fort Hamilton, New York. At the time American Episcopalians were debating the "High Church" theology advanced in England by Edward Bouverie Pusey. Lee attempted to stay out of the debate over Puseyism. One evening some fellow officers became especially insistant. Henry J. Hunt, a lieutenant who had also refused to take sides in the doctrinal dispute, recalled that Lee addressed him in mock seriousness and said:

> I am glad to see that you keep aloof from the dispute that is disturb-ing our little parish. That is right, and we must not get mixed up in it; we must support each other in that. But I must give you some advice about it, in order that we may understand each other: Beware of Pussyism! Pussyism is always bad, and may lead to unchristian feeling; therefore beware of Pussyism![19]

Freeman insists that Lee was responding to the "feline character" of the quarrel and states that on the evening Lee spoke of "Pussyism," the dispute was "very catty." It is true that Puseyites were called "pussy-cats" in the slang of the time. It is also true that "pussy" and "pussy-cat" were nineteenth-century vulgarisms for the vulva and by extention for women as sex-objects. The latter meaning of "pussy" seems to make more sense in Lee's little exhortation to Hunt. If he did speak to the cattiness of the debate, perhaps he intended a triple entendre. Whatever he meant, he repeated, "Beware of pussyism!" whenever he saw Hunt for some time thereafter. And the meaning behind "pussyism" is even more intriguing than "Canadian snake."[20]

II

As an example of an existential appreciation of Lee, let me cite one letter, written in 1845 to his oldest child Custis who was thirteen at the time and away at school. Much of the letter is about Lee's second son William Henry Fitzhugh (Rooney) Lee who was then eight years old.

The letter begins with some remarks about Custis's school work:

> I am pleased with your progress so far & the last report sent me by Mr. Smith gave you a very good standing in all your studies. I was surprised to see that you were lower in Algebra than in any other. How was that, for I thought you had some talent for mathematics.[21]

This is the classic parental comment. Never mind all those "A's," let's concentrate on this "B." And students have read and heard words to this effect probably forever.

Then Lee writes about Rooney:

> You may possibly not have heard of the accident that has happened to our dear Rooney. Last Monday afternoon (24th Inst.) while I was in N.Y. & your Mother had gone out to tell the neighbors goodbye, preparatory to her leaving for Arlington, he feeling lonesome, went down to the...barn where they were putting in some hay for the horses & got up in the loft & before Jim was aware of it commenced to cut some hay with the straw cutters & took off the ends of the fore & middle fingers of his left hand. The first just at the end [?] of the nail—the second at the first joint. Jim took him immediately into the fort to the hospital, but unfortunately Dr. Eaton was also in N.Y. So that more than one hour & a quarter elapsed before they could be dressed. All that time he sat in the hospital with his fingers bleeding profusely without complaining & frequently scolded Jim for making a fuss about it...
>
> I hope my dear son this may be a warning to you to meddle or interfere with nothing with which you have no concern & particularly to refrain from going where you have been prohibited, or have not the permission of your parents or teacher. Fearing that some accident might happen to Rooney...I had prohibited his leaving the yard without permission & never to go to the stables without my consent & Jim had told him never to go near the cutting box. Notwithstanding all this he did both & you see the fruits of disobedience. He may probably lose his fingers & be ruined for life. You cannot conceive what I suffer at the thought. Do take warning from the calamity that has befallen your brother. I am now watching by his bedside lest he should disturb his hand in his sleep. I still hope his hand may be restored. Since the accident he has done all in his power to repair

his fault. He has been patient & submissive, giving no trouble & never complaining. He has been more disturbed at my & your mother's suffering than his own & says he can do very well without his fingers & that we must not mind their loss. Although he is at times heedless obstinate & disobedient, which are grave faults, he has some very good qualities which gives us much pleasure. I hope this will be a lesson to him & that in time he will correct his evil ways."

In many ways this is a dreadful letter— "the fruits of disobedience" — "ruined for life"—"evil ways." This is a father writing about an eight-year-old child who must have been sufficiently penitent in the midst of his pain! Lee was following the nineteenth-century parental pattern of making moral lessons of common events, and he surely went to great lengths to try to make something good come from poor Rooney's misfortune.

Eventually the child's fingers healed, and he was not "ruined for life." But what about the father? Amid Lee's heavy moralizing, it is easy to overlook an important sentence: "I am now watching by his bedside lest he should disturb his hand in his sleep." While he was writing didactic doom, he was acting out something quite different. As it happened Lee stayed with Rooney for several nights, acting out loving concern even while writing down judgement.

Freeman speaks briefly to this incident. He makes it an example of Lee's concern for physical perfection. "As a man and as a parent, Lee was singularly sensitive to personal beauty and always seems to have had an inward shuddering at any deformity." Freeman also notes that, "For years his messages to his boys were full of solemn preachments...." But Freeman does not empasize Lee's actions, only his words.[23]

I confess when I rethink Lee's letter to Custis and focus upon deeds beyond words, I recall the concluding pages of a modern novel which is truly a celebration of parenthood. The character Jem is a boy who has suffered trauma and injury. The narrator is his sister.

> As I made my way home, I thought what a thing to tell Jem tomorrow. He'd be so mad he missed it he wouldn't speak to me for days. As I made my way home, I thought Jem and I would get grown but there wasn't much else left for us to learn, except possibly algebra.
> I ran up the steps and into the house. Aunt Alexandra had gone to bed, and Atticus's room was dark. I would see if Jem might be reviving. Atticus was in Jem's room, sitting by his bed. He was reading a book.
> "Is Jem awake yet?"
> "Sleeping peacefully. He won't be awake until morning."
> "Oh. Are you sittin' up with him?"
> "Just for an hour or so. Go to bed, Scout. You've had a long day."

And finally:

> He turned out the light and went into Jem's room. He would be there
> all night, and he would be there when Jem waked up in the morning.

The novel, of course, is Harper Lee's *To Kill a Mockingbird.*[24]

III

To emphasize Lee's humanity, let me begin by posing that Lee was considerably more multi-dimensional than Americans have yet imagined. One of those unacknowledged dimensions was ambition. Lee's humanity did not only involve writing thoughtful notes to gentlewomen. He could be ruthlessly anxious for the loaves and fishes of favor and rank. In the aftermath of the Mexican War Lee wrote a revealing letter to his father-in-law George Washington Parke Custis. Although Lee addressed Custis as "My dear father," the two men were all but polar opposites. Custis dabbled in many things to the detriment of his once considerable fortune. He died in 1857, and Lee was still trying to pay the debts of the estate and complete his charge as executor when he himself was near death in the late 1860s.

But Custis retained his connections with prominent men, and he lived just across the Potomac from Washington. So Lee wrote Custis from Mexico City in April of 1848 and vented frustration, false modesty, and covetousness.

> I hope my friends will give themselves no annoyance on my account or any concern about the distribution of favors. I know how those things are awarded at Washington & how the President will be besieged by clamorous claimants. I do not wish to be numbered among them. Such as he can conscientiously bestow I shall gratefully receive, & have no doubt that those will exceed my deserts. I cannot consider myself very highly complimented by the brevet [temporary promotion] of 2 grades. They were bestowed on two officers at Palo Alto, ..., for one single effort on the part of each. I have never seen an officer yet, present at the engagement, that thought they deserved more than one. Genl. [D.E.] Twiggs in an official letter to Genl. [Winfield] Scott which has fallen under my eye & endorsed by Genl. S. recommended me for the brevets for the battles of Cerro Gordo, 17 & 18 of April. So that if I performed any services at Vera Cruz, or at the battles around this capital, they will go for nought. The Secy.'s rule [limiting the number of brevets] did not seem to prevent Lt. [John C.] Fremont from being advanced 3 grades from a Lt. of Engrs. to a Lt. Col. of Rifles.

Lee offered other examples of rapid advancement among his brother officers and continued, "I presume however that their services exceeded mine, which

I know to be small. Only one of these however, had been previously in an engagement...."[27]

Alive, Lee was very much a human being; only later did he suffer apotheosis. I suggest that, Douglas Freeman to the contrary, there is indeed mystery in that "coffin there in front of the windows that look to the sunrise."

The first time I ever met my professional mentor Frank E. Vandiver, he informed me in matter-of-fact tones, "Douglas Freeman is God." And my friend Tom Connelly, for all his iconoclasm toward Freeman and Lee, once proclaimed in public, "*R. E. Lee* is the greatest biography in the English language." Nevertheless, I believe it is time to reponder Freeman's "Lee," to reexamine stock stories and standard solibeths.

Almost every morning in his life Douglas Freeman paused in his drive to walk along Richmond's Monument Avenue to salute Lee's statue. Connelly's bold work has offered Lee as that same statue in flawed marble. The time is ripe for someone to fill in Benét's blank verse and present Lee off the pedestal—as a human being whose essence was action; as a hero who fashioned greatness from the human condition.

Endnotes

1 In the course of preparing this essay I have picked the brains of several people. My colleague Jean Friedman, fellow graduate students from long ago Tom Connelly, Judy Fennar Gentry, and Jon Wakelyn, and Virginia Historical Society reference librarian Frances Pollard all contributed. And Michael O'Brien offered what became an insightful challenge: "Tell us a Lee joke."

2 Robert E. Lee Headquarters Papers, Virginia Historical Society, Richmond, Virginia.

3 John Gignilliant, "A Historian's Dilemma: A Posthumous *Footnote* for Freeman's *"R. E. Lee,"* Journal of Southern History, XLIII* (May, 1977), 217-236.

4 *Ibid.*, 221-23.

5 *Ibid.*, 234-36.

6 Douglas Southall Freeman, *R. E. Lee: A Biography* (4 vols., New York, 1934-35), *IV*, 494.

7 Thomas L. Connelly, *The Marble Man: Robert E. Lee and His Image in American Society* (New York, 1977).

8 *Ibid.*, XIV.

9 See Thomas L. Connelly and Barbara L. Bellows, *God and General Longstreet: The Lost Cause and the Southern Mind* (Baton Rouge, 1982), 73-106.

10 Stephen Vincent Benét, *John Brown's Body* (New York, 1927), 171.

11 *Ibid.*, 173.

12 J. Bryan, III, *The Sword Over the Mantel: The Civil War and I* (New York, 1960), 42-43.

13 R. E. Lee to Sarah Beaumont, Ft. Hamilton, N.Y., March 11, 1843, in Robert E. Lee Papers, Virginia Historical Society, Richmond, Virginia.

14 R. E. Lee to Martha Custis Williams, Baltimore, May 10, 1851, printed in Avery Craven, ed., *"To Markie:" The Letters of Robert E. Lee to Martha Custis Williams: From the Originals in the Huntington Library* (Cambridge, 1933), 24-27.

15 R. E. Lee to Elizabeth and Matilda Mason, St. Louis, August 31, 1840, Lee Family Papers, Virginia Historical Society, Richmond, Virginia. As it happened, Gaines was sixty-three, not seventy, and he did live to become seventy-two.

16 Craven, ed., *"To Markie,"* v-vi.

17 Freeman, *Lee*, I, 451.

18 My reading of this material is informed by Peter Gay, *The Bourgeois Experience: Victoria to Freud* (2 vols., New York, 1984, 1986).

19 A. L. Long, *Memoirs of Robert E. Lee* (reprint edition, Seraucus, N.J., 1983), 66-67.

20 Eric Partridge, *A Dictionary of Slang and Unconventional English*, Edited by Paul Beale (Eight edition, London, 1984), 938.

[21] Robert E. Lee to G. W. Custis Lee, Ft. Hamilton, N.Y., November 30, 1845, Lee Family Papers, Virginia Historical Society, Richmond, Virginia.

[22] *Ibid.*

[23] Freeman, *Lee*, I, 196, 198.

[24] Harper Lee, *To Kill a Mockingbird* (Popular Library Edition, New York, 1962), 282-84.

[25] R. E. Lee to G. W. P. Custis, City of Mexico, April 8, 1848, Robert E. Lee Papers, Virginia Historical Society, Richmond, Virginia.

Lincoln's Tarnished Brass: Conservative Strategies and the Attempt to Fight the Early Civil War as a Limited War

Joseph L. Harsh

One of the most venerable platitudes in Civil War History is the old saw that George Brinton McClellan is a puzzle. The most widely held view today is that the solution to that puzzle can only be found through posthumous psychoanalysis. We are told that McClellan was vain, egotistical and pompous; that he was timid and lacked the iron will to carry through on the battlefield; and that, while he might have contributed something to the war effort with his organizational talents, he was not much more than the first of a series of sorry candidates to try the patience of the Job-like Lincoln.

In an article which appeared in *Civil War History* in June of 1973, after surveying the various views which have been held on McClellan for the past one hundred years, I took issue with the current interpretation of the General. I suggested we remove McClellan from his merry-go-round of controversy by paying *some* attention to his strategy and somewhat *less* attention to his personality. I found it almost incredible that inspite of the gallons of ink spilled in debate, no one, not even his friends and biographers, had grasped what it was McClellan was trying to do, nor how his strategy, once understood, explains many of his actions which are otherwise puzzling.*

In the restrictive limits of that article I could give only a brief summary of McClellan's military program:[1]

> The heart of McClellan's policy was to wage war within the limits of the Constitution and "to do nothing to render ultimate reconciliation and harmony impossible, unless such a course were imperative to secure military success."[2]

McClellan believed that the deleterious effects of the war could be kept to a minimum only if the popular passions on both sides were conscientiously damped. On the one hand, Southerners should be treated firmly but gently, as prodigals soon to be home and forgiven. While their armies were defeated, their prisoners of war should be handled humanely and their civilians' property scrupulously protected. On the other hand, Northerners should not be called on to wage an overly long war checkered with battlefield reverses—which, unfortunately, had been exactly the presagement of Bull Run. In all cases, he hoped to avoid a "useless effusion of blood."[3] To implement this policy, McClellan devised his strategy of "overwhelming." He wanted the North to undertake massive preparation and then launch a vast, irresistible offensive to end the war in one, continuous campaign. McClellan was cautious (at least in part), because he believed caution, or to use his own phrase "reasonable certainness," was the proper course for the North to pursue to achieve its war aims.

In this paper I wish to expand upon the latter part of that thesis and to examine in more detail both the theory and practice of McClellan's conservative, or limited war strategy.

*   *   *   *   *

In the rush to condemn the North's early generals and their strategies, military historians have ignored the reasons the North went to war. In the first year or so, there was widespread agreement among Northerners about what they wanted from the struggle. There was an amazing consistency in the statements of the President, his cabinet, both houses of Congress, newspaper editorials, letters home from the volunteer soldiers, residents of the border states, Democrats, and the conservatives and moderates which comprised the vast majority of the Republican party. Northern war aims were literally conservative. Northerners wished to conserve the Union and the Constitution and to restore the *status quo ante bellum*. They were not interested either in destroying the South or in engaging in experiments in social reform. They took up arms not to bring about change but to keep things the way they had been.

It was in this atmosphere and against this national consensual mandate that the early Northern generals were called upon to devise their strategies. And it was within this shared definition of victory that they were called upon to formulate their plans for winning the war.

Not surprisingly, there was at least some understanding that there should be a correlation between what the North wanted and how it went about getting it; a correlation, in other words, between aims and strategy. In fact, before McClellan came to Washington on July 26, 1861, there had already been two attempts to implement limited-war strategies more or less suited to achieving the North's conservative war aims.

Winfield Scott, General-in-Chief at the start of the war, had offered the first. Appreciating the armed potential of the new Confederacy, Scott believed that the military subjugation of the South, even if successful, could come only after the expenditure of billions of dollars and hundreds of thousands of lives. More importantly, Scott feared (I am tempted to call it Scott's dread) that the passions aroused in such a war by what he called "exasperating attacks" would

GEORGE B. McCLELLAN, *Harper's Pictorial History of the Civil War*

undermine the federalism of the Constitution and would make it impossible to restore the Union as it was. He proposed, therefore, a strategy that was essentially passive: institute a blockade of the southern coast and send a flying column down the Mississippi to capture and hold strong points along the river. He then proposed to do nothing but wait until, under the economic pressure, the strong latent Unionism in the South reasserted itself.

Scott's plan was dubbed the "Anaconda" by the press, and it was misunderstood then and it has been misunderstood since. Historians have ridiculed the old General himself for falling asleep during dinner, for needing a ladder to mount his horse, and for devising such a silly strategy. Yet, his plan was a limited-war strategy that harmonized with the North's war aims and on that basis alone deserves more serious attention than it has received.[1]

Scott's program was never given a chance to succeed, because it contradicted, almost totally, the second conservative strategy, and because that second strategy was put forward by none other than the President of the United States. Although Abraham Lincoln was thoroughly in tune with the North's original war aims, he decided early on, sometime in May of 1861 and probably under the influence of Congressional radicals and the Blair family, that the key to reestablishing the Union on a pre-war basis was the speed with which the South could be compelled to lay down its arms. His conservative strategy was to end the war quickly and before much change had a chance to occur or become permanent. For this reason he rejected Scott's prolonged plan and against all professional military advice hurried Irvin McDowell's column forward into Virginia to disperse the rebels at Manassas Junction. At the battle of Bull Run the North reaped the harvest of its haste. As the routed bluecoats scurried back to Washington, Lincoln and the North was left without a military plan.[5]

At this point, McClellan was called to Washington. Shortly after his arrival, the President asked him for his thinking on a grand strategy for winning the war, and McClellan replied in a memorandum dated August 2nd. All of the essentials of McClellan's strategy, which I have called the strategy of overwhelming, are present in that document; and, although he would amplify and somewhat modify the details, the basic ideas would remain constant to be reasserted in his famous Harrison's Bar letter in July, 1862, and again in his memoirs after the war, as the plan he still thought the best the North could have followed.[6]

McClellan's was a conservative strategy, as had been Scott's and Lincoln's, in that it sought to conduct the war in such a way as to insure reconciliation. He agreed with Scott that great losses of men and money could well prove to be counter-productive, but he disagreed that the war could be won without hard fighting. McClellan agreed also with Lincoln that the length of the war would affect the reconstruction of the nation, but he understood that moving too quickly and without adequate preparation could lead to reversals which would, ironically, lengthen the war. This, indeed, had been the hard lesson learned at Bull Run.

McClellan proposed, therefore, a compromise: to win the war in as little time *as was possible* and with as little loss *as was possible*. And he devised a strategy that minimized time and casualties within what he believed to be a reasonable assessment of Southern resistance. The three keys to McClellan's plan were: immense forces, thorough preparation, and the exertion of constant pressure on the enemy at many points simultaneously. In the first place, McClellan wanted the North to mobilize its great human and material resources and to translate its preponderant odds from paper to the battlefield. It is in this regard that he writes a number of times of "overwhelming" the South. In the second place, McClellan wanted to take the time, before beginning his campaign, to drill, season and discipline the men and officers to a high level of efficiency and dependability.

He wanted a superior degree of discipline not only because he wanted to be reasonably certain of victory in battle, but also because the behavior of Northern soldiers toward Southerners and their property was another essential to reconciliation.

In the third place, McClellan devised a strategy for the deployment of Northern forces that exerted constant and growing pressure all along the perimeter of the Confederacy. The net effect of McClellan's plan was to be this: on the one hand, to make Southern resistance seem foolish if not impossible; while, on the other, to make returning to allegiance seem easy and attractive. Of all of the early, conservative strategies, McClellan's was the most realistic. It was also, it might be added in passing, surprisingly "modern" approach to waging limited war.

It might be even more surprising to speculate that McClellan may have found inspiration for his strategy in the writings of the Baron Jomini, the 19th century military theorist who today is judged to have been so obsolescent as to have crippled the abilities of those who followed his advice. Reflecting upon the Napoleonic campaigns on the Iberian peninsula, where the French had sought to crush the Spanish nation in arms, Jomini had counseled:[7]

> If success be possible in such a war, the following course will be most likely to insure it. Make a display of a mass of troops proportioned to the obstacles and resistance likely to be encountered, calm the popular passions in every possible way, exhaust them by time and patience, display courtesy, gentleness, and severity united, and (particularly), deal justly.

*   *   *   *   *

McClellan's specific strategy for the deployment of troops to "overwhelm" the South called for the main effort to be made in Virginia. Here, the Army of the Potomac, augmented by forces from elsewhere, was to capture Richmond in one continuous but cautious campaign, knock Virginia out of the war and severely maul, if not destroy, its counterpart, the main Confederate army. McClellan was probably correct to choose Virginia as the main theater for the kind of war he wished to wage. If one wants a relatively short war, it probably is right to slash for the jugular. And indeed Virginia was just that, possessing not only the capital of the Confederacy, but also more of its people, wealth and industry than any other state. After finishing with Virginia, the Army of the Potomac was to pursue the remaining Confederate forces through the Carolinas to Chattanooga and thereafter wherever necessary.

A secondary column was to be formed in Kentucky to drive on Nashville and thence to Chattanooga to form a junction with the Army of the Potomac. While these main columns advanced, pressure was to be kept up elsewhere. Forces in Missouri and western Virginia were to be reduced to support the field armies, but enough troops were to be retained to pin down sizable numbers of Confederate soldiers. Additionally, and this was an important part of his strategy, in a series of south Atlantic coastal operations, combined army and navy forces were to capture southern ports and then serve as flanking enclaves to threaten the rear of the retreating main Confederate army and finally to join the Army of the Potomac as it advanced southward.

*   *   *   *   *

McClellan was never able to implement his strategy in a totally systematic way. When he submitted his proposal, he commanded only the Army of the Potomac. Not until November 1st did Scott retire and McClellan become General-in-Chief, with authority to carry out such a broad and sweeping strategy. In the meantime, McClellan did what he could. He worked feverishly to drill and equip the Army of the Potomac and to increase its numbers as much as possible. He had, in fact, largely completed this task by the time of his elevation to overall command, and he probably could have commenced his campaign against Virginia in early December.

He did not do so for one simple reason. Upon moving into Scott's office, he discovered that the Army of the Potomac alone, of all the forces of the Union, was even near to being ready to take the field. Elsewhere there was chaos—discipline and morale were wretched, essential supplies were ungathered, and most regiments had not even been brigaded let alone armies formed. McClellan decided not to move forward with the Army of the Potomac, when it could not be supported by movement in any other theater. He decided, instead, to take the time to bring these other areas up to operations and to implement as best he could at this late date his strategy of overwhelming. If the right men could be found to organize and lead in the other theaters, McClellan believed his plan could be launched as an early spring offensive and the war ended in late 1862 or early 1863.

This decision to delay was for McClellan the beginning of the end. During the subsequent four months, Northern frustration and impatience would build to such an extent as to ruin his effectiveness as General-in-Chief and, indeed, end with his removal from that office. It is ironic, of course, that McClellan, even though he was responsible for the decision to delay, was not responsible for the waste of time prior to November which compelled the delay. It is equally ironic that he wasted virtually no time during the four months he was General-in-Chief, for four months would be all of the time allowed him to mount and undertake his strategy of overwhelming.

*   *   *   *   *

McClellan moved first to organize the middle theater, comprised of Kentucky and Tennessee, which was to yield the other main field army for his grand offensive. By-passing William T. Sherman, whom the administration had adjudged "unreliable," McClellan merged the departments of the Cumberland and the Ohio into a new and larger Department of the Ohio and named to its command Don Carlos Buell. On November 15, Buell assumed his new command, bringing with him detailed orders and the sort of policy guidelines that McClellan alone ever provided to his subordinates. As a legacy of Kentucky's period of neutrality, virtually nothing had been done in that state, and, indeed, only fourteen regiments had been brigaded in the new department. Buell was an excellent organizer and administrator, however, second only to McClellan in this respect, and in three months' time, that is by mid-February, he had pulled his command together and readied the middle theater for active operations.[8]

Elsewhere, in Missouri and the Department of the West, McClellan had inherited a mess that was even worse than in Kentucky. Not only was there disorganization but also demoralization following the Federal defeat at Wilson's Creek, the discovery of rampant corruption in army purchasing, and the removal of the popular John C. Fremont from command after his abortive attempt to emancipate slaves. McClellan divided the cumbersome Western Department, creating from the plains states a Department of Kansas, minor command which he used to shelve David Hunter, who had assumed temporary command after Fremont's removal.

A new command, its area of active operations including Missouri, Arkansas and Kentucky-Tennessee west of the Cumberland River, and denominated the Department of Missouri, was given to Henry W. Halleck. Although Halleck was not of the caliber of either McClellan or Buell, he assembled an able corps of subordinates, including Ulysses Grant, William Sherman and John Pope, and his department was also ready to contribute to the offensive by February. While most of Halleck's assignment involved the pacification of Missouri, he was requested to provide a field force in western Kentucky to cooperate with Buell. This column, commanded by Grant, had moved into Tennessee and captured Forts Henry and Donelson by February 16th.[9]

By early March 1862, therefore, McClellan could be satisfied that the west was ready to take its part in his grand invasion of the Confederacy. Kentucky had been cleared of rebel forces; Grant held nearly all of west Tennessee; Buell had occupied Nashville in the center of the state; and George Thomas' smashing victory at Logan's Crossroads, near Mill Creek, had opened the way to Knoxville and east Tennessee.

*   *   *   *   *

One other series of events contributed to the bright Union prospects of March 1st, for McClellan had not devoted his attention exclusively to the preparation of the mainland armies during the four months period of delay. In fact, nearly from the beginning McClellan seems to have been impressed with the contribution the U.S. Navy ought to play in the suppression of the rebellion. Beyond its role on the high seas in protecting Federal commerce and in blockading the Confederate Atlantic and Gulf coasts, McClellan envisioned using the massive Northern superiority on the waters to reenforce and support land operations.

In the working outline used by McClellan to draft his strategy memorandum of August 2, 1861, he summarized his ideas in two contiguous points:[10]

11. Line of its [i.e. the main column in Virginia] operations so directed as to avail of water transportation.
12. Naval force and flanking expeditions on the coast.

In this earliest expression of his concept of combined operations can be seen the origins of both McClellan's peninsula campaign against Richmond and the several joint army-navy expeditions against the Confederate coastline. It is interesting and significant that these two strategies, which were later developed independently, originally were part of one, unified program and were meant to interact and be mutually supportive. It is clear that McClellan saw these combined operations as a critical contribution in achieving the North's war aims through a limited war strategy because they helped to economize on both the time and money needed to defeat the rebels and restore the *status quo ante bellum.*

In expanding upon his outline in the full memorandum to Lincoln, McClellan argued that Northern naval superiority could be used to neutralize the Confederate advantage of interior lines of operations, an advantage he recognized was even more dangerous since the development of the railroad. McClellan argued that by seizing strategic points behind the Confederate armies on the frontier, each Southern state would "be forced, but the necessity of its own defense, to diminish its contingent to the Confederate Army." Thus, he intended to use combined operations both to strengthen the Northern invasion of the South and to weaken Southern resistance. He would accomplish this by so planning the advance of the main column (what would become the Army of the Potomac) to be partly by water, simultaneously: (1) shortening his route; (2) making his lines of supply and communication more secure, while reducing the number of troops needed for their protection; and (3), isolating and neutralizing large chunks of Confederate territory.[11]

In addition, an "essential feature" of his strategy called for an amphibious force to move ahead of the army, on its flanks, jumping "from point to point" on the enemy's seacoast, "thus either creating diversions and rendering it necessary for them to detach largely from their main body in order to protect

BUILDING HUTS FOR THE ARMY OF THE POTOMAC, *Harper's Pictorial History of the Civil War, December, 1861.*

such of their cities as may be threatened, or else landing and forming establishments on their coast at any favorable places that opportunity might offer. This naval force," McClellan concluded, "should also cooperate with the main army in its efforts to seize the important seaboard towns of the rebels."

*   *   *   *   *

McClellan never achieved the desired simultaneity of these combined operations: (1) because before November 1st they lay outside his area of authority; and (2) because of his decision as General-in-Chief to delay the advance of the column in Virginia. Through a series of fortuitous occurrences the coastal expeditions were undertaken independently of one another in the fall and winter of 1861-1862. In all there were three: the Port Royal, South Carolina expedition of DuPont and Thomas Sherman; the Burnside expedition to New Bern, North Carolina; and Ben Butler's operations in the Gulf against New Orleans. All three owed much to McClellan, and all were incorporated by him into his strategy for overwhelming the South.[12]

The Port Royal expedition, the first of these coastal operations, did not originate with McClellan. It was conceived while he was still in western Virginia, ordered immediately after his arrival in Washington, and launched a week before he became General-in-Chief. It grew directly from the report of a special board studying ways to support the blockade, and initially it was intended only to establish a coaling and supply station within easy distance of ships on duty far from friendly shores. McClellan was on intimate terms with Professor Alexander Bache of the Coast Survey and John G. Barnard, chief engineer of the Army of the Potomac, two of the three members of the board. It is likely he heard of the expedition upon his arrival in the capital, and it is possible that it was the source of his inspiration for the flanking enclaves. It is also likely that McClellan's thinking influenced the shape of the expedition, because as it developed it became less a coaling station and more of an enclave. After Sherman and Dupont had successfully established themselves on the South Carolina coast by November 8, McClellan, who was now General-in-Chief, sent additional troops and artillery and encouraged the capture of Fort Pulaski to close the harbor of Savannah, Georgia. McClellan also hoped that in the future the expedition could serve as the base for operations against Charleston.[13]

The North Carolina expedition was a different story altogether. Well planned and excuted, it was McClellan's project from the start. In early September, shortly after he had begun to build the Army of the Potomac, McClellan applied to Cameron for permission to organize a marine division of some ten regiments. The men enlisted were to be from New England and to be familiar with ships and the sea. The division was to be "an integral part of the Army of the Potomac." McClellan wanted authority to select its commander and determine its use. He also wanted each regiment to have its flank companies armed with "Dahlgren boat-guns, and carbines with water-proof cartridges." The division was also to have its own permanent fleet of troop transports. While the main army was forming, the division was to operate in the Chesapeake Bay. Its main purpose, however, as McClellan pointed out, was "to follow along the coast and up the inlets and rivers the movements of the main army when it advances."

On September 12, 1861, McClellan sent orders to his old friend Ambrose Burnside to organize the division which had been approved as proposed. Because of difficulty in raising the specialized troops and in collecting transportation, nearly four months passed before Burnside was ready to move with his force. In the meanwhile, the situation had changed and McClellan's thinking had crystallized. Once he became General-in-Chief, he was free to plan in larger terms. He saw that the movements of the Army of the Potomac against Richmond could be facilitated by a Federal force in place at New Bern. Such a force could cut railroad links between the Confederate capital and the south Atlantic states and be in position to drive northward to close a pincer movement as well. On January 11, 1862, Burnside left Fort Monroe. By February 8 he had captured Roanoke Island and a full Confederate brigade, and five weeks later he occupied New Bern.[14]

The last of the seacoast operations had the motliest origins. It was, in fact, the marriage of two ideas, separately conceived and independently launched. The first of these might be called the Butler ego expedition, for seemingly its chief aim was the gratification and glorification of Benjamin Franklin Butler, Massachusetts Democrat and Major-General of Volunteers. After his stint as commander at Fort Monroe, Butler cast about for occupation of his restless ambition. Receiving War Department permission to raise a division of Democrats in New England, Butler found it difficult to settle on a target. At one time or another, he considered Virginia's eastern shore, Cape Hatteras and Mobile, Alabama.

At this juncture a series of parallel developments intersected with Butler's operations. The navy had from the first recognized the importance of New Orleans as a port to the Confederacy. In September, with virtually no opposition, it had occupied Ship Island, near the mouth of the Mississippi, as a landfall for the Gulf blockading squadron. About a month later Commander David Dixon Porter advanced the argument that New Orleans could be reduced with primarily naval forces and as little as 10,000 or so infantry support. It was inevitable that the two ideas would soon be joined.

McClellan's support of the New Orleans expedition varied from time to time. For awhile, when the cloud from the *Trent* affair cast shadows on Anglo-American relations, he felt the need to retain Butler's force as the only mobile reserve available to the nation. He also doubted that so small an infantry force could accomplish such a major objective. By early February 1862, the threat of a foreign war had abated, and the easy victories at Henry and Donelson had induced the euphoric belief in the Federal high command that Confederate resistance might be less than had been anticipated. At this point, McClellan adopted the expedition fully into his grand invasion. He gave Butler nine additional regiments and sealed instructions which envisioned captured New Orleans becoming the focus for a thrust up the Mississippi.

On February 25, the troops of the expedition left Fort Monroe. By the middle of March, Farragut was ready to cross the outer bar of the Mississippi. Five weeks later, Federal officers would set foot in New Orleans and claim the city for the United States.[15]

*   *   *   *   *

As the spring of 1862 approached, therefore, McClellan's strategy of overwhelming had been well launched. Halleck had made Missouri largely secure. Grant held northwest Tennessee and had advanced to Pittsburg Landing, within ten miles of the Mississippi state line. Buell occupied Nashville, and the way into east Tennesse and Chattanooga were open to him. Sherman held Port Royal and was preparing to move on Fort Pulaski. Burnside held New Bern and would soon be ready for interior operations in North Carolina and for cooperation against Richmond from the south. Farragut was entering the mouth of the Mississippi, and in Virginia the Federals' major thrust was about to be made. Lander occupied Winchester at the head of the Shenandoah Valley. Near Washington McClellan held about 150,000 reasonably drilled soldiers ready to march—and to sail; for it was with the Army of the Potomac that McClellan had decided to undertake his most extensive combined operations.

McClellan never doubted that he could move directly forward against Johnston's army at Manassas. He simply never believed it was wise. He had always assumed that a frontal attack on the Confederate entrenchments would be much too costly even if successful and that the chances of success were not high enough. He had further assumed that some sort of turning or flanking movement would be necessary to dislodge the enemy before a great battle was to be fought. Then, sometime around December 1st, an idea began to take shape. Why not make the turning movement a large one? Why not put the entire army aboard ships, sail down the Chesapeake and up one of the many Virginia rivers to land at a point behind enemy lines and nearer to Richmond? This would at once shorten his own land based supply lines, and it would also shorten the distance between his army and the chief enemy prize. The enemy would have to abandon his carefully prepared fortifications at Manassas and fall back, and McClellan could try to hit him while off balance.

The origin of this plan is somewhat hazy. It resembled in broad outline Winfield Scott's amphibious campaign against the Mexican capital, in which McClellan had participated some fifteen years earlier. Also, some of the advice he had received from Rush Hawkins and other officers stationed at Fort Monroe had pointed in the same direction. Still, there is no reason to look beyond McClellan. The germ of the idea can be found in the August 2nd memorandum and, more particularly, in the first intended use of Burnside's marine division.

Sometime near the end of November, McClellan broached the idea to his chief engineer, John G. Barnard and asked for advice. Barnard's memorandum, dated approximately December 1st, reveals that McClellan's thinking was just then in transition. While still tenuously connected to the Burnside expedition, the size of the operation had grown to 30,000 or more troops and three or four landing sites were being considered. During December, but before the onset of his illness of the 20th, McClellan came to adopt the proposed flanking movement as the major thrust of the Army of the Potomac. He also selected Urbana as the landfall. He intended to carry some 140,000 troops about 100 miles by water from Annapolis to the mouth of the Rappahannock and thence fifteen miles up river to Urbana. He would thus be some ninety miles behind Johnston's position at Manassas and within forty-five miles of Richmond.[16]

It was preeminently a sound strategy. It seized the initiative and compelled the enemy to act on the defensive; and it used Federal naval superiority to overslough the Confederate advantage of interior lines. It moved the scene of battle from the vicinity of the Northern capital to that of the Southern, and, therefore, it promised greater fruits in the event of victory. At the same time, by eliminating the long overland lines of supply and communication in favor of a river base, it not only minimized the disasters of defeat, it also freed additional troops which could be employed at the front.

While the idea was a good one in any event, obviously there were tremendous advantages to be gained if its major details could be kept secret. No doubt the collection of a huge fleet of transports would warn the Confederates that a great amphibious expedition was imminent. But, if they did not know its destination— and it could be going anywhere from the lower Potomac to Galveston—they would be virtually powerless to react to it. The very least that could happen would be this: if Johnston decided to gamble that the Federal destination were the vicinity of Richmond, the element of time would dictate that he must prematurely abandon all of northern Virginia and march south. A large hunk of rich enemy territory would thus fall without a battle into McClellan's hands.

*   *   *   *   *

At the very outset McClellan found it necessary to modify his strategy, although the first change was the most beneficial of the many to come. So long as Johnston had remained at Manassas, some ninety-five miles from Richmond, it was neither necessary nor desirable for the flanking movement to be made farther south than Urbana. On March 9, however, when Johnston retired southward and reestablished his line along the Rappahannock-Rapidan rivers, Urbana was no longer an attractive landing point. Rather than abandoning his plan—and McClellan seems never to have considered returning to the overland route—he simply shifted his point of attack farther south.[17]

McClellan had three options before him in mid-March as he revised his plans. He could advance by the James River, the Yorktown peninsula or the York River. Undoubtedly, the James offered the best route of invasion. The river flowed directly into Richmond from the southside, providing not only a water route to the very doorstep of Jefferson Davis, but also severing the Confederate capital's rail links with Petersburg and the south. Only one factor militated against the James River route, but so fearsome was it as to negate the approach altogether. From the burned hulk of the abandoned frigate U.S.S. *Merrimac*, the Confederates in the Norfolk navy yard had constructed the powerful ironclad, the C.S.S. *Virginia*. In early March this iron behemoth had steamed into the Federal fleet at Hampton Roads, destroyed two ships-of-the-line and caused a serious panic in Washington. Although the Yankee's own little *Monitor* appeared capable of neutralizing the *Virginia* and stopping her up in the James, it seemed sheerest folly to plan a campaign up that river at the present.

The second option, advancing up the Yorktown peninsula, was inherently the weakest of the three. Indeed, its only significant advantage lay in the Federal possession of Fort Monroe at the tip of the peninsula, which would provide a friendly haven for landing. Not only would Federal shipping still be relatively close to the *Virginia*, but the overland distance to Richmond was some seventy miles, or about the same march as Johnston's own army was from its capital.

McClellan chose, therefore, the route that was second best in theory but most attractive in his present circumstances, the York River. It was his intention to land a large portion of his army at West Point, at the head of the York and about thirty-five miles from Richmond. McClellan's revised strategy was also a sound one. He would bypass by water the Confederate forces at Gloucester Point and, more importantly, Magruder's Army of the Peninsula at Yorktown. He would thus thrust his Army of the Potomac between two smaller enemy forces at a point from thirty miles nearer Richmond than the main Confederate army. It is a somewhat bolder plan than McClellan is credited with ever having devised. Magruder would be faced with two unattractive alternatives. Either he must scurry up the peninsula to safety, thereby clearing the York of obstacles and facilitating McClellan's rapid advance on Richmond—perhaps, before Johnston could arrive to defend it; or, to slow McClellan's advance by threatening his rear, Magruder must hold at Yorktown and risk the capture of his entire force.

There were two drawbacks to be overcome in this, McClellan's revised, or second strategy. First, Confederate batteries would have to be run between Yorktown and Gloucester Point, thus necessitating naval cooperation. On the basis of several meetings and of sending Barnard to Hampton Roads to consult with Flag Officer Louis Goldsborough, McClellan believed he had full naval assurances that the *Virginia* could be bottled up in the James and the enemy batteries could be run on the York.

Secondly, because landfall would be made in enemy territory, it would be necessary, or so McClellan believed, to land no less than an entire army corps at once in order to secure the beachhead. It was on this point which the revised strategy foundered within days of its conception. Unaccountably, Stanton, the new Secretary of War, had not ordered the collection of water transportation until February 27th. By mid-March there were boats enough to transport any one division at a time. As the "great impatience of the Government grew apace," McClellan decided he could wait no longer. For the third time he revised his strategy, although this time the revision was intended to be moderate. He wanted to avoid landing a single division at West Point, but he also did not want to remain idle until three times the number of boats had been collected.[18]

Hence, McClellan struck a compromise. He would use the ships at hand to transport by divisions the bulk of the Army of the Potomac to Fort Monroe. He hoped, with the number of boats increasing daily, this could be accomplished in two to three weeks. He would save his largest corps, McDowell's 15,000 men, until last. He assumed that McDowell could by then be carried entire and landed at West Point. This third plan was not so good as the second. It was safe enough to be sure. It still promised the entrapment of Magruder at Yorktown. But it vastly reduced the possibility that McClellan could reach Richmond before Johnston had settled in for its defense.

*   *   *   *   *

The most crushing blow to McClellan's overall strategy, the one which was after all lethal, came on March 11th, when Lincoln issued his Presidential War Order No. 3, abolishing the office of General-in-Chief and restricting McClellan's command to the Army of the Potomac. At its floodtide, the grand invasion lost its controlling hand, and the Army of the United States lost unity of command. The land columns in Virginia and Tennessee became uncoordinated, independent operations, and the coastal enclaves endured as isolated outposts stripped of most of their strategic importance.

There was nothing in the Presidential Order which changed the North's war aims, nor was any new strategy announced to replace the one McClellan had been pursuing. Lincoln simply abolished professional military direction at the national level and left the pieces to struggle on uncoordinated. Since unity and concert of operations were the very heart of the strategy of overwhelming, however, the President's action effectually destroyed McClellan's program.

McClellan's grand invasion dwindled to his campaign on the Yorktown peninsula—and kept on dwindling. Lincoln fearing for the safety of the capital, detached the entire 1st Corps and gave McDowell an independent department. Goldsborough changed his mind and decided the navy could not run the batteries on the York River. Burnside's enclave in North Carolina, no longer under McClellan's authority, would play no role in the campaign against Richmond. By April 4th, virtually nothing remained of McClellan's plans for the use of the water route to surprise the enemy and shorten the war. In the end, his net gain comprised some forty fewer miles of overland communications to be protected and another thirty-five, being on the peninsula, which were much more easily guarded. Even the advantage of carrying the war away from Washington and to the suburbs of Richmond were negated by Lincoln's overweening fear for his capital's safety.

McClellan's campaign on the peninsula and against Richmond took a shape almost opposite the one he had planned. He never commanded more than 90,000 men, and when the climactic battles came he was possibly outnumbered by 10-20,000. He lost rather than gained mobility; first on the narrow Yorktown peninsula, divided by a rain swollen river that ran at right angles to its course on the maps provided him by Wool's engineers; and then, from mid-May onward, by War Department orders which nailed his right flank to the north bank of the Chickahominy. McClellan failed to take Richmond, and he may have failed to make the most of the resources and opportunities which were his. His strategy did not fail, however, because it was abandoned and never tested.

It is fruitless to speculate in the brief space of this paper about the causes for the abandonment of McClellan's strategy of overwhelming. Over the years many historians have spent much time and energy demonstrating that McClellan's "flawed" character brought on his downfall. Even if this hoary interpretation is true, the time has come to distinguish McClellan from his strategy and to recognize that the latter, at least, contained many points of merit.[19]

After McClellan, there would be another General-in-Chief, but not for two more years would there be another conprehensive strategy for winning the war and coordinating the military forces of the North in concerted actions. In the meantime, of course, with the issuance of the Emancipation Proclamation, the North's war aims would change. And, thereafter, the North would no longer be fighting to restore the "Union as it was," and conservative generals and limited war strategies, no longer appropriate, would be relegated to the junk heap of history—which is pretty much where historians have allowed them to languish ever since.

Endnotes

*AUTHOR'S NOTE:
A careful reading of the newly published biography by Stephen W. Sears, *George B. McClellan: The Young Napoleon* (Boston, 1988), has not induced me to make any emendations in the present paper.

1 "On the McClellan-Go-Round," *Civil War History*, XIX, (June 1973), 117-118.

2 George B. McClellan, *McClellan's Own Story* (New York, 1887), p. 35.

3 *The War of the Rebellion. A Compilation of the Official Records of the Union and Confederate Armies* (Washington, 1880-1901), ser. 1, XI, pt. 3, 345-346. Hereafter cited as *O.R.*; all are series 1, unless otherwise stated.

4 Erasmus D. Keyes, *Fifty Years' Observations of Men and Events, Civil and Military* (New York, 1884), pp. 427-428; Winfield Scott, *Memoirs of Lieut.-General Scott* (New York, 1864), II, 610-626; Edward D. Townsend, *Anecdotes of the Civil War in the United States* (New York, 1884), pp. 6, 13 *et seq.*, 55-56, and 249-255; Charles W. Elliot, *Winfield Scott: the Soldier and the Man* (New York, 1937), *passim*; and *O.R.*, LI, pt. 1, 339 and 369-370.

5 Roy P. Basler (ed.), *Collected Works of Abraham Lincoln* (New Brunswick, N.J., 1953-1955), IV, 431-432, and V, 145-146 and 388-389; William E. Smith, *The Francis Preston Blair Family in Politics* (New York, 1933), II, 144-145; and Allan Nevins, *The War for the Union* (New York, 1959-1960), II, 151-152.

6 McClellan, *Own Story*, pp. 101-105 and 487-489.

7 J.D. Hittle (ed.), Jomini and His Summary of the Art of War (Harrisburg, 1947, p. 51; see also 46 and 68-70.

8 *O.R.*, IV, 247, 251, 254, 313-314, 332-334, 342 and 348; and, VII, 443-444, 447-449, 457, 460-461 and 467.

9 *O.R.*, III, 568-569; and VIII, 369, 382, 408, 409, 419 and 463.

10 These were points eleven and twelve of a sixteen point outline, August 2, 1861, McClellan Papers, Library of Congress.

11 McClellan, *Own Story*, pp. 101-105.

12 *Official Records of the Union and Confederate Navies* (Washington, 1849-1927), XII, 195-206; also, Robert U. Johnson and Clarence C. Buel (eds.), *Battles and Leaders of the Civil War* (New York, 1956), I, 671-674.

13 *O.R.*, VI, 133-167, 168-171, 173-174, 179-181, 184, 192-196, 198, 203-204, 207-208, 219, 224-225 and 306; McClellan, *Own Story*, pp. 103-105; and *Battles and Leaders*, I, 676 and 682-691.

14 *O.R.*, IV, 566-721; V, 36; IX, 352-353; also series 3, I, 500 and 535-536; McClellan, *Own Story*, p. 205; *Battles and Leaders*, I, 600-669.

15 *O.R.*, VI, 677-678, 684, 685, 691-693 and 694-695; and series 3, I, 646, 652, 658, 815 and 834; *Battles and Leaders*, II, 23-25, 25-26 and 91; Benjamin F. Butler, *Autobiography and Personal Reminiscences of Major-General Benjamin F. Butler* (Boston, 1892), pp. 294-298, 299, 323-324 and 330-336; and Gideon Welles, *Selected Essays...Civil War and Reconstruction* (New York, 1959), pp. 126-127 and 132-134.

16 *Battles and Leaders*, I, 639-640; *O.R.*, V, 671-673; and *Report of the Joint Committee and the Conduct of the War* (Washington, 1863), I, 122-130 and 170-178.

17 *Battles and Leaders*, II, 167.

18 *Battles and Leaders*, II, 168.

19 Rowena Reed in her perceptive study, *Combined Operations in the Civil War* (Annapolis, 1978), p. xviii, has observed: "Of the men in the Federal high command, professional and civilian, during the first two years of the war only General McClellan envisioned the use of combined operations as the foundation of a comprehensive plan to paralyze the South.... Had McClellan's brilliant strategy been fully implemented, it would have ended the Civil War in 1862, as intended."

Jefferson Davis
and the Historians

Herman Hattaway

Jefferson Davis believed that history eventually would do him justice. It seems not yet to have done so, and this despite a one-and-a-quarter century-long period during which has poured forth a plethora of writing about him.[1] Ranging the entire gamut: good and bad, hostile or favorable, sometimes artfully researched and intelligently construed, the outpourings of countless historians and would-be-historians still leave Davis something of an enigma.*

T. Harry Williams, to whom we dedicate our proceedings, and honor with this symposium, suggested that an explanation of Davis's "inner self" is the needed but missing ingredient. "Either the authors" or previous biographical efforts, Williams indicated, "were incapable of explaining, or there was something in Davis that caused him to elude explanation."[2] That may indeed be the case, and the problem may prove ultimately to be an unsolvable one, though I am willing to wager otherwise. Nevertheless we have now, as was the case a decade ago when Williams wrote these words, a huge body of extant writings, and despite them, still, we do not have an adequate and convincing—certainly nothing even closely approaching universal agreement within the profession—assessment of Jefferson Davis—neither of the man, nor of his contributions to the outcome of events.

It is, of course, not a matter of whether Davis was flawed, *assuredly* he had personal flaws, the crucial matter is to be convincing as to what was the specific effect, and, rather, what was Jefferson Davis really like, what were his motivations, and his true limitations? How well did he face things and what should he, or *could* he, perhaps have done differently, with any more desirable result? To add to the efforts expended in the past, a goodly number of scholars already have indicated their intent to wrestle in the future with these and other questions about Davis.

I am sure that likely I am not informed about, nor aware of, *all* of the new work now underway. Let me here indicate that which I *do* know about. Richard E. Beringer and I have a contract with the Kansas University Press to produce an administrative history of the Davis presidency, which will be a companion volume to their "American Presidents Series." We plan, too, after completing that to attempt something longer and more ambitious. There may be a crowded shelf full of new Davis studies by that time! William Cooper, the LSU Graduate School Dean, has an NEH Fellowship for 1988-1989 to support his sabbatical-year project, a new Davis biography.[3] Richard Beringer heard news of others,

142

too, at the 1987 meeting of the Southern Historical Association, and this has been corroborated in a telephone conversation which I had on June 1, 1988, with Lynda Lasswell Crist and Mary Seaton Dix—co-editors at Rice University of the *Papers of Jefferson Davis*. There are perhaps as many as five—and possibly even still more than five—new Davis biography projects underway (and while I am not sure about the identity of all the would-be authors, the names Frank Vandiver [and sometimes any of several of his former students], have been mentioned, as well as Grady McWhiney [rumored to be under contract with the University of South Carolina Press], William C. Davis, Peter Walker, and Richard

MARY SEATON DIX and LYNDA LASSWELL CRIST
co-editors of "The Papers of Jefferson Davis," flank the oil portrait of Davis at Rice University.
Courtesy of Herman N. Hattaway

Marius—*him* sure to be an interestingly different Davis student, for he previously has written a life of Sir Thomas More), and three studies are being done on Varina Howell Davis.

Lastly, there have been several doctoral dissertations, a few of them provocative, done on Davis, any of which may eventually be published, in some revised form. I should like to comment upon two of them.

The first is a formidable and respectable attempt at modern psycho-biography, by one of Fawn Brodie's students, Phyllis Sanders, completed at UCLA in 1976.[4] Based upon an impressive array of sources, nevertheless the work relies for vital underpinning upon crucial material in the first two volumes of the new edition of Davis Papers—the only ones then yet published when Sanders wrote—and so is limited to being a study only of Davis's pre-Civil War years.

Beautifully written and intelligently construed, the dissertation is marvelously interesting to read, intellectually stimulating and valuable, although perhaps somewhat too speculative. By far the author's most-often used phrase is "must have been." Possibly the most jolting of her many interpolative suggestions is that the reason the widowed Jefferson Davis stayed unremarried, as he did, for the unusually long period of ten years was because his sexual needs were being fulfilled by various female slaves. In any event, should Sanders complete the work, rendering it a full biographical treatment, assuredly it would merit publication, as well as serious consideration by Davis scholars. She may not be correct in all of her inferences, I personally doubt that she is, but she certainly seems convincing at least in some of them.

To be sure, Sanders could not completely escape being hampered by the inevitable problem that inhibited any earlier psycho-biographical investigation of Davis: the severe dearth of appropriate documentary material, particularly from the time of Davis's youth. That, it seems doubtless, is why there was no Freudian biography of Davis, a genre which was very popular during the 1920's and early 1930's, the very time that four Davis biographies were completed.

The second dissertation is that of Stephen E. Woodworth, who in 1987 completed his doctorate at Rice University under the distinguished military historian, Ira Gruber. It is the long-awaited and long-needed monograph (a counterpart for one of T. Harry Williams' best-known volumes) "Jefferson Davis and His Generals."[5] All of us who hope to do any work pertinent to Davis do envy Woodworth his long and convenient access to the rich treasure trove of Davis-related material gathered at Rice University. I am afraid, however, that I am among those who will be disappointed with his finished product, for he appears to have become somewhat anti-Davis in bias. Of course, his *may* be the true position, for he asserts that he began with what he thought "was a slight bias in favor of Davis," and was impelled toward harsher conclusions by "the weight of evidence."[6] In any event, Woodworth's is doubtless a worthy addition to the growing list of fresh Davis inquiries.

What will be different and valuable about this new body of work? It will, we trust, continue the trend set by the better outpourings produced during the publication-rich era of the Civil War Centennial, and more especially since 1971, when appeared the first volume of the new edition of Davis Papers.[7] Probably to be based upon richer and more subtle research, it may employ inter-disciplinary or other elevated techniques of analysis.

An able corps of authors long since has begun to etch, as Frank Vandiver put it in his 1976 presidential address to the Southern Historical Association, a more sophisticated and complex image of an "emerging Davis." This new historical image is still yet to be so fully sharp and clear as we hope it can become. "Much of the new Davis," Vandiver said, no doubt correctly, "will have to come from shading, from analyses of things he did that were untypical..."[8]

This is because we already know the broad outlines of Davis's life, and because now little more of significance or value can be said, *if* simply in attack or detraction, admiration or defense. Vandiver himself did an exemplary job of thumbnail-sketching the extant Davis scholarship up through 1976, and a few of my passages which follow still echo part of the essence of his speech, but I have a number of different things to say.

In a sense, all of the earlier—and, even if hard to define how, unsatisfactory—work on Jefferson Davis can be traced to the writings, and reactions to them, of Edward Alfred Pollard: wartime Richmond newspaper editor, early historian of the war[9] and biographer of Davis,[10] bitter and acerbic critic of the Confederate president, and—in the priceless words of Frank Vandiver—"curmudgeon extraordinary."[11] Pollard but thinly veiled his hostility and all of his works are seriously marred by venomous anti-Davis feeling and bitter anti-Northern prejudice. He charged Davis with incompetence, self-delusion—and responsibility for the Confederacy's failure. A veritable legion of subsequent readers and later historians have believed much of what Pollard said, and cited it, giving him a much greater than deserved historiographical significance. Pollard was, after all, merely a biased contemporary critic who said and wrote much that was hyperbolic, distorted, and unjustified. But plausibility played its role, and in Vandiver's words, "things he saw wrong with the President had the power of popularity and the ring of repetition."[12]

So, much subsequent historical writing either followed Pollard's lead, or it attempted in near-eulogistic, and therefore in overly-simplistic, fashion to refute Pollard. Such, for an example of the latter, was the 1868 biography by Frank H. Alfriend—the last editor of the *Southern Literary Messenger* (which had ceased publication early in 1864) and a personal friend of Davis.[13] While Alfriend deserves no more credit for his adulation than does Pollard for his bitter prejudice, at least Alfriend tried to support his case by including extensive quotations from Davis's letters and speeches. Thus this early and bias-blinded pro-Davis biographer pointed the way that years later at last would be taken, only after which—in Vandiver's pithy phrasing—"as any scholar could have guessed, research revealed a fuller man than Pollard's shabby mannequin."[14] Or the shabby mannequin for that matter of the adulators, a genre added to in 1890 with the eulogistic joint tribute to Davis and to Stonewall Jackson by Markinfield Addey.[15]

Such eulogistic works as Addey's had their welcoming readership, of course, especially among the then newly formed United Confederate Veterans and the soon-to-be ancillary organizations, and to anyone who might be steeped in the growing myth of the Lost Cause.

It is an irony that as interest in, enthusiasm for, and devotion to that body of myth, the Lost Cause enthusiasts, and also most of the later historians who wrote about Davis while under any of Pollard's influence, turned the former Confederate president into a "scapegoat," or even—as Vandiver suggested—"they have, of course, made him more than a scapegoat—he is a kind of southern Barabbas."[16] Thomas L. Connelly described the phenomena in his clever 1963 spoof of the Civil War Centennial, buffs, re-enactors, and Round Tables, *Will Success Spoil Jeff Davis?*[17] In it Connelly offered a list of ten requirements for amateur standing as a neo-Confederate: you have to do things like "cry during *Gone With the Wind*," and "have a great-grandmother who buried silver under the smokehouse." But most interesting of all is that you must "hate Jefferson Davis."

Emory M. Thomas used this tidbit, in 1971, as a point of departure for his chapter on "The Davis Administration and State Rights," in the significant and thoughtful little book, *The Confederacy as a Revolutionary Experience.*[18] In suggesting an image of Davis as a much stronger and abler leader, and of the Confederacy as unique—and more revolutionary than previous scholars had perceived—, Thomas sketched the outlines of a concept that the Italian scholar, Raimondo Luraghi, would in 1978 carry much farther.[19] Thomas to a degree and Luraghi to a stark extent wrote of Davis's clear-mindedness, creativity, genius, high deserved rank as a statesman, intelligence, iron will, capability in facing and solving appalling problems.

But, in fairness, Thomas used Connelly's little joke out of context, and gave it a different meaning—that of Confederate citizens having chafed at Davis's revolutionary measures which they found uncomfortable. The real reason why latter-day neo-Confederates have to "hate Jefferson Davis" is that, while *beatified*, perhaps, and early, Davis did not become *sainted* by the civil religion which the Lost Cause eventually spawned.[20] *Somebody* has to be blamed for the Confederate defeat, and Davis is so conveniently available. I am suggesting here that Connelly, and his disciple William Piston, are correct in their most crucial assertions concerning R. E. Lee and James Longstreet: and, I am interpolating, that following the war, Davis was very popular with a great many—quite possibly always at least a majority—of the Southern people for the remainder of his lifetime, and even for some time thereafter; Davis's false mantle as "scapegoat" or even "Barabbas" plausibly seems to be, in large part at least, an anti-thetical corollary to the "sainting" of R. E. Lee and the hatchet job done on truth by J. William Jones, Jubal Early, and their company of dedicated distorters of history, which have been written about so brilliantly by Connelly and Piston.[21]

This context for the timetable relating to Davis's varying levels of post-war popularity, or lack thereof, seems to me compatible with the data in two recent and brilliant pieces of scholarship: Michael B. Ballard's *A Long Shadow: Jefferson Davis and the Final Days of the Confederacy* and Gaines M. Foster's *Ghosts of the Confederacy: Defeat, the Lost Cause, and the Emergence of the New South, 1865 to 1913*. It is, on the other hand, not compatible with the mindset of Edward K. Eckert in *"Fiction Distorting Fact": Prison Life, Annotated by Jefferson Davis*, but I join Ballard in expressing opinion that Eckert is incorrect on that one supposition. Otherwise, Eckert's too is a modern work of genuine merit.[22]

To be sure, some of the relatively early authors who wrote about Davis did produce meritorious work. Such a one was William E. Dodd—a great pioneer among professionally trained historians dedicated to study of the South—, who wrote—and published in 1907—what fairly may be termed the first truly scholarly biography of Davis.[23] Although fundamentally sympathetic in tone, it is judicious in judgment and well written, lean, clean, crisp, and elementally informative. Frank Vandiver called it a "near classic [which] still rings truer than most studies of Davis in its unadorned try for the truth."[24] But while it still can be read with profit, a number of factors render it less than adequate to most modern needs.

One limitation is that Dodd was more keenly concerned with things political, and tended to show less interest in things military. The ultimate limitation is the thinness of underlying research. Dodd did the best he could do with what he had, he measured up well to the standards of his time; but those standards have changed, and the available appliances have evolved. To be blunt, a look at his sources suggests an elementary depth and scope of research that we now might see in the work of merely a promising neophyte. Hence, Dodd's work continues to deserve mention, it is memorable because of his artful and graceful attempt simply to find and depict the real Davis, but it is haplessly too thin in underpinning, and it is dated.

Dodd himself, in a situation not totally dissimilar to the one I and the other current Davis scholars now find ourselves, knew that there soon would be more work done on his subject. He had learned before the completion of his own biography that three other students had entered the field. He expressed hope that a more just estimate of Davis's services might be the result, and he believed that future discussions of Davis would take place "with less acrimony than in the past."[25] In both of these, he was to be disappointed. He lived to see seven more biographies of Davis published. Although levels of research did advance, none of these biographies truly transcended, some scholars might even say equalled, Dodd's in noteworthiness; and all were somehow tainted with one kind of distorting influence or another from Pollard or Alfriend.

These biographies were, in the chronological order of their appearance, written by Armistead Churchill Gordon, Morris Schaff, Hamilton J. Eckenroad, Allen Tate, Elisabeth Cutting, Robert W. Winston, and Robert McElroy.[26] While far from being ideal, McElroy's stands above, and fairly separate from, the group; the other six, while quite divergent one from another, are about equally superficial and lacking in objectivity. I shall deal briefly with each of the seven.

A native of Charlottesville, Virginia, and a lawyer of some repute, Gordon was a prolific writer of popular historical articles for several leading magazines. Because of his reputation, Scribner's editors asked him to attempt the Davis work, to be a part of their series, *Figures From American History*. He, like Dodd, seems only to have had a passing interest in Davis, but commendably, Gordon sought help from numerous scholars who were able to provide him with much good data. Nevertheless, he opted, however, to attempt no new interpretation of Davis, and worse, he occasionally lapsed into journalistic license. So, while his biography was rather well received in some circles, in truth it was neither as penetrating nor as thorough as Dodd's.

The next Davis biographer, Northern-born Morris Schaff, was an octogenarian by the time he wrote on Davis. Schaff had graduated from West Point in 1862 and had served in the Union Army during the Civil War. Following retirement from the military, he wrote several books. As a devoted West Pointer, he had come to be an admirer of Davis, and believed that justice had not been done, that Davis's image unjustly had been distorted. With an obvious enthusiasm for his subject, he wrote a defensive Davis biography, but his argument and his underpinning both were rather shallow. The work attracted rather little attention, nor did it deserve to do so.

Eckenrode, a native of Fredericksburg, Virginia, won a Ph.D. from Johns Hopkins in 1905, and served as State Archivist of Virginia from 1907 to 1914, when he went to the University of Richmond as professor of economics. His Davis biography is of interest primarily for his racist interpretation of the Civil War. Frank Vandiver called it a "strange Nordic polemic," in which "Eckenrode sees Davis as the leader of a failed racial crusade and hence as bearing guilt far beyond his time...."[27] But interestingly, and I think perplexingly peculiar (especially when considering further that Eckenrode actually introduced no new

Davis material, and in many respects railed at Davis somewhat as had Pollard), Clement Eaton—a famed historian of the South, and later also a Davis biographer—thought it was the best of the group![28]

Can we look through Eckenrode's rubble of Nazi-like ugliness and find any of the redeeming value that Eaton believed was there? It is significant that Eckenrode was the first Davis scholar to make extensive use of the *Official Records*.[29] That may explain why he overemphasized military study, equally as Dodd had sacrificed it for political consideration. But in that excursion, one impressive thing that Eckenrode did was to long-predate Tom Connelly in suggesting that R. E. Lee's campaigns had been over-emphasized, at the expense of analyzing adequately the Civil War in the West. And, *if* Frank Vandiver's conceptions of Davis as an archetypical antebellum Southern gentleman-planter be correct, then Eckenrode touched a true track there as well, for as such so too did he depict Davis.

There, however, is where Eckenrode veers into his "Nordic protest." It had been *the planters*, he believed, who had *created* the republic. Denizens of the antebellum South represented a desirable, and spiritually elevated, strain of the Nordic race, and the Confederacy constituted the final hope of preserving that race and the marvelous socio-governmental form it had inherited. In the years since the end of the Civil War, he believed it had proved impossible to "Nordicize—or Americanize—aliens," thus "the American people of today are no longer adapted to American institutions." He concluded that "success depended, in the last analysis, on Jefferson Davis. He failed...and with him faded the last hope of the Nordic race."

But that said, and one might hope ignored, Eckenrode's analyses of Davis's failure would make sense, to some modern critics, and be possible points of departure for fuller argument. Eckenrode believed the Southern armies should have been directed, more than they were, with a common purpose. He inferred a stern disapproval of the military department system. He gave credit to Henry W. Halleck's and Ulysses S. Grant's superior strategic ideas, but asserted that the South nevertheless had two great strategic opportunities, which *could* have engendered victory. These were: to invade the North following the First Battle of Bull Run, and to have achieved better results in the West by establishing unity of command (throughout the Confederacy) and a general staff system. If one man had been in control of all, in 1863 for example, the Pennsylvania invasion never would have taken place and Vicksburg would have been relieved. If Davis had *managed* the war better, and he *could* have done so, but only if he had delegated more, and insisted on more modern staff organization, and been more revolutionary in his actions, then things would have gone better in the West and the war would have lasted a little longer, resulting in an eventual Union capitulation.[30]

Less seriously, Eckenrode took it upon himself to do a little plastic surgery on Davis's name. "Beyond Doubt," Eckenrode asserted, with no justifying evidence, "his name was originally Thomas Jefferson [Davis], but, like Woodrow Wilson, he dropped the Thomas, giving himself a sonorous and distinctive name. It had something to do with his success in life."[31] Here, though, is the appropriate moment which we can seize logically to refute another apocryphal story concerning Davis's given name. It *may* have been the creation of one Hudson Strode, that since Davis was the last of ten children, his middle name was "Finis"— Latin for "finished" or "last." Lynda Lasswell Crist and Mary Seaton Dix have asserted, in an interview with Dick Beringer and me, that no sources known to be extant—nor likely now ever to be discovered—prove that Davis had any middle name at all, let alone what it might have been (although he did sign his name "J. F. Davis" until the early 1830's, and some family members continued to address and refer to him as Jefferson F. Davis as late as 1893).[32]

To continue with consideration of the next biography, one by a man who was more a man of letters than an historian, Allen Tate, we find an author who, like Eckenrode, also used Davis for his own purposes. Tate is kinder in his treatment of Davis, and occasionally offers tantalizing perceptions of character. Tate consciously tried to stand on the shoulders of his predecessors, to combine the best features of the works by Dodd and Eckenrode, and also to incorporate the essence of several pieces of article length monographic work on Davis which had been produced by Walter Lynwood Fleming. Very significantly, Tate was the first Davis biographer to have access to and make use of the 1923 Dunbar Rowland ten volume edition of Davis Papers.[33] But, Tate's tracks are hard to retrace, because he did not footnote. And his work ultimately is flawed by his vague disappointment over what he perceives was lost with the war's outcome— "the original America...soul and substance from the hope of the founding fathers"—, and his subtle condemnation of Davis "who lost a world he lacked the vision to grasp."[34]

The next Davis biographer, Elisabeth Cutting, wanted to produce a sympathetic as well as sound biography. The Brooklyn-born Miss Cutting had since 1910 held various editorial positions with *The North American Review*, and apparently became interested in attempting a Davis biography when her European travels led her to discover in Paris some previously unpublished materials relating to the Confederacy. She was rather an impressively industrious scholar, paid good attention to the previous Davis studies, had numerous personal conferences with Eckenrode, and made a laudable attempt to sweep archival repositories, especially foreign ones, in England and France. Her extensive footnotes and bibliography remain useful.

But she too could not escape the lingering legacy of Pollard's prejudice, nor could she much transcend Eckenrode's general critical line. Something of a divided mindset, displayed throughout her work, ruined her analysis. She did not really have the familiarity with historical context that one might hope to find in a professional. Knowing that she liked Davis, she struggled to be fair, to attain a scholarly impartiality; yet, that very process led her into a self-creating distortion. Ultimately she tended to agree that Pollard largely had been correct in delineating Davis's shortcomings, and if anything, her book became something of a monument to Pollard's interpretation. And so she concluded of Davis:

> Only in a restricted sense was he a statesman....He was not a great executive. He could not delegate...his vanity must be fed....[He was] neither resourceful nor foresighted in his capacity of Commander-in-Chief...unequal to...the magnitude of the task...always...the egoist....His vanity admitted of no rebuke....He was a leader of a cause but not of men.[35]

Doubtless having been at work at the same time as Cutting, Robert W. Winston, in his *High Stakes and Hair Trigger*, which appeared later the same year, unhappily fell far short of his stated goals. He wanted, of course, to produce an exemplary biography, and he wanted "to interpret the New South to the Nation and the Nation to the New South."[36] At the age of sixty he had retired from a legal career and commenced studies in history as a freshman at the University of North Carolina. He lived to be eighty-four, and during his final decades garnered rather a lot of attention for his biographies of Andrew Johnson, Davis, Robert E. Lee, and others. His work on Lee, which emphasizes human qualities, character and personality, is better than that on Davis, which despite being based upon commendable exploitation of some fresh sources, notably numerous contemporary newspapers, is undistinguished.

Avery Craven, observing that Winston's earlier Andrew Johnson biography had been "creditable," suggested that the author now had "forsaken the sober approach and gone in for popular writing."[37] To be sure, Winston did want to sell books, and perhaps believing that a little pizzazz might help, his chapter titles are groaners almost as bad as what he chose to name the book itself, but the work reflects more scholarliness than initially meets the eye. I suspect that Winston's definitions were blurred. His perception of the essence of the Nation was more accurate than was his understanding of the New South. He was enamored with the Civil War's outcome, and with the industrialization which he believed came as a result, and which would not have come had the Confederacy prevailed, and so he wrote critically, depicting Davis as an aspiring pseudo-aristocrat. In some respects, Winston too, sounded like a modern day Pollard.

But this notwithstanding, Winston did have one significant insight. He perceived that the Reconstruction experience, the humiliation of the proud Southern people, and the early post-war persecution of Davis, combined to render the former Confederate President a symbol for the cause which after 1865 had become more holy than it had been before

Still, even if we do admire Winston's occasional manifestation of craftsmanship, his ultimate assessments of Davis are somewhat strange: "Jefferson Davis's 'vice'...was a failure to interpret progress and civilization." Davis's weakness was his inability "to sink himself in the cause." And in the end, "pride and self-will were Jefferson Davis's destruction." But:

> Was Jefferson Davis fitted for his job? Undoubtedly he was—no one better. His was an impossible task, the task of Sisyphus, a task for no one but himself. Before the foundations of the earth were laid, the finger of fate had pointed to Jefferson Davis as the leader of the Lost Cause. None other could have filled that place.[38]

And, so now, to Robert McElroy's 1937 biography.[39] In two volumes, this was the most extensive treatment of Davis yet to appear, and thus it left the legacy of an enlarged body of readily-available factual data about Davis. Most unfortunately, the published work is not footnoted, although the well-annotated bibliography is as exemplary as it is useful. For researchers willing and able to make the sacrifice to consult it, a copy of the original *and annotated* manuscript was deposited at the New York Public Library. Phyllis Sanders suggested, however, in her dissertation, that McElroy had a "tendency toward superficiality," and this quasi-suppression of the annotation was intended to veil that superficiality.[40]

McElroy was a native of Perryville, Kentucky, and received a Ph.D. in 1900 from Princeton University, where he subsequently held a professorship until 1925. He then was invited to be Rhodes Professor at Oxford and served there until 1939, save for a series of appointments, as a visitor, at several Far Eastern universities. He was an admirer of Dunbar Rowland and of Walter Lynwood Fleming (to whom jointly he dedicated his work on Davis). McElroy personally believed that the accusations made against Davis were unduly hostile or unjustified, and he rather consciously attempted to vindicate, though he hoped to do so in a convincingly intellectual way. While previous authors had *used* Rowland's edition of Davis's papers, McElroy made a painstaking sifting of them. He also had access to, and exploited well, a large collection of materials which Fleming, dead by that time, had gathered for his own projected life of Davis.

Walter Lynwood Fleming (1874-1932) deserves special notice for his truly outstanding contributions to Davis scholarship. This eminent pioneer professional historian of the South long harbored the dream of completing an exhaustive biography of Davis, and began collecting pertinent material as early as 1907. He placed an advertisement in the New Orleans *Picayune* asking for information about Davis, and this was copied by a number of other Southern newspapers; and he also distributed widely a printed circular describing the types of data he wanted. He heard from at least 125 people, and a vast collection resulted: of letters, diaries, scrapbooks, pamphlets, books, newspapers, relics, reminiscences, and—most valuable—many theretofore unknown photographs and other illustrations.

Between 1908 and 1924 Fleming published sixteen articles on Davis, but because he had the habit of sometimes slightly revising and reprinting various of his papers, only ten of the articles were singularly original.[41] Collectively they constitute perhaps twenty per cent of the dream, the comprehensive Davis biography, that ill-health and and early death denied his fulfilling, but they are of lasting importance, invaluable contributions on obscure aspects of Davis's life. Settling and clarifying many points long held in controversy, they touch on Davis's earliest years, his time at West Point, the first marriage, his relations with Negroes, Davis's involvement with the army's famous experiment with camels, and Davis's religious life.[42] Thus, McElroy had access to materials, the articles as well as the Fleming collection of data, which put him into the position of having much more with which to work than any previous Davis scholar.

McElroy, incidently, cited one arcane source which he found in the Fleming collection that, discussing now, allows us to mention again the historical work of the honoree of this symposium: T. Harry Williams. Professor Williams served on the first Board of Advisory Editors for the new edition of Davis Papers, but in his own scholarly work he, himself, did not do a *lot* that touched directly upon the probing of Jefferson Davis, devoting himself so much the more to Lincoln...and to "Lincolnand." But he did sometimes turn his attention to Davis, and I shall touch upon that, here and there, in this paper. In 1943, in collaboration with James S. Ferguson, Williams published in *The Journal of Mississippi History* an informative little "note and document" type of article on *"The Life of Jefferson Davis* by M'Arone."[43] M'Arone was the *nom de plume* of George Arnold, a wartime journalist and poet who worked in New York City. His piece is an insulting caricature of Davis's life, published originally in the July, 1865, issue of the magazine, *Comic Monthly*, and reissued later the same year in enlarged form as a pamphlet. If Pollard saw it, and probably he did, it no doubt warmed his heart. It made much over the grossly distorted charge that Davis had been captured in woman's garb, and it had a running theme alleging that Davis achieved social and professional success chiefly because he was a maker of good cocktails. And as regards Davis's education:

> ...Little Jeffey was sent to Transylvania College, where he learned reading, writing, arithmetic, geometry, syntax, botany, secession, hydrography, nullification, trigonometry, mendacity, and a variety of other useful knowledge.

. . . .

> He used convincing arguments, and undoubtedly advanced some of
> them in the form of a V, or may be an X....[44]

The reference to the "V" is, of course to the famous and unorthodox forma-
tion that Davis once had employed with his regiment during the Mexican War.
Ridiculing it provided grist for generations of Davis critics, beginning with
Pollard, who suggested that the Confederacy had "Died of a V."[45] T. Harry
Williams found it useful humor to enliven many of his lectures, and we who
knew and loved him can almost hear him again: Davis "never ceased to recall
his action at Buena Vista, and in Richmond during the Civil War anti-administra-
tion wags quipped that the Confederacy was dying of an inverted-V. A later critic
sneered that at Buena Vista, Davis learned enough about war in five minutes
to defeat the Confederacy."[46]

But this sort of thing is an extreme example of that from which McElroy tried
to rescue Davis. Perhaps to a degree he succeeded, for several later scholars
did admire, and make use of, McElroy's work. But it somehow has not remained
well suited to our modern needs, possibly because while trying to show that
the earlier historians erroneously had made Davis "a scapegoat," McElroy himself
ultimately and unwittingly did the same thing. Frank Vandiver perceived this
in his 1976 speech: terming McElroy's "...an awful sterility of achievement...an
episodic, oddly discursive book." Because "Davis's views of America...were of
lasting value in McElroy's eyes,...he, too, makes Davis a scapegoat, makes him
the stout champion of dying ideals, dear to McElroy."[47] Too, McElroy consciously
was addressing his British audience, and he made undue and awkward attempts
to equate and relate issues of the Civil War era to issues of his own day.

In the two decades that intervened between the appearance of McElroy's
biography and the beginning of the Civil War Centennial celebration, the image of Davis that he projected tended to prevail, although the better historians
sometimes tried to improve on synthesizing that which was most worthwhile
in the previous scholarship, and on occasion they at least glimpsed the more
complex Davis. We see that, for example, by contrasting the 1939 somewhat
sketchy though enduring contribution to Confederate history by a rather biased
New Englander, Burton J. Hendrick, *Statesmen of the Lost Cause; Jefferson
Davis and his Cabinet*[48], with the more complex and significant early favorable
assessment of Davis as a war leader which came five years later, in 1944, with
Rembert W. Patrick's *Jefferson Davis and his Cabinet*.[49] A young South Caroli-
nian, working on a dissertation at the University of North Carolina under the
famed Southern historian, Fletcher M. Green, maintaining scholarly detachment,
Patrick did a remarkable job of hinting at some of the aspects that seem
characteristic of the more recent newly emerging Davis.

Basically what we had during the ensuing years of transition in Davis scholarship was a rather stark division among historians: some still looking back toward

the old simplistic Davis, others—perhaps only tentatively at first—toward the new. Among those who continued to espouse the old depiction of Davis, Clifford Dowdey and Bell I. Wiley have to be noted as the harshest and most Pollardesque his modern critics.

Dowdey began his negative interpretation in his 1946 fuzzily-construed book *Experiment in Rebellion,*[50] continued it in his 1955 general history of the Confederacy,[51] and warmed still more to the task in his numerous and sympathetic, possibly even adoring, studies of R. E. Lee and that general's specific campaigns. What more would anyone need to know to perceive the nature of Dowdey's bias than that he titled a short chapter which covers R. E. Lee's appointment to army command, "The God Emerges"![52]

To Dowdey, Davis was always the villain: Davis thought of himself as a military genius...tried to run both the Government and the armies as he might have run his plantation...always standing on his own dignity, unwilling to accept advice ...treated members of his Cabinet as if they were mere office boys...neglected the needs, and also ill-used the sterling abilities, of R. E. Lee...displayed, countless times, his bull-headed self-delusion. Lastly, and most thoughtful—*if* developed within a scholarly context—, Dowdey opined that Davis lacked the *instincts* of a Southern planter. Not having been *born* to the manor, Davis had *acquired* both his status and his property, thus his patterns were rigid and fixed. And *that* was the explanation for Davis's hopelessly inferior capability.

This might be the best place to observe that, aside from Dowdey, the authors of the other standard histories of the Confederacy have not been major interpreters of Davis. With one obvious exception—Frank Vandiver's 1970 rendering, *Their Tattered Flags*, which is noted for its fresh, and kind, evalutions of Davis—, monographic Confederate histories have not typically been outlets for the introduction of new Davis-oriented original research, although of course the authors invariably did wrestle with attempting to synthesize extant scholarship. These include works by J. C. Schwab, in 1901; Nathaniel W. Stephenson, in 1919; Robert S. Henry, in 1931; Ellis Merton Coulter, in 1950; Clement Eaton, in 1954; Albert D. Kirwan, in 1959; Charles P. Roland, in 1960; and Emory M. Thomas, in 1979.[53]

Too, this seems an appropriate moment to point out that, until quite recently, Davis did not fare very well in the hands of biographers of other individuals, especially biographers of generals, unless their work happened to be a debunking one. Douglas Southall Freeman was more friendly than most. Still, even Freeman wrote of Davis's excessive sensitivity, his inclination to claim to a maximal degree *all* due authority, and his proclivity to dispute theoretical points merely to win an argument of logic.

But to return now to the more "head on" Davis critics, Clifford Dowdey's more incisively scholarly soul mate, Bell I. Wiley, took two particularly bitter swipes at Davis. The first in a 1954 lecture at Memphis State College, which he published in 1956 and republished with added comment in 1968 in *The Road to Appomattox*,[54] wherein Wiley said, Davis "lacked the wisdom, the boldness, the magnanimity, the flexibility and the stamina to lead the Southern revolt of the 1860's." Indeed, Wiley opined that Robert E. Lee was the *only man* who could have handled the Southern presidency! Otherwise, ironically, the lecture contained some useful data on the human side of Davis. Wiley continued his basic theme, more succinctly but also more sharply, in an introduction to a reprint edition of Davis's memoirs[55] in which he charged Davis with (1) inability to get along with people; (2) lack of administrative capacity; (3) aloofness from the people; and (4) neglect of civil functions in favor of military matters. Wiley regarded Davis as inadequate for his job, simply "beyond his depth."

One who strenuously argued otherwise, and whose labors on the largest of all the Jefferson Davis biographies[56] were done during years which coincided with the mature career of Bell Wiley, was Hudson Strode. An English professor, at the University of Alabama, Strode wrote lovingly of Davis, recapturing in three hefty volumes only in grander scale the simple idolatry of the early eulogizers. "Almost a benchmark of excess," said Frank Vandiver, "pleasant and interesting," wrote Clement Eaton, but "all-admiring and written in a political vacuum"; and my favorite observation of Strode's work always has been that of William Adams, long-time History Department Head at Nicholls State University: "every page reeks of Magnolia blossoms."[57]

Still, Strode's enormous research, and monumental literary effort, left us a potentially useful inheritance of data. Unfortunately, however, in that respect, it is not easy to use because he did not footnote his work. Strode managed to acquire many important private family letters, previously unknown to scholars, and also gathered much useful data from legends and testimony collected from Davis's descendants and collateral relatives. In addition to his three volumes of narrative biography, Strode also published the noteworthy compendium, *Jefferson Davis: Private Letters, 1823-1889.*[58] Bringing many of Davis's opinions into sharper focus than ever before, the collection reinforces what Strode consistently had maintained: that Davis was a leader of great ability, lofty principles, and boundless courage, and also a warm-hearted human being, a devoted husband and father, a man of great kindliness, patience, charm, and even-tempered fortitude, who faced bitter difficulties, disappointments, and incredible odds. I think Strode had more of the truth in his grasp than he was able to handle subtly, or succinctly.

It may be, though, that Strode's work on Davis has been a significant part of the inspiration impelling other thoughtful scholars, in the post-World War

II years, to conceive and to describe Davis's new historical image. We see this, perhaps most interestingly, in the evolving attitude of Allan Nevins. In his 1950 book *The Emergence of Lincoln,*[59] Nevins presented a very unfavorable portrait of Davis, describing him as proud, arrogant, and austere, observing—apparently in agreement—that Davis's political foes thought him too much of a martinet, too moody, and too metaphysical. In *The Statesmanship of the Civil War,* published in 1953, Nevins emphasized Davis's lack of great passion, and supposed that this rendered the president incapable of stirring his nation.[60] But in the eighteen years that remained to him—he died March 5, 1971—, Nevins became more and more convinced that history had been unfair to Davis, and Nevins shared the lead with Frank Vandiver—who in earlier writings also had been harsh with Davis—in urging, and launching in late 1965, the new Davis Papers project.[61] Further, Nevins's later work—a major multivolume narrative history of the war period—emphasized the difficult context in which Davis struggled.[62]

This emphasis upon context has been the primary vehicle wherein several relatively recent writers, as Frank Vandiver phrased it, have begun to "set the new Davis mold."[63] Before the 1971 advent of Volume I of the new edition of Davis papers, the vanguard of this group seems to me to have moved toward their better vision of Davis—like Nevins, that is, more from changing their own interpretive attitudes and gradually widening the breadth of their considerations,—while the writers since 1971 have had potential access to richer sources.

Vandiver's own conversion seems to have begun during the late 1950's. Before that, Vandiver, like many biographers of other Confederate personalities, had been influenced negatively toward Davis while studying the life of Josiah Gorgas.[64] Vandiver still held the same views at mid-decade, when in *Rebel Brass* he wrote of Davis's ideas being limited by "prejudice" and inferior strategic thinking that "grew smaller and smaller," because Davis's mindset was narrow and parochial.[65] But by the end of the 1950's Vandiver had begun to reverse himself on Davis, and in April 1959 at Hampden-Sydney College, in an oral presentation, subsequently published, offered some very perceptive and pathbreaking new ideas about the formulation and evolution of Confederate strategy.[66]

In addition to Nevins and Vandiver, outstanding examples of the new interpreters of Davis who are contemporary to our own times and have contributed to shaping the "new Davis mold," include Shelby Foote with his three volume narrative, *The Civil War,* David Herbert Donald in his revised textbook, Archer Jones, William Cooper, Thomas B. Alexander, and Richard Beringer.[67] A novelist turned historian, Foote brilliantly and exhaustively exploited a goodly body of printed material, the *Official Records* and several hundred well-selected books, and in the process came to perceive that "the underrating of Jefferson Davis is almost like a giant conspiracy."[68] Donald earlier had observed that "much of the criticism of the Confederate President fails to take into account the insuperable difficulties of his position and to realize that no other Southern political leader even approached Davis in stature."[69] Jones, Cooper, Alexander and Beringer all have done much to empasize consideration of context and—while, to be *sure*, they are not totally uncritical of Davis—all have tended to exonerate the Confederate president as being primarily responsible for the Confederate defeat, or at least somewhat to rehabilitate his image.

At the same time, there continued to be a corps of critics who remained convinced that the final assessment of Davis truly should be a negative one. These historians, from an early date, included David Potter and T. Harry Williams, and joining them soon was Grady McWhiney. Potter and Williams both used as their matrices, as others did both before and since, a comparison and contrast of Davis and Abraham Lincoln as war leaders. As one might expect, it is a strong temptation to make Davis look bad when he is depicted as a foil for Lincoln, a phenomenon that was described and ridiculed by Ludwell Johnson in a compellingly interesting 1981 essay, "Jefferson Davis and Abraham Lincoln as War Presidents: Nothing Succeeds Like Success."[70]

Potter, admittedly overstressing his case for the sake of good argument, suggested that Davis's shortcomings alone best answered the question posed by the title of the fascinating 1960 book, *Why the North Won the Civil War*, which contained the essay wherein Potter said that "Davis failed in three important ways—in his relations with other Confederate leaders and with the people, in his fundamental concept of his job as president, and in his specific handling of his politico-military role as commander in chief."[71] I disagree with one statement made by Vandiver in his "Leader Without Legend" speech, I do not agree that Potter elsewhere softened his negative assessment of Davis while giving more attention to the context of Confederate weakness.[72]

In the same vein as Potter, T. Harry Williams first dismissed Davis, in 1952, as a "mediocre" war president in *Lincoln and His Generals*,[73] but Williams did his real job on Davis in a speech, entitled "Two War Leaders: Lincoln and Davis," delivered at Springfield, Illinois, on Lincoln's birthday, in 1972.[74] In his delightfully engaging manner, Williams talked about the myths intertwining the early lives of Lincoln and Davis, discussed the apocryphal allegations that perhaps they were half-brothers,[75] and stressed revealing differences between perceptions and observations reported by foreign observers and those made by Americans. Williams seemed impressed with Clifford Dowdey's inference concerning Davis's lack of patrician instincts, and elaborated upon the subject, as somewhat the springboard of Williams's main thesis concerning Davis, that Davis did not know much about people nor, especially, anything about their *feelings*. "He had had much applause and little critcism," Williams said, "he was gracious to inferiors and polite to equals and probably did not realize that he had any superiors."[76]

There, my fellow historians, is an insight of considerable import. It well may be that Jefferson's brother, Joe, was the *only* superior to whom Jefferson ever inwardly deferred.

Continuing now with Williams's analysis, in numerous ways, but especially politically, things had come much easier for Davis than they had for Lincoln, and hence Lincoln had *learned* much in the process whereas Davis had not. This rendered Lincoln much abler than Davis "to lead people in a crisis."[77] From that, Williams modulated toward Davis's (not only relative to Lincoln, but outright) inadequate ability to *say* anything memorable, let alone something stirring. Williams then flirted with Allan Nevins's earlier suggestion that Davis had no *passion* for anything, even embellished it by supposing that perhaps Davis simply was not a passionate person, but finally rejected this track because he believed it misleading. Indeed, Williams concluded, the reason was simply because Davis "really did not know what people were like."[78]

Williams also talked about the "average and even mediocre capacity" of Davis's advisors, opining that possibly "some unsureness in himself impelled him [Davis] to place 'little' men in his entourage." And Williams waxed elaborative on Davis's excessive conservatism, alleged that this prevented a more offensive military strategy which should have been employed, and that Davis "disliked the new, the unorthodox." Thus, the crux: Davis was the ultimate product of his society and his class, not adequate "to the discipline that modern war demands." And so, in the end, Williams suggested a certain impossibility about the Southern war effort, for even if (by *accident*, because that is the only way the people would have allowed it to occur) a proper revolutionist—unlike Davis—somehow had captured the Confederate presidency, he would have been rebuffed, for "the Southern people could not possibly have understood what he was trying to do."[79]

Williams's assessments harmonize with those of Grady McWhiney.[80] Cited in the June 1975 issue of *Civil War History* as then "completing a study of Jefferson Davis and His Generals," McWhiney apparently put that particular work aside in order to concentrate on several other distinguished productions, but he has published several stimulating article-length foretastes.

In his 1973 article, itself entitled "Jefferson Davis and His Generals," McWhiney argued subtly that Davis suffered chronically from poor health, but even more telling, perhaps, Davis had a penchant for picking sickly people to be around him, and even sickly men to lead the Confederacy's armies. "Sickness is after all an aspect of weakness," McWhiney observed, "and there is abundant evidence that Davis liked to surround himself with weak subordinates." Furthermore, Davis had bad luck, but occasionally Davis himself had much to do with bringing that bad luck, for "at times Davis also used his appointing power to punish his enemies," and even more to the point, the president might retain or dismiss on a purely personal basis: Davis like people who agreed with him. If they did not, they usually left his administration." And the crux is that Davis *could not* have done otherwise, "because he was imprisoned by his own character and background. And so was the Confederacy." The true failure of the Confederacy's leaders was their very selection of Davis.[81]

Subsequently, in his 1975 article, "Jefferson Davis and the Art of War," McWhiney stressed the complexity of attempting new assessments of Davis, then proceeded to make several intriguing suggestions. First, rejecting the often-repeated assertion—and a favorite theory of T. Harry Williams—that militarily Davis was a Jominian (hence Davis's military failings could be explained in light of the inevitable wrong-headedness in such a person—or at least according to misinterpretations of Jomini, which commonly prevailed until the brilliant later work of Archer Jones elaborated clearly on what a Jominian truly was), McWhiney probed what he understood precisely to be Davis's ideas about war-making. Davis believed "that it could be glorious and just"...,but if so, it had to be "fought only between organized armies," and this "prevented him from encouraging extensive espionage, sabotage, or guerilla warfare." Davis believed "that white Americans, and especially white Southerners, were a martial people generally superior...," but this not only gave him a false confidence in Southern prowess, it meant that "his strong racial prejudices kept him from supporting the use of slaves in the Confederate army until it was too late." Davis believed that a navy was of minimal importance in warfare, and so, with bitter result, he neglected it. Lastly, Davis's concept of how wars should be fought combined with the ideals which guided him in choosing generals, to impel him to pick men who tended to be too aggressive—"indeed, sometimes reckless"—and hence the war was lost[82]—because all too often they attacked...and they died.

McWhiney has won a goodly number to his point of view; I and my recent collaborators, Archer Jones, Richard Beringer, and William Still, stand in an opposite camp.[83] The better of the Davis scholarship during the most recent two decades or so has been enticingly interesting and intellectually experimentive. It has, I like to believe, thrust forward in the best spirit and traditions of those urged early in this century by William E. Dodd—with fair and honest inquiry, and without acrimony. But it *typically* has veered away from attempts to describe the whole Davis, and into special, tangential—but I think fruitful—directions. Worthy of particular mention, it includes a goodly number of monographic articles, most of them provocative and helpful, on various aspects of Davis studies. Many of these have been published from time to time in the *Journal of Mississippi History*, and otherwise that distinguished state journal does a fine job of keeping up with and presenting reference notes to Davis material published elsewhere.

Among the untypical few of the recent studies of Davis that fairly may be termed eclectic, the kindest assessments have come from Frank Vandiver's pen.

JEFFERSON DAVIS, Photographic Portrait by Washburn, New Orleans, 1888.
Eleanor S. Brockenbrough Library, The Museum of the Confederacy, Richmond, Virginia.

We see this especially in his 1970 book, *Their Tattered Flags*, which Emory Thomas hailed in *Saturday Review* as "while not a biography, it ranks as the best biographical treatment of Jefferson Davis to date."[84] Most importantly, it is well balanced. In it, an heroic Davis, often brilliant, but sometimes foolish, succumbs ultimately to his fatal flaw: he cannot inspire in others devotion which equals his own.

By 1976 Vandiver had still more sharply etched his vision of the "new Davis." Inescapably, in some degree, parts of the old Davis must remain, but they now are more interesting, because our knowledge and understanding has become more nearly complete. The new Davis is a different person in private than in public, warm, witty, and able to charm. Davis's love for his new country was an "anguished" one, and he was filled wth it, as deeply as Lincoln was filled with love for the Union. Perhaps it was this that limited Davis somewhat, because it kept him from taking a more pragmatic stance. But he did grow, he did learn. And the men that Davis picked were "better than his critics admit," especially at the lower managerial levels. "Davis deserves praise as an executive," he "showed courage, considerable flexibility and imagination," and he was an impressive, enthusiastic, innovator.

But, perhaps admitting that his own ultimate conclusions were yet to become final, Vandiver closed, first by asking rhetorically if Davis had been "a man who rose to challenge," and answered only that "certainly he rose to crisis." Lastly, the ultimate question was whether Davis had succeeded "in making a Confederate nation." *That* would make Davis deserve rank with the "handful of *legendary* Americans who changed history." Vandiver thought the answer was Yes.[85]

A graduate student earlier at Duke, Paul D. Escott, thought it was No, and for his dissertation wrote a masterly treatise to that effect, subsequently revised and published in 1978 as *After Secession Jefferson Davis and the Failure of Confederate Nationalism.*[86] Escott's is an impressive intellect, his presentation is formidable and intricate. Certainly no heir of Pollard, Escott's description of Davis is in places intensely favorable; his Davis has many strengths, however they weigh too lightly when balanced against defects, and in the end Escott does blame Davis for the Confederate defeat because the president did too little to elevate, or sustain the spirits of the common masses—and *their* tenacity had been essential.

Escott lauds Davis's strategy, particularly at the war's outset, when already it contained the element of painting a popular picture that the United States was waging uncivilized warfare, and subsequently even to "change the South's image of the North," by exploiting a theme of "northern barbarity." Davis's attempts to define the South's ideology were validly on track, and Davis made good psychological and manipulative use of naturally-occurring loyalties, such as to one's home state, and to the church.

Davis himself *was* truly a revolutionary, however,—and here Escott's interpretation becomes unique—Davis's dedication to achieving independence needs notice. Davis probably failed clearly to perceive the process, and the cost, wherein waned the support of the common people of the Confederacy. Ideology meant less to the common masses than it did to Davis, or to most of the upper class Confederates. State rights sentiment has been a misunderstood force; in part it was beneficial to the Confederate war effort, and its power could have been, and should have been, manipulated more than it was. Davis deserves censure for having chosen, on the whole, to "put the needs of the army and the preferences of the planter class ahead of the urgent problems of nonslaveholding southerners," and, even in that, he too-often failed adequately to placate anyone, so "to many advocates of states' rights Davis played the role of a despot."

But Davis was *not* a despot, the problem was his nationalism: *it* was so intense, he neglected fuelling it in others; and he was so fixed, and so certain, in his goals, that he "banished" all "idea of compromise." Davis, and a few insightful souls who thought somewhat similarly, made alterations in their thinking about necessary subsequent southern racial adjustments, because it was *not race* which motivated Davis, independence served that purpose. But, although he tried, belatedly, he did not, perhaps he could not, communicate these societal alterations, or make them seem as acceptable as they were necessary.

While not totally so, Davis seems to have been relatively unaware of "the importance of internal morale. The spirit of the people...a vital factor...." At any rate "any assessment of him as Confederate president must rest to a great degree upon his sensitivity to problems of morale and his effectiveness in eliciting the enthusiasm and energies of the people. It is in this area," Escott concluded, "that the judgment of Davis must be most harsh." Davis "proved insensitive to the problems of ordinary southerners, who suffered greatly...," and for this, the blame for losing the war *must* lie on Davis's shoulders.[87]

Published in 1977, the year between Vandiver's speech and Escott's book, was a new attempt at a full Davis biography by the then retired eminent Southern historian, Clement Eaton.[88] (Apparently, neither Vandiver nor Escot had access to Eaton's work when they were preparing their own studies, for they make no mention of it.) Eaton's is a graceful presentation, to be sure, but unsatisfying. The book's most striking quality is its conciseness, and in that well-packed brevity it does pleasantly present the essential facts about Davis, making it a good modern introduction for uninitiated enthusiasts.

With few exceptions, for scholars Eaton's story is a familiar one. While some of his new probes reflected current contemporary concerns, such as a consideration of Davis's "relations with women," and on the qualities of slave life on the Davis plantation; the most interesting chapters are those which deal with Davis as a national political figure and subsequently as Confederate president. Eaton delineates Davis as more conservative than have Vandiver or Escott, and he concludes that while Davis did grow as a war leader, it was not enough, and that can be taken as at least one of the key reasons why the Confederacy failed.

While coming a little closer than previous Davis biographies in explaining the inner man, ultimately the book falls flat. I think, in the end, for Eaton, too, despite his long study, deep learning, and mature reflection, Davis still remained an enigma—"The Sphinx of the Confederacy," as Eaton named his final chapter.

Robert Penn Warren, in a written meditation which was prompted in part by the restoration of Jefferson Davis's citizenship in the United States, during the Carter Administration, indicated that he thought Eaton was right. Being Sphinx-like, Warren said, "We can ultimately only guess about Davis." And *Warren's* guess about Davis was that the man had been "certainly neurotic in some undiagnosable way (perhaps suffering from an inner struggle of values)...that Davis "lacked the indefinable sense for 'handling' men, the intuitive understanding of others, and, ultimately, perhaps, self-confidence."[89]

And others, too, continue to guess—as has James M. McPherson in his newly-published highly acclaimed best seller, *Battle Cry of Freedom*.[90] To McPherson Davis is the prime scapegoat, not, however, for personality defects but for lack of managerial skill. I and my collaborators wrote otherwise in *How the North Won*, and subsequently in *Why the South Lost the Civil War*. We believe that Davis managed well, and that viewpoints like this particular one of McPherson's probably form only because there still remains an elusive inadequacy in Davis scholarship. No one has been able yet to fit *everything* that is available and pertinent into an adequate, acceptable, and artful whole. And it seems a bit ironic that the considered guesses which have come from poets and literary people have struck more resonant notes than have the guesses of most historians. The enticing question still stands, unresolved, and the task beckons: how indeed shall Jefferson Davis properly be profiled?

What the near future may bring, no one with any certainty can say. But there *will* be more Davis scholarship. And it seems justified to assert that this yet-to-be scholarly body of material shall transcend that which already has appeared: in quality and value, and—we do dare hope—also in insight and analytic assessment.

Endnotes

*This paper is part of a larger biography of Jefferson Davis which the author is writing with Richard E. Beringer.

1 For an elaborative summary, up to 1970, see John Junior Jones, "A Historiographical Study of Jefferson Davis" (Ph.D. Dissertation, University of Missouri-Columbia, 1970). This dissertation is especially important to Davis scholars, and useful, because of the wide range of works which the author considered.

2 T. Harry Williams, "Review of *Jefferson Davis* by Clement Eaton," in *Alabama Review*, 31: (October, 1978), p. 309.

3 *Louisiana History Newsletter* 14: Spring, 1988, 3.

4 Phyllis Sanders, "Jefferson Davis: Reactionary Rebel 1808-1860" (Ph.D. Dissertation, UCLA, 1976).

5 I believe this dissertation, in the form in which I was able to read it, was well done in some respects, poorly in others, and in need of strenuous revision and addition. I know the author already to have revised some, to be working on more, and to be negotiating with a press. Of course, the Williams work referred to here is *Lincoln and His Generals* (New York, 1952).

6 Steven E. Woodworth to Michael Briggs, January 11, 1988; Kansas University Press readers's evaluations of *Jefferson Davis and His Generals*, copies of all documents in my possession.

7 *The Papers of Jefferson Davis*, published by the Louisiana State University Press for the Jefferson Davis Association, five volumes have been published to date: 1971, 1974, 1981, 1983, and 1985, originally edited by Haskell M. Monroe, Jr. and James T. McIntosh, and now by Lynda Lasswell Crist and Mary Seaton Dix.

8 Frank E. Vandiver, "Jefferson Davis—Leader Without Legend," *Journal of Southern History*, 43: February, 1977, pp. 7-8.

9 Each year as the war progressed he did a history of that annum's wartime events. In 1866 he published a condensation of the earlier four volumes, *The Lost Cause; a new southern history of the war of the Confederates* (New York and other cities). Pollard is thus the effective originator of the phrase "Lost Cause," though not the creator of the full-blown mythic form which later developed. It strikes me as both amusing and somehow strangely significant that the book remains perennially in print, apparently a durable seller in the large chain-bookstores.

10 *Life of Jefferson Davis, with a Secret History of the Southern Confederacy Gathered "Behind the Scenes in Richmond"* (Philadelphia and other cities, 1869).

11 "Leader Without Legend," p. 3.

12 Ibid., p. 3.

13 *The Life of Jefferson Davis*, (Cincinnati and other cities).

14 "Leader Without Legend," p. 5.

15 *Life of Jefferson Davis, with an authentic account of his private and public career, and his death and burial; together with The Life of Stonewall Jackson...including his glorious military career and his tragic death on the battlefield.* (Philadelphia). The year 1890 was an interesting one with respect to Davis scholarship for several reasons. A group

of Davis's friends published a useful compendium of their recollections about him: *Life and Reminiscences of Jefferson Davis* (Baltimore). Secondly, Mrs. Davis published her quite important two-volume memoir, *Jefferson Davis, Ex-President of the Confederate States of America* (New York). And the year also marked the occasion for the only significant evaluation of Davis to be done by an historian who was black. William E. B. DuBois graduated that year from Harvard, and as one of six commencement speakers, he orated on "Jefferson Davis as a Representative of Civilization." DuBois regarded Davis with reluctant admiration, noting particularly his extraordinary a condemning conclusion concerning Davis and that for which he had stood, primarily placing the blame upon flawed societal standards and tenets of human justice. DuBois had an able and facile mind, and this was a worthy piece, but it is doubtful that he changed the minds of any of his hearers. The speech apparently was not published. Sanders says that a microfilm copy is in the Research Library at U.C.L.A., and she cites it in her dissertation, "Jefferson Davis: Reactionary Rebel," pp. 17-18, 27n29.

[16] "Leader Without Legend," p. 6.

[17] Thomas L. Connelly, *Will Success Spoil Jeff Davis?* (New York, 1963), p. 12.

[18] Emory M. Thomas, *The Confederacy as a Revolutionary Experience* (Englewood Cliffs, New Jersey, 1971.

[19] *The Rise and Fall of the Plantation South* (New York and London).

[20] See Charles Reagan Wilson, *Baptized in Blood The Religion of the Lost Cause, 1865-1920* (Athens, Georgia, 1980); Lloyd A. Hunter, "The Sacred South: Postwar Confederates and the Sacralization of Southern Culture," (Ph.D. dissertation, St. Louis University, 1978); and Herman Hattaway and Lloyd A. Hunter, "The War Inside the Church," *Civil War Times Illustrated*, 26: (January, 1988), pp. 28-33.

[21] In Thomas L. Connelly's *The Marble Man Robert E. Lee and His Image in American Society* (New York, 1977); and William Garrett Piston, *Lee's Tarnished Lieutenant James Longstreet and His Place in Southern History* (Athens, Georgia, 1987).

[22] Michael B. Ballard, *A Long Shadow: Jefferson Davis and the Final Days of the Confederacy* (Jackson, Mississippi, 1986); Gaines M. Foster, *Ghosts of the Confederacy: Defeat, the Lost Cause, and the Emergence of the New South, 1865 to 1913* (New York, 1987); Edward K. Eckert, *"Fiction Distorting Fact": Prison Life, Annotated by Jefferson Davis* (Macon, Georgia, 1987); Michael B. Ballard, "Review of Eckert, 'Fiction Distorting Fact," in *Louisiana History* 28: Fall, 1987, pp. 415-17.

[23] Dodd, *Jefferson Davis* (New York, 1907). Born in North Carolina in 1869, Dodd won a Ph.D. from Leipzig in 1900, and had a professorship at Randolph-Macon College. Otherwise it is perhaps a bit surprising that he did such a good job on this volume, or even that he did the work at all, for in truth he never was more than casually interested in Davis: he was invited to do the volume by Ellis Paxson Oberholtzer, editor of *The American Crisis Biographies* series, because Oberholtzer was impressed with his earlier biography of Nathaniel Macon. Just a few years previous, in 1904, Landon Knight—an Akron, Ohio newspaperman—had attempted a scholarly Davis biography, *The Real Jefferson Davis* (Battle Creek, Michigan). Short, rather uncritical, it is shallow, poorly organized, and marred by numerous errors of fact.

[24] "Leader Without Legend," p. 5.

25 Dodd, *Jefferson Davis*, p. 7.

26 Gordon, *Jefferson Davis* (New York, 1918); Schaff, *Jefferson Davis: His Life and Personality* (Boston, 1922); Eckenrode, *Jefferson Davis, President of the South* (New York, 1923); Tate, *Jefferson Davis: His Rise and Fall, a Biographical Narrative* (New York, 1929); Cutting, *Jefferson Davis Political Soldier* (New York, 1930); Winston, *High Stakes and Hair Trigger The Life of Jefferson Davis* (New York, 1930); and McElroy, *Jefferson Davis, the Unreal and the Real* 2 volumes (New York, 1937).

27 "Leader Without Legend," p. 5.

28 Eaton, *Jefferson Davis*, (New York & London, 1977), p. 317. That is, the best of the first four that he listed—McElroy stood apart. Eaton did not list Gordon's nor Schaff's at all, apparently either failing to find them or simply regarding them as not worthy of any notice.

29 *War of the Rebellion: A Compilation of the Official Records of the Union and Confederate Armies* (70 volumes in 128 parts, Washington, D.C., 1880-1901). Of course, Eaton did not really like Davis very much either, and that could be a partial explanation for Eaton's favorable opinion.

30 Eckenrode, *Jefferson Davis, President of South*, pp. viii, 4-7, 9, 12-14, 18, 34-35, 340-45, 348-51, 355, 359, 361-63, 366.

31 Ibid., p. 29.

32 Lynda J. Lasswell, (ed.), "Jefferson Davis Ponders His Future, 1829," *The Journal of Southern History*, 41: November, 1975, pp. 517-22.

33 Dunbar Rowland (ed.), *Jefferson Davis, Constitutionalist*, 10 volumes (Printed for the Mississippi Department of Archives and History, 1923). In large volumes of some 600 pages each, this noteworthy compilation, completed with the help of Rowland's historian wife, Eron, constitutes a monument to Davis of major proportions. The Rowlands did assemble the collection in such a way as to present Davis in the most favorable light possible, and since numerous additional documents subsequently have come to light, the collection deserves to be replaced by a more modern edition, but due to the unfortunately necessary down-scaling of the scope of the still-being-published new edition of Davis papers, the Rowland volumes will continue to be necessary tools for Davis scholars.

34 Tate, *Jefferson Davis: His Rise and Fall, a Biographical Narrative*, p. 303 and *passim.*; Vandiver, "Leader Without Legend," p. 5. A native of Kentucky, and only thirty years of age, Tate was one of the "Nashville Agrarians," a group of literary critics, authors, and poets, who expressed uneasiness about what they felt the South had become since the antebellum era.

35 Cutting, *Jefferson Davis, Political Soldier*, pp. 323-24, 326-27.

36 Obit., in *American Historical Review* 50: (January, 1945), p. 432.

37 Avery O. Craven, "Review of Winston's *High Stakes and Hair Trigger*, in *American Historical Review* 37: (January, 1932), pp. 384-85.

38 Winston, *High Stakes and Hair Trigger; the Life of Jefferson Davis* (New York, 1930), pp. 259-62.

[39] Robert McElroy, *Jefferson Davis: The Unreal and the Real* (2 vols., New York and London, 1937).

[40] Sanders, "Jefferson Davis: Reactionary Rebel," p. 18.

[41] Walter Lynwood Fleming, "Jefferson Davis, the Negroes and the Negro Problem," *Sewanee Review*, 16: October, 1908, 407-27; "Two Important Letters by Jefferson Davis Discovered," Southern Historical Society *Papers* (Richmond), 34: 1908, 8-12; "Jefferson Davis at West Point," Mississippi Historical Society *Publications* (University, Oxford, & Jackson), 10: 1909, 247-67; "Jefferson Davis's Camel Experiment," *Popular Science Monthly* (New York) 74: (February, 1909), 141-52; "Jefferson Davis and Andersonville," Southern Historical Society *Papers* 36: 1910, 8-12; "The Religious Life of Jefferson Davis," *Methodist Quarterly Review* (Louisville & Nashville), 61: (April, 1910), 325-42; "Jefferson Davis's First Marriage," Mississippi Historical Society *Publications* 12: (1912), 21-36; "The Early Life of Jefferson Davis," Mississippi Valley Historical Association *Proceedings*, 1915-18 (Cedar Rapids), 9: (1919), 151-76; "Some Documents Relating to JeffersonDavis at West Point," *Mississippi Valley Historical Review* 7: (September, 1921), 146-52; "Concerning Jefferson Davis," *Bookman*, 59: (March, 1924), 82-85. Several of these studies were reprinted as *Bulletins of Louisiana State University* (Baton Rouge).

[42] There is an important lecture series named for Fleming at Louisiana State University, where for a decade he was a professor. He himself was the subject of one such lecture, by Wendell Holmes Stephenson. See Stephenson, *The South Lives in History   Southern Historians and Their Legacy* (Baton Rouge, 1955), Chapter IV, and especially section 4 thereof for a full narration about Fleming's Davis project. Fleming's poor health forced him into retirement at the age of 54 and he died four years later.

[43] 5: (October, 1943), pp. 197-203.

[44] I have drawn all of this from Williams's and Ferguson's article and have not myself seen the pamphlet.

[45] *Richmond Enquirer*, January 9, 1865, quoted in Eckenrode, *Jefferson Davis: President of the South*, p. 45.

[46] T. Harry Williams, *Two War Leaders: Lincoln and Davis* (Springfield, Illinois, 1972), p. 10.

[47] "Leader Without Legend," p. 6.

[48] Hendrick, *Statesmen of the Lost Cause* (Boston, 1939). The term "enduring" applies to its readability and appeal as an introduction; historiographically it is hopelessly out of date.

[49] Patrick, *Jefferson Davis and his Cabinet* (Baton Rouge, 1944).

[50] Dowdey, *Experiment in Rebellion* (Garden City, New York, 1946). The work purports to be a general history of the Civil War from the Southern viewpoint, in many respects it is a quasi Davis biography, and in fact it mainly is a fragmented and incomplete story of embattled Richmond.

[51] Dowdey, *The Land They Fought For; the story of the South as the Confederacy, 1832-1865* (New York, 1955).

[52] Dowdey, *Experiment in Rebellion*, Chapter 16.

53 Schwab, *The Confederate States of America, a Financial and Industrial History of the South During the Civil War* (New York, 1904); Stephenson, *The Day of the Confederacy; a Chronicle of the Embattled South.* (Vol. XXX of *The Chronicles of America*, edited by Allen Johnson, New Haven, 1919); Henry, *The Story of the Confederacy*, originally published 1931, new and revised edition with a foreword by Douglas Southall Freeman (Indianapolis, 1936); Coulter, *The Confederate States of America 1861-1865 (A History of the South, VII*, Wendell Holmes Stephenson and E. Merton Coulter, eds., Baton Rouge, 1950); Eaton, *A History of the Southern Confederacy* (New York, 1954); Kirwan, *The Confederacy* (New York, 1959); Roland, *The Confederacy* (Chicago, 1960); Vandiver, *Their Tattered Flags: The Epic of the Confederacy* (New York, 1970); and Thomas, *The Confederate Nation 1861-1865 (New American Nation Series*, ed. by Henry Steele Commager and Richard B. Morris, New York, 1979).

54 Wiley, *The Road to Appomattox* (New York, 1968).

55 Bell I. Wiley (ed.), *The Rise and Fall of the Confederate Government by Jefferson Davis* (New York, 1958), 2 volumes, I, Foreword.

56 Hudson Strode, *Jefferson Davis*, 3 volumes (New York, 1950-1964).

57 Vandiver, "Leader Without Legend," p. 7; Eaton, *Jefferson Davis*, p. 317; William H. Adams, "Review of *Jefferson Davis, Tragic Hero*" [Volume 3], in *Louisiana History*, 7: Winter, 1986, pp. 86-87. Phyllis Sanders observed more bluntly that Strode "masked his white supremacist bias very subtly." See Sanders, "Jefferson Davis: Reactionary Rebel," p. 22. Another more humorous assessment came from the pen of reviewer Gerald M. Capers, who suggested that instead of having an axe to grind, Strode had proved that he didn't even have a hatchet. Capers, "Review of *Jefferson Davis: American Patriot*," [Volume 1] in *The Journal of Southern History*, 22: (February 1956), p. 112.

58 *Jefferson Davis: Private Letters, 1823-1889*, selected and edited by Hudson Strode (New York, 1966). Alas, it is true, and important for scholars to know, that there *are* in an unknown number of the letters here reproduced, certain unindicated omissions; and some of the letters have disappeared since Strode saw them, making verification impossible. The collection can never be used as conclusive evidence.

59 Nevins, *The Emergence of Lincoln*, I [*Ordeal of the Union*, Vol. III] (New York, 1950).

60 Nevins, *The Statesmanship of the Civil War* (New York, 1953), especially Chapter three.

61 Lynda Lasswell Crist, "From Quill to Cume: Editing the Papers of Jefferson Davis," Paper read on September 30, 1983 at the Grand Forks, North Dakota, meeting of the Northern Great Plains Historical Association, copy in my possession.

62 Beginning in 1959, and during the remainder of his life, the last appearing posthumously, Nevins produced four volumes of grand narrative history which covered the entire Civil War period, continuing *Ordeal of the Union*, his New Nationalist School remake of the pioneering multivolume *History of the United States From the Compromise of 1850* (7 volumes, New York, 1893-1906) by James Ford Rhodes. For explanation and elaboration on the various schools of Civil War historiography, see Thomas J. Pressly, *Americans Interpret Their Civil War* (revised edition, New York, 1962).

63 Vandiver "Leader Without Legend," p. 6.

64 Frank E. Vandiver, *Ploughshares into Swords Josiah Gorgas and Confederate Ordnance* (Austin, 1952).

65 Frank Vandiver, *Rebel Brass The Confederate Command System* (Baton Rouge, 1956), especially pp. 19, 23, & 25-6.

66 Frank Vandiver, "Jefferson Davis and Confederate Strategy," in Bernard Mayo (ed.), *American Tragedy: The Civil War in Retrospect* (Hampden-Sydney, Virginia, 1959).

67 Shelby Foote, *The Civil War: A Narrative* (3 volumes, New York, 1958-1974); J. G. Randall and David Donald, *The Civil War and Reconstruction* (Second Edition, Revised, Lexington, Massachusetts, 1969)—this being a substantially unchanged reprint of the 1961 edition, the year in which Donald originally made his statement; Archer Jones, *Confederate Strategy from* Shiloh to Vicksburg (Baton Rouge, 1961); Thomas Lawrence Connelly, *Army of the Heartland: The Army of Tennessee, 1861-1862* (Baton Rouge, 1967) and *Autumn of Glory: The Army of Tennessee, 1862-1865* (Baton Rouge, 1970); Thomas Lawrence Connelly and Archer Jones, *The Politics of Command; Factions and Ideas in Confederate Strategy* (Baton Rouge, 1973); William J. Cooper, Jr., "A Reassessment of Jefferson Davis as War Leader: The Case from Atlanta to Nashville," *The Journal of Southern History*, 36: (May, 1970), pp. 189-204; Vandiver, *Their Tattered Flags* and "Leader Without Legend"; Thomas Alexander and Richard E. Beringer, *The Anatomy of the Confederate Congress: A Study in the Influences of Member Characteristics on Legislative Voting Behavior, 1861-1865* (Nashville, 1972). I purposely omitted Tom Connelly from this particular textural list, adhering to a suggestion made to me by Archer Jones, a sometime collaborator (although on separate projects) with both Connelly and myself.

68 *Mississippi Writer Talking*, John Griffin Jones, Interviewer and Editor (Jackson, 1982), pp. 62-63.

69 Randall and Donald, *The Civil War and Reconstruction*, p. 273.

70 Ludwell H. Johnson, "Jefferson Davis and Abraham Lincoln as War Presidents: Nothing Succeeds Like Success," *Civil War History*, 27 (March, 1981), pp. 49-63.

71 David Donald, ed., *Why the North Won the Civil War*, p. 101.

72 David Donald, ed., *Why the North Won the Civil War* (Baton Rouge, 1960), pp. 91-114, the quote is on p. 101; David M. Potter, *The South and the Sectional Conflict* (Baton Rouge, 1968); and, although containing nothing new on Davis, but distinguished for its recapitulation of historiography concerning the Fort Sumter episode, *The Impending Crisis 1848-1861* (completed and edited by Don E. Fehrenbacher, *New American Nation Series*, edited by Henry Steele Commager and Richard B. Morris, New York and other cities, 1973).

73 Williams, *Lincoln and His Generals*, p. 7.

74 T. Harry Williams, "Two War Leaders: Lincoln and Davis," (address presented on February 12, 1972 to the Abraham Lincoln Association, Duplicated by the Association, Springfield, Illinois, 1972).

75 The origin of this fanciful allegation—that Lincoln actually was the bastard offspring of Nancy Hanks and Samuel Davis—has been traced to J. M. Gibson, a Mississippi newspaper editor, born in 1856, and neighbor of Davis. Sanders, "Jefferson Davis: Reactionary Rebel," pp. 171, 180*n55*.

[76] Ibid., p. 10.

[77] Ibid., p. 12.

[78] Ibid., p. 13.

[79] Ibid., pp. 13-18.

[80] Grady McWhiney, "Jefferson Davis and His Generals" in *Southerners and Other Americans* (New York, 1973), pp. 83-101; "Jefferson Davis and the Art of War," *Civil War History*, 22: (June, 1975), pp. 101-112; "Jefferson Davis—The Unforgiven," *Journal of Mississippi History* 42: (May, 1980); and most recently in "The Divided Union," television series, produced for the BBC by Peter Battey.

[81] McWhiney, "Jefferson Davis and His Generals," passim. The quotes are on pp. 89, 95, and 100.

[82] McWhiney, "Jefferson Davis and the Art of War," passim. The quotes are on pp. 105-06 and 111.

[83] Herman Hattaway and Archer Jones, *How the North Won   A Military History of the Civil War* (Urbana and London, 1983), especially Chapter 20; Richard E. Beringer, Herman Hattaway, Archer Jones, and William N. Still, Jr., *Why the South Lost the Civil War* (Athens, Georgia, 1986), especially Appendix Two.

[84] Emory Thomas, "Review of Vandiver's *Their Tattered Flags*," in *Saturday Review* 53: March 28, 1970, p. 33.

[85] Vandiver, "Leader Without Legend," passim. The quotes are on pp. 7-12 and 18.

[86] Paul D. Escott, *After Secession   Jefferson Davis and the Failure of Confederate Nationalism* (Baton Rouge and London, 1978).

[87] Escott, *After Secession*, pp. 46-47, 51, 73, 90, 99-104, 115, 127-28, *137*, 144, 148-49, *154*, *178-80*, 181, 184, 196, *197*, 207-08, 215-16, 219, 221, 223-24, 228, 235-37, *239*, 245, 252-55, *256*, 257, 259, 261-64, 266-67, *268-69*, 270-74. The italicized page numbers are those from which I have taken quotes. Archer Jones and I, while continuing to admire and to value Escott's scholarship, have in our own studies of Davis's military management been led to our belief that Escott's context is too limited to political considerations, and this in turn leads him to an overall conclusion concerning Davis which we believe to be too harsh.

[88] Clement Eaton, *Jefferson Davis* (New York and London, 1977). A native of Winston-Salem, North Carolina, Eaton was educated at the University of North Carolina and at Harvard. He spent his career at the University of Kentucky.

[89] Robert Penn Warren, *Jefferson Davis Gets His Citizenship Back*, originally published in *The New Yorker* (1980), republished in book form (Lexington, Kentucky, 1980)—which I have used to obtain my quotes, pp. 51. 53; and republished still again, in excerpted and editorialized form, in *Civil War Times—Illustrated* 26: Summer, 1987, pp. 22-74 ff.

[90] McPherson, *Battle Cry of Freedom: The Civil War Era (The Oxford History of the United States, Vol. VI* New York, 1988).

Appendix A

Books and Articles by T. Harry Williams

Books

Lincoln and the Radicals. Madison: University of Wisconsin Press, 1941.

Editor, *Selected Writings and Speeches of Abraham Lincoln.* Chicago: Packard and Company, 1943.

Lincoln and His Generals. New York: A. A. Knopf, 1952.

P. G. T. Beauregard, Napoleon in Gray. Baton Rouge: Louisiana State University Press, 1955.

Editor, *With Beauregard in Mexico.* Baton Rouge: Louisiana State University Press, 1956.

A History of the United States, with R. N. Current and Frank Freidel. 2 vols. New York: A. A. Knopf, 1959.

Americans at War: The Development of the American Military System. Baton Rouge: Louisiana State University Press, 1960.

Romance and Realism in Southern Politics. Athens: University of Georgia Press, 1961.

Editor, *Military Memoirs of a Confederate,* by E. Porter Alexander. Bloomington: Indiana University Press, 1962.

McClellan, Sherman and Grant. Brunswick, N.J.: Rutgers University Press, 1962.

The Union Sundered. New York: Time, Inc., 1963.

The Union Restored. New York: Time, Inc., 1963.

Hayes: The Diary of a President. New York: David McKay Press, 1964.

Hayes of the Twenty-third: Civil War Volunteer. New York: A. A. Knopf, 1965.

Huey Long. New York: A. A. Knopf, 1969.

The History of American Wars, from 1745 to 1918. New York: A. A. Knopf, 1981.

The Selected Essays of T. Harry Williams. Baton Rouge and London: Louisiana State University Press, 1983.

Chapters in Other Works

"Abraham Lincoln: Pragmatic Democrat." In *The Enduring Lincoln*, edited by Norman A. Graebner. Urbana: University of Illinois Press, 1959.

Introduction to V. L. Bedsole and Oscar Richard, *Louisiana State University: A Pictorial Record*. Baton Rouge: Louisiana State University Press, 1959.

"Lincoln: The Military Strategist." In *Abraham Lincoln: A New Portrait*, edited by Henry B. Krantz. New York: Putnam's, 1959.

"Lincoln and the Causes of the Civil War." In *Lincoln Images*, edited by O. Fritiof Ander. Rock Island, Ill.: Augustana College Library, 1960.

"Lincoln and the Committee on the Conduct of the War." In *Lincoln for the Ages*, edited by Ralph G. Newman. Garden City, N.Y.: Doubleday, 1960.

"The American Civil War." In *The Zenith of European Power*, edited by J. B. Bury. Vol X of *The New Cambridge Modern History*. Cambridge: Cambridge University Press, 1960.

"The Military Leadership of the North and the South." In *The Harmon Memorial Lectures in Military History, 1959-1987*, edited by Harry R. Borowski, Washington, DC: Government Printing Office for the Office of Air Force History, 1988.

"The Military Leadership of North and South." In *Why the North Won the Civil War*, edited by David Donald. Baton Rouge: Louisiana State University Press, 1960.

"P. G. T. Beauregard: The South's First Hero," in *The Unforgettable Americans*, edited by John A. Garraty. New York: Channel Press, 1960.

"Disruption of the Union: The Secession Crisis, 1860-1861." In *Major Crises in American History*, Vol. I, edited by L. W. Levy and M. D. Peterson. New York: Harcourt, Brace and World, 1962.

"Lincoln and the Radicals: An Essay in Civil War History and Historiography." In *Grant, Lee, Lincoln, and the Radicals*, edited by Grady McWhiney. Evanston: Northwestern University Press, 1964.

"The Gentleman from Louisiana: Demagogue or Democrat." In *The Pursuit of Southern History*, edited by George Brown Tindall. Baton Rouge: Louisiana State University Press, 1964.

Introduction to *Every Man a King: The Autobiography of Huey P. Long*. New York: Quadrangle Books, 1964.

"Trends in Southern Politics." In *The Idea of the South*, edited by Frank E. Vandiver. Chicago: The University of Chicago Press, 1964.

"The Military Leadership of North and South." In *American Defense Policy in Perspective*, edited by Raymond G. O'Connor. New York: John Wiley and Sons, 1965.

"The Military Systems of North and South." In *Patterns in American History*, Vol. I, edited by Alexander De Conde *et al*. Belmont, Calif.: Wadsworth Publishing Company, 1965.

Foreword to A. J. Liebling, *The Earl of Louisiana*. Baton Rouge: Louisiana State University Press, 1970.

"The Politics of the Longs." In *Huey Long*, edited by Hugh Davis Graham. Englewood Cliffs, N.J.: Prentice-Hall, 1970.

"Huey Long and the Politics of Realism." In *Essays on Recent Southern Politics*, edited by H. M. Hollingsworth. Austin: University of Texas Press, 1970.

"The Civil War." In *Interpreting American History*, edited by John A. Garraty. New York: Macmillan, 1970.

THW with others. *The Meanings of American History*, Vol. II. Glenview, Ill.: Scott, Foresman, 1972.

"The Coming of the War." In *Shadows of the Storm*, Vol. I, edited by William C. Davis. Garden City, N.Y.: Doubleday, 1981.

Articles

"General John C. Frémont and the Politicians." *Journal of the American Military History Foundation*, II, No. 4 (Winter, 1938), 179-91.

"Benjamin F. Wade and the Atrocity Propaganda of the Civil War." *Ohio Archaeological and Historical Quarterly* (January, 1939), 33-43.

"The Attack upon West Point During the Civil War." *Mississippi Valley Historical Review*, XXV, No. 4 (March, 1939), 491-504.

"General Banks and the Radical Republicans During the Civil War." *New England Quarterly*, XII, No. 2 (June, 1939), 268-80.

"The Committee on the Conduct of the War." *Journal of the American Military Institute*, III, No. 3 (Fall, 1939), 139-56.

with Helen J. Williams. "Wisconsin Republicans and Reconstruction." *Wisconsin Magazine of History*, XXIII, No. I (September, 1939), 17-39.

"The Navy and the Committee on the Conduct of the War." *United States Naval Institute Proceedings*, LXV, No. 12 (December, 1939), 1751-55.

"Andrew Johnson as a Member of the Committee on the Conduct of the War." *Proceedings of the East Tennessee Historical Society*, No. 12 (1940), 70-83.

with James Ferguson. *"The Life of Jefferson Davis* by M'Arone." *Journal of Mississippi History*, V (October, 1943), 197-203.

"Precedent Exists for Congressional War Committee." New York *Times*, January 10, 1943.

"Civil War Papers Spilled Secrets." *The Quill*, January-February, 1944, pp. 5-12.

"Free State Government of Louisiana." *Journal of the Illinois State Historical Society*, XXXVII (March, 1944), 85-86.

"Voters in Blue: The Citizen Soldiers of the Civil War." *Mississippi Valley Historical Review*, XXXI (September, 1944), 187-204.

"The Louisiana Unification Movement of 1873." *Journal of Southern History*, XI (August, 1945), 349-69.

"General Ewell to the High Private in the Rear." *Virginia Magazine of History and Genealogy* (April, 1946), 157-60.

"An Analysis of Some Reconstruction Attitudes." *Journal of Southern History*, XII (November, 1946), 469-86.

"The Macs and the Ikes." *American Mercury*, LXXV (October, 1952), 32-39.

"Abraham Lincoln: Principle and Pragmatism in Politics." *Mississippi Valley Historical Review*, XL (June, 1953), 89-106.

"Robert E. Lee." *Compton's Encyclopedia*, 1954.

"The Changing History of Our Civil War." *Commentary*, XVIII (August, 1954), 161-65.

"Investigation: 1862." *American Heritage*, VI (December, 1954), 16-21.

"Freeman, Historian of the Civil War: An Appraisal." *Journal of Southern History*, XXI (February, 1955), 91-100.

"Beauregard At Shiloh." *Civil War History*, I (March, 1955), 17-34.

"Thaddeus Stevens: An American Radical." *Commentary*, XXI (June, 1956), 578-83.

"The Civil War Letters of William L. Cage." *Louisiana Historical Quarterly*, XXXIX (January, 1956), 113-30.

"The Reluctant Warrior: The Diary of N. K. Nichols." *Civil War History*, III (March, 1957), 17-39.

Eighteen essays on Union generals for *World Book*.

"George B. McClellan." *Encyclopedia Americana*.

"The Civil War." *World Book*, 1960, pp. 472-93.

"Reconstruction." *World Book*, 1960, pp. 166-71.

"Abraham Lincoln: The Military Strategist." *Civil War Times*, October, 1959.

"The Military Leadership of the North and the South." Harmon Memorial.

Lectures in Military History, No. 2, U.S. Air Force Academy, 1960.

"The Hard School of Experience." Louisville *Courier-Journal*, November 20, 1960, pp. 53-54.

"Grant Moves In." Louisville *Courier-Journal*, November 20, 1960, pp. 73-74.

"A Real Good Hearty War Dies Hard." *New York Times Book Review*, March 12, 1961.

"Impact of Leadership on Planning and Strategy." *The Official Army Information Digest* (August, 1961), 15-21.

"The Politics of the Longs." *Georgia Review*, XV (Spring, 1961), 20-33.

with Stephen Ambrose. "The 23rd Ohio—Regiment of Presidents." *Civil War Times Illustrated*, III, No. 3. (May, 1964), 22-25.

"Badger Colonels and the Civil War Officer." *Wisconsin Magazine of History*, XLVII, No. I (Autumn, 1963), 35-46.

"The Gentleman from Louisiana: Demagogue or Democrat." *Journal of Southern History*, XXVI, No. I (February, 1960), 3-21.

"Huey, Lyndon, and Southern Radicalism." *Journal of American History*, LX, No. 2 (September, 1973), 267-93.

"Now, Maybe, We Can Begin to Appreciate Lyndon Johnson." *Southern Voices* (May, 1974), 66-71.

"The Return of Jomini—Some Thoughts on Recent Civil War Writing." *Military Affairs*, XXXIX, No. 4 (December, 1975), 204-206.

Appendix B

Thomas L. Connelly—Chair, Department of History at the University of South Carolina and author of numerous books, including *Army of the Heartland*, *Autumn of Glory*, and *The Marble Man*.

Joseph Harsh—Associate Professor of History at George Mason University, director of the Northern Virginia Association of Historians, and editor of *The Civil War Monitor*.

Herman M. Hattaway—Professor of History at the University of Missouri at Kansas City and author/co-author of *General Stephen D. Lee*, *How the North Won*, and *Why the South Lost*.

Lawrence L. Hewitt—Associate Professor of History at Southeastern Louisiana University and author/editor of several books, including *Port Hudson, Confederate Bastion on the Mississippi*.

Archie P. McDonald—Professor of History at Stephen F. Austin State University and author/editor of nearly two dozen books, including *Make Me a Map of the Valley: The Journal of Jedediah Hotchkiss, 1862-1865*.

Richard Sommers—Chief Archivist-Historian at the U.S. Army Military History Institute and author of several books, including *Richmond Redeemed: The Siege of Petersburg*.

Emory M. Thomas—Regents Professor of History at the University of Georgia and author of several books, including *The Confederacy as a Revolutionary Experience*, *The Confederate Nation*, and *Bold Dragon: The Life of J. E. B. Stuart*.

Frank E. Vandiver—Director, Mosher Institute for Defense Studies at Texas A&M University and author of numerous books, including *Mighty Stonewall*, *Rebel Brass*, *Jubal's Raid*, *Ploughshares into Swords*, and *Their Tattered Flags*.

Jon L. Wakelyn—Chair, Department of History at the Catholic University of America, co-editor of the American Biographical History Series by Harlan Davidson, Inc., and author/editor of several books, including the *Biographical Dictionary of the Confederacy*.

INDEX